THE CHILD WITHIN
LYNN NEW

Published by

An Imprint of Melrose Press Limited
St Thomas Place, Ely
Cambridgeshire
CB7 4GG, UK
www.melrosebooks.com

FIRST EDITION

Copyright © Lynn New, 2011

The Author asserts her moral right to
be identified as the author of this work

Cover designed by Hannah Belcher

ISBN 978 1 907732 31 7

All rights reserved. No part of this publication may be reproduced, stored in a retrieval system, or transmitted, in any form or by any means electronic, mechanical, photocopying, recording or otherwise, without the prior permission of the publishers.

This book is sold subject to the condition that it shall not, by way of trade or otherwise, be lent, re-sold, hired out or otherwise circulated without the publisher's prior consent in any form of binding or cover other than that in which it is published and without a similar condition including this condition being imposed on the subsequent purchaser.

Printed and bound in Great Britain by:
CPI Group (UK) Ltd, Croydon, CR0 4YY

Foreword and Acknowledgements

I started writing *The Child Within* for no reason other than that I needed to recognise how big a part my childhood played in my past. I needed to acknowledge that as an adult I could draw on the strengths and let go of the weaknesses formed through the period of my life during the fifties and sixties. I had consciously denied my childhood of pain and embarrassment and sometimes over-protective love; I had now reached a time of reflection and crisis and was looking to make sense of it all.

Once I had begun my story and the autobiographical facts started to unfold, I realised that there was an underlying spiritual strength within this child. Her innocence was my own; I began to acknowledge myself, though I could hardly recognise the child who was beginning to stand before me.

Having written the original manuscript in the third person and changed the name of the child to make it possible to write about myself, I became again that child and every episode is factual and poignant. I needed to weave myself and the child that I once was into a position where they could converse with each other at the 'junction of understanding'. These are the only examples of storytelling that I have used in my autobiography. It was a hugely humbling experience.

Once I had completed the manuscript, I realised that I was partially failing in my admission of the truth. How could I encourage others to view their childhood when I would not admit to my own name? The underlying aim of my work had been to help, by admission, readers to face their past and to recognise its importance – however traumatic, simple or loving it had been. A diamond has many facets. I pressed *'find; replace'* on my keyboard and made my final admission: my name is *Lynn*.

This book is a true autobiography written within the framework of storytelling. All events and characters are real, though most names have been changed – with the exception of those holding special merit – and deserve acknowledgement for the help, direction and comfort they have supported me with. I apologise to those unmentioned yet unforgotten.

I dedicate this book to all these people but, more especially, to my brother who shared my early childhood and who now, on completion of my manuscript, has shared his own memories and has encouraged me with the publication of *The Child Within*.

The locket on the front cover shows a photo and lock of hair of the author.

CHAPTER 1

It was the evening before her fifty-ninth birthday. She turned round in the room and smiled at the many cards; they all smiled back at her. They were as friends of good cheer; each one held a wish, a promise of love sincere. Some were sent as a token of friendship, some held greater meaning. The carded "Care Bear" smiled soulfully from the window sill, next to the parchment paper bouquet. The pinks and blues and "Old Masters" scenes soldiered across the bookcase, the cabinet and the coffee table.

She carried her mug of evening tea and smiled at them as she passed. 'Thank you, dear friends and family, for wishing me happy birthday and for being pleased to know me.'

She glanced along the line and her eyes alighted on one of the cards. A soulful spaniel puppy looked out at her. The words along the bottom conveyed a wish for health. She had missed it when taking down the other cards that were now stacked within the bookcase, pressed tightly between her favourite volumes as if she were trying to lose the imagery of sympathy between the pages. To make room for her birthday cards she had removed the many "get well" cards from display. This one had escaped but the wording was similar to the kind and genuine wishes of all the others. Lynn picked it up and opened it. Inside it simply read, "Please get well soon". She smiled at the irony and her resolve melted for the first time since her return home from hospital. A single tear escaped her control.

Don't cry now, she thought, brushing it away, it's bad luck to cry around the time of your birthday, Nevertheless, another fell as she turned away.

She took the tea to bed with her and as she climbed the stairs from the lounge the friends she knew, and had known, climbed with her. The higher she climbed the more friends joined her in thought. The cards downstairs were written by the living but the well-wishers now were those whom she had known and loved and who had gone before her. It didn't disturb her to feel this so strongly for she had an understanding of the thin veil between life and death – indeed, she found it somewhat comforting. To her mind love should be unconditional and able to conquer all unseen barriers and that would include death itself. Why she should feel it so strongly that night she did not know but she wrapped the warm feeling around her and pushed open her bedroom door. Her bed was large, the covers co-ordinated, the large chocolate-coloured teddy bear held his arms wide. She put down her mug and pulled the bear to her, burying her face in its soft fur.

She didn't want to be alone; it was not of her choice or making. Those who comforted her now could not hold or caress her. They could not kiss away her tears or make her feel safe from an unknown future. Her bed lay before her, the sheets cold and unwelcoming.

'I don't want to be alone,' she whispered to the bear. 'Not now, not ever, but what choice do I have, what choice have I ever had?'

She wondered what had turned in her life, what had made her the way she was. When did the dream of marriage, children and total happiness change? When did she cease waiting for her Cinderella dream to come true and realise that what she had was what she was? When did she stop hoping that life would be responsible for her and realise that she had to be responsible for herself? She had eventually realised that she could no longer blame circumstance or fate for the way life had worked out, although she could not let go of the thought that destiny wound its way through her life like some strengthened golden thread, delicate and transparent to the naked eye. She had not set out to walk a chosen path, nor had she seen the pitfalls along the path she had walked. She had learned how to turn and adapt, but without conscious effort and always as a way of surviving without falling into pits of self-pity or self-destruction.

Yes, she thought as she looked around the room, this is where I am and I am here because of who I am and how life has schooled me. She could not apologise for who she was, nor make excuses for herself or the hand that life had dealt her. She sank against the pillows unaware that her guardian spirits gathered round as exhausted sleep overtook her. 'Never alone,' they whispered unheard. 'Never alone.'

The child was puzzled; it was as if she had been woken from a deep sleep. A sleep that had encouraged her to think that she had been neglected by the adult she now saw before her, as if for the first time. She paused, gathering her senses and her short memories around her. She knew she had a past, yet somehow also a remembered future. How could that be? Perhaps this was why the woman in the bed, now strangely familiar, had called her again to consciousness. What would the woman ask of her?

She stood, wanting to touch her yet fearing to do so in case she should lose her own identity and become that woman, so close did they seem to be bound. She resisted and remained standing at a distance.

Little Lynn had been asleep for a long time, all her adult life, in fact, so she only knew herself as that child. She lived in the twilight world of memories; unable to place herself with any right to exist any more. It was as if she had played out her purpose and now, living in limbo, was unable to warrant a reason for any future part of the woman she saw before her; the woman she had become. She was indeed "The Child Within".

Many times she had watched with fascination from a distance as she called to the woman from a place called Memory. But the woman, if she heard her at all, never understood why she called. She would play with her as with a doll, for amusement, and then put the child back in a darkened box for another time. Little Lynn only seemed to be remembered as a plaything to be toyed with. The woman owed the child so much more than that.

Gradually, the woman shunned Little Lynn, denying her existence; she put away childish things, turning herself into the adult who now lay in crisis. The child waited on the edge of her twilight for the opportunity of recognition. It came on the evening before Lynn's fifty-ninth birthday. Lynn the adult was looking for answers that only Lynn the child could supply. At last she was needed.

Chapter 2

Little Lynn was fully awake now, reliving her young life. She wondered why the woman had woken her in recall but she seemed to understand what must be done. Her memory was short but obviously important to the woman who had called her.

The Zealey family moved to Dunstable in the early 1950s. They relocated from Jersey, the largest of the Channel Islands, where Lynn's mother Joyce and her two children had been born. Her brother Bill was three years older than Lynn who was just a toddler. Their father Syd resumed his occupation as printer for the *Luton News* and had managed to secure a family flat above the offices of another paper, the *Dunstable Gazette*. They were a perfect family, intent on the discovery of a new life while Lynn's parents let go of the memories of the Second World War, now some years behind them.

The newspaper offices and flat above were positioned on the corner of the High Street and Albion Street, where the view of the town centre was extensive. Lynn, held by her mother, would look down on the busy street and watch people hurry into shops or stop to talk to one another. Cars and lorries passed in clouds of exhaust fumes along the road and shoppers and children had to cross at the zebra crossing now that the flow of traffic through the old town had escalated. On rainy days the children would look down at the growing puddles and enjoy the whoosh of water being displaced by the car tyres. It was like being in heaven. The child was so high up that nothing could harm or disturb her; she could watch everything from the safety of her mother's arms. She would enjoy early childhood without anticipating the future. Even at that early age the child was insecure from seemingly forgotten episodes of hospital experiences. She liked nothing better than being cuddled and held by her mother who, in turn, must have been comforted by the nearness of the daughter she had already nearly lost. Good health, though, was intermittent and visits to the hospital were regular and distressing for the family.

To reach the street from their lofty home the big metal pushchair had to be bumped down the many stairs. Her mother would call in at the newspaper's office and say hello to Mr Philbrow who worked there. Lynn could remember very little about the man except that he always wore a suit and she was threatened by her mother with his disapproval all through childhood. If Lynn cried when having her hair washed she would be told that Mr Philbrow could hear her. It had great effect on Lynn's behaviour for she never ever liked to be disapproved of! Even when they moved to the new house it was still a good deterrent.

Once in the street the little family stayed close while Joyce shopped for bread at Coombes bakery and bought meat at Baxter's the butchers. There were no supermarkets and everything had to be bought fresh although Lynn enjoyed going to the Co-op and standing by the counter while her mother shopped. Upon paying for her purchases her mother's pound notes were put in a small cylinder-shaped container and hooked on to a wire. The shop assistant only had to pull a lever, sending it across the ceiling to an office somewhere above them and then wait for it to return, as if by magic, with her mother's change. When she was older, Lynn always asked if they could shop at the Co-op. She also liked a dress and fabric shop which sold ladies' fashions and pretty dresses as well as coloured ribbons and threads and Lynn, always fascinated by bright colours, would stand in front of the racks, mesmerised, while her mother talked to the assistant. She thought her mother knew everybody in the town!

Sometimes as a special summer treat their mother would take them into the sweet shop run by Mr and Mrs Tubb. They would choose which of the home-made ice creams they would like and Mrs Tubb, a lovely friendly lady, would lean over the chrome container and scoop out the flavour they wanted; strawberry, vanilla, chocolate – the variety seemed endless. They could only have one scoop but that was enough. Anything bigger and Lynn would find it melting before she had eaten it down to the cornet. The delicious aroma from the barley sugars, sherbet lemons and acid drops spilled out through the shop doorway tempting the children in even before they had reached the shop. Lynn had never found another ice cream shop like it and she quite loved Mrs Tubb. When the couple retired she thought her mother missed them badly for they had become her friends.

Lynn's first memories of the upstairs flat were of the high ceilings and a large main room with tall sash windows. There was an open fireplace and coal was the only form of heating, having to be brought up the stairs every day. She remembered the chimney breast because a bird flew down it one spring and as her father was at work Mr Philbrow was called from his office downstairs and asked to open all the windows and help it escape. There was an awful lot of soot everywhere and her mother had to clean it all up; she wasn't very happy and Lynn played quietly on her own for the rest of the morning.

Christmas was cosy with all the magic of the tree decorated in the corner. Her mother built a snow scene with cotton wool around the base of the small pine tree. Every year she would add little Christmas ornaments taken mostly from previous cake decorations and parcel adornments that came from Lynn's great-aunt in Canada. Gradually over the years the scene grew to cover a larger corner table and when they moved to the new house the snow scene extended to the window sill. In the early days all the ornaments in the scene were of plaster and chalk-based material. The tree ornaments were of glass and very fragile metal and the candles were real, though they were only lit when an adult was in the room and for short periods only. Lynn loved Christmas then; everyone seemed very happy and excited. Each year Great-aunt Nan would send gifts from Canada. One year she sent a set of candles that were like choirboys with the wicks coming out of their heads and a wax tree to match. The following January her father made a mistake when the family wrote their thank-you letters. He mentioned that the nuts she had sent him were his favourite. After that first year he would receive the same monotonous gift of peanuts, which he never actually enjoyed. Lynn knew that they caught under his false teeth and hurt his gums. He became sick of them, but didn't have the heart to say so. Christmas was made for children and in the 1950s it held for Bill and Lynn the magic of a united family.

Dunstable was a growing town. The end of the war brought with it the end of an era and the plans for new growth. By its historic layout the town was quartered by the two ancient roads that dissected it. Watling Street built and paved by the Romans, was crossed by Icknield Way, also an ancient road. Signs of habitation dated back to Neolithic times and there were many sites located in the surrounding area. History meant little to the children but they loved the family outings on Saturdays or Sundays either by train from Dunstable station or later by the family's own transport. It was a great disappointment and inconvenience when the railway station and local line to Dunstable was closed. Bill and Lynn loved tumbling down Totternhoe Knolls on such outings and picking wild flowers on the chalk downs was another favourite. In the winter they could all toboggan down the Dunstable Downs on the red sledge her father had made, and laugh at her mother as she rolled off the sledge, tumbling over and over until she lay at the bottom of the hill, looking rather like an upturned snowman. Lynn loved the countryside just as much as the beach; even more so, if she was honest with herself.

The town itself held a weekly market in the square, designated for that purpose. Lynn would be pushed in the pram to see the animals. She was afraid of the size of the cattle and bulls but liked the calves and sheep. She wasn't so keen on the sweet smell of dung and straw but always enjoyed the short outing. Her mother once told her as she was growing up of the time a bull escaped from its pen and she had to shelter with her children in a doorway until the animal was caught. Although it stayed vividly in her mother's mind, Lynn could remember none of it.

Life continued quietly for a while in the family household. Her brother started school and Lynn led a cocooned existence. She was too young then to realise that she was a sickly child, needing prescribed drugs and hospital appointments to give her young life some form of normality. Theirs was a happy family, or so it seemed to the children.

Lynn was not party to the conversations and whisperings over the months after Christmas until eventually the children were told they would all be moving. Lynn did not like change and couldn't settle to sleep; change to her meant insecurity.

One cold winter's day they all piled in to "Old Lob", their family motorbike and sidecar, and their father drove them to the new house. At that time the building didn't have a roof, nor could it realistically be called a house. Fifty-four First Avenue was a building site with ladders up against the unfinished walls and mud where there would eventually be a garden. The day was bitterly cold and a Chiltern mist hung dank over the area. There were a few houses along another road and also some buildings on the road they had driven up. Apart from that the semi-detached pair of houses stood alone and aloof. As far as the eye could see there were fields, roughly ploughed and barren. That view carried towards a hill and the horizon on two sides, while the town was starting to encroach on the others. Lynn was cold and tired but she had picked up on the excitement of the family and loved to hear her mother laugh even while scolding her brother for climbing the ladder the builders had left.

The next few months saw many trips to the house. They all watched it grow and while Lynn was happy to crack the ice in the frozen puddles and play make-believe, her brother and parents were planning for the family's future. Their new house was in the south-west quadrant of the town boundaries but to all intents and purposes it stood proudly on the edge of the countryside that became Lynn's natural environment. Some forty-five years later the area would be unrecognisable, laid under concrete like a spreading cancer for the benefit of others like Lynn's family who needed homes. But nothing could change the very thing that became the child's backbone. Ingrained in her personality was her love of wildlife. In growing up on the edge of the Chilterns she would experience the countryside at its most limitless and a childhood of freedom without fear.

The town now meant little to the child. Once the family had moved from the flat over the newspaper office she had lost her bird's-eye view of all that was going on below her in the street. Lynn and her brother could no longer watch the world from the seat in the window and Lynn's trips to town now either meant her being taken in the pushchair or managing the long walk with her mother once she became a little older. She had no yearning to be taken into shops for her mother told her children that treats were for birthdays and special occasions only and there was not enough money to be frivolous. Generally, shopping was for food and supplies. However, a currant bun from Coombes the bakery or an ice cream from Tubbs was always a great incentive and the long hill that climbed up First Avenue was soon forgotten when her mother opened the front door of their new home and set a small bottle of orange juice that the milkman had delivered in front of her daughter. Lynn would take it on to the front porch and sit on the step to drink it while watching the sparrows feed on the front lawn. It didn't take Lynn long to forget she was ever a town girl.

Once a year the fair came to Dunstable town. Lynn thought it happened as if by magic. One day the market square in the centre of town was no more than just that, but by the next day it became a bustling noisy centre of attraction. The Stati fair was allowed by an old decree to set up one day a year, while passing through the town. The law stated that if for any reason the fair missed its allotted time, they would lose the right to ever set their stalls and amusements up again. It was also law that they would dismantle and leave the town by the following morning.

Lynn and her brother always went to the fair with their father and mother and while Bill enjoyed the dodgems and faster, noisier rides, Lynn preferred the stalls. She hated the swinging seats and the helter-skelter and her mother even found it hard to persuade her daughter on to the carousel. She liked the painted horses and how they went up and down, but she hated going round and round; she would feel a little giddy but knew there was no getting off once the music and the engine that drove the horses started up. She would only go on the dodgems with her father but hated to get bumped. Her brother thought she was no fun at all and preferred it when his friend Jimmy went to the fair with them.

The little girl liked the "hoop-la" stall and, although she was too small to throw the hoops for herself, she squealed with delight when her father nearly hooped a square wooden box on which stood a cuddly doll with big felt eyes; perhaps next time he would be lucky. Her favourite stall was one which she could enjoy without the aid of a grown-up. Having paid the pennies her father had given her, she was handed a long bamboo pole with a hook on the end. The big man who gave it to her smiled a toothless grin and wished the child lots of luck. It took several visits to the fair over the years for Lynn to master the knack of hooking the ring on the back of a wooden yellow duck. Too many times the duck, which was bobbing in the circular tank of water, would sink with the pressure of the rod, only to bob up again a few inches further away. It took her until she was nearly eight years old to master the skill. Lynn eventually caught a duck, hooking it expertly, and lifted it out of the water for the man to turn it over and read the number on its tummy.

'Seventeen, little lady, lucky you; let's see what you have won.' The man had smiling wrinkles round his eyes and a moustache that looked like a droopy mouse. It partially hid the toothless grin. He reminded her of the bad guy in the cowboy films, but she liked his twinkling eyes. He was talking to her again. 'You've won a goldfish, my dear.'

He handed her a plastic bag, part filled with water. It was one of many placed on a circular shelf in the middle of the stall. The little goldfish swam to the bottom, trying desperately to hide and prevent being sloshed around the bag. Lynn reached out and took it, looking nervously at her father to see whether she could keep her prize.

'We'll have to buy a bowl, Lynn, and you will have to look after it.' Her father took the bag gently from her and held it up to make sure the fish was still alive. He could see that it would be more trouble than it was worth but his daughter was thrilled that she had won something and even more pleased that she now had a pet to call her own. Her father, although not a domineering man, controlled all home and family decisions until the children were in their midteens. They respected him and never queried his disapproval of his children owning a family pet. However, that day, he could not refuse his daughter the pleasure of winning the goldfish. By the time the family had got home she had christened it Cleo, though she rather thought it was more at her mother's suggestion than her own.

True to form, the next day, when Lynn was taken to town with her mother to buy fresh bread, the fair had gone. A street sweeper was pushing his huge broom along the paving stones but apart from a little rubbish there was no sign that the fair had ever been in town.

Lynn secretly hoped all the goldfish had been won, otherwise they would have disappeared like magic too and found themselves in another town on another day. There was an air of sadness about Lynn that day; she hated it when things changed or ended without reason. She trailed behind her mother who had hold of her hand tightly and showed no enthusiasm until her mother promised to buy the bowl for Cleo to swim in to replace the old washing-up bowl now being used, and the food flakes the fish would need.

Her father was of course proved right. The little fish did not live its solitary life very long. He breathed a sigh of relief that Lynn hadn't found the fish floating tummy up some weeks later. She was told the truth and so began to learn the brutal facts of life. Cleo was given a nice funeral and was buried in the garden. The ceremony was watched intently by the neighbours' ginger tom cat! Lynn mourned for half a day and then wondered if her father would allow her to have a hamster. She thought she could bargain down for a mouse but in truth her family thought they should wait until she was older and more responsible before allowing her to have another pet to look after. Lynn was consoled by being presented with a small brown paper bag. Inside were two currant buns, one for her and one for her brother. He wondered what all the fuss was about but ate the currant bun anyway!

Chapter 3

Lynn was born at the end of August and because of the structure of the educational system starting in September she was one of the youngest in her class. She was dreading starting what should have been a new adventure but, at five years and a few days, she walked to her new school with her mother, her brother having left for school earlier. Icknield Primary school was built on the corner of Burr Street on the edge of town and involved an easy walk along the neighbouring streets that passed Bennett's Recreational ground. An alley way dividing the allotments cut through to the road again. Suddenly the school was in front of mother and child; they crossed the road and joined all the other mothers and young children at the grey iron gates. The youngsters wore the red and black school uniforms, big and uncomfortable, allowing for growth and some were already crying. Before the introduction of nursery and playschool, the children's fifth birthday was the first encounter with authority and the educational system. Some had never been away from the family home before; others like Lynn held memories of being torn away from family under different circumstances and were aware that this occasion would be none the less traumatic. Lynn was one of the children already crying.

Once their parents had left their youngsters, they were seated in their first class room and introduced to their teacher. Many of the children had stopped snivelling; Lynn looked around. The rooms were partitioned from the main hall by half-glassed walls making up the classrooms. A series of unframed pictures hung all round these walls in a sequence. Some matched numbers with amounts of fruit while another set matched the letters of the alphabet with types of animals. Lynn immediately liked the Z for zebra drawing. Her eyes followed the pictures round the room; her sobs subsided, but didn't stop. Her heart ached and her eyes were sore and all the time she cried she felt she was getting smaller and smaller; it was like being back in hospital and she wanted to go home. The other children seemed to be getting on with something now but Lynn hadn't been listening and didn't know what to do.

The time seemed to pass very slowly and eventually even Lynn was getting tired of crying. She looked at all the other children and to her horror there was only one other child who was sniffing and bubbling. Tears were coming from his eyes and his nose was so moist that it was running in thick and pendulous mucus. He wiped it on his sleeve. The poor miserable child wore National Health round-rimmed glasses with Elastoplast round one spectacle arm. He looked an unhappy wretch; he had tousled hair and his face was smudged, dirty even, and his uniform wasn't brand new. She studied him; he squinted back at her like a frightened animal. Lynn had no compassion; she did not want to be compared with such a creature. Everyone was looking at them; this was survival and Lynn stopped crying. She never cried in class again and, just as she adapted to later hospital life, she thrust her chin forward and gradually turned her living nightmare into achievement. She was no different to her classmates and occasionally was told to stand in the corner. It rarely dawned on her that she had been naughty and she was pleased to stand facing the wall for shamefully she hoped no one would notice her disgrace.

Her primary school teacher was a homely lady – almost cuddly in her big, shapeless cardigans that she always wore. If she hadn't been so nervous of authority, Lynn would have taken to her kindly. She was a good teacher, and with encouragement, Lynn had settled down in class, eager to learn. She loved drawing and painting and writing her daily diary. In this subject she excelled for she was able to describe in good handwriting something that had happened at the weekend and then draw and colour the picture of the event above the writing. The exercise book would be handed in and if she had really done well she would receive a gold or silver star for her effort. Lynn was very proud to show her mother how well she had done. She wished she could do so well at sums, but she just didn't understand how to add up and subtract and, when reciting her times table in one voice with the class, she would mouth the words and follow behind the others. She was terrified to be asked to stand up and recite some of it out loud. Sums didn't seem to hold any meaning for Lynn and she was nearly at the bottom of the class when it came to test time.

Spelling for her was difficult but she persevered and managed with great effort to come midway in the class. She would enjoy the class-reading of the series of "Old Lobb". The stories revolved around the life of the farmer and his animals'. This book character lent his name to the family's motorbike and sidecar – at Lynn's insistence.

Once Lynn was old enough to choose a book from the foldaway library case in the class, she began to understand the importance of spelling and gradually improved. However, when the end of the school year came and she took her school report home to her parents, it read, "Tries hard constantly and is a pleasant member of the class." Throughout her primary schooling, her attendance was poor because of her fragile health; Lynn seemed always to be in the position of trying to catch up with her lessons. Each school report became an echo of the first. She invariably was too tired to play when she came out of school and liked nothing better than to see her mother at the school gates to walk her home at the end of the school day.

During her primary education a monitor system was in practice. Each month children were allocated different tasks, probably to give them a sense of responsibility within their class. At the beginning of January Lynn became "straw monitor". She was allowed to stand beside the big metal crates of milk placed in the corner of the classroom and hand a straw out to each child at morning break time. The milk bottles were small with silver tops and although Lynn didn't like milk very much she did like the importance of her designated role. She thought one day she might become milk monitor, a position that all the children held in high regard. When the weather became icy, the milk would freeze in the bottles and the foil lid would be lifted off the top by the expansion of the milk. The children were unable, of course, to drink their government ration. Likewise if, in summer, the weather was too hot, the milk would sour and be equally wasted. Lynn couldn't really understand why they had to drink it, but she did like break time. Once the milk had been drunk the children deposited their bottles back in the crate and were then allowed out to the playground for their break.

Lynn stayed for school dinners. On a Monday morning the money her mother had given her in an envelope was collected by her teacher, allowing her to have five school dinners. The responsibility of her mother's money in her school bag didn't sit easily with Lynn for she was fearful she would lose it. Her brother stayed at the school for meals too, but they were usually in different sittings. Now Bill was a "big" brother and played with his own friends at play time and dinner hour. Sometimes someone would ask Lynn if she was Bill's sister but, apart from the odd glimpse across the playground, they could have been on different planets. They didn't walk home together but once the school day had ended they became brother and sister again, playing and teasing each other. Bill was very good at his lessons and was growing up fast. It was good, though, because Lynn had met Jane and her brother; Jimmy was Bill's age. Gradually as the school year progressed the four of them became playmates out of school hours.

The schoolchildren played in the playground before lunch. They were then divided into two sittings and when the hand bell rang, the first large group made their way to queue outside the dining hall. Dinner took about three quarters of an hour and started with grace. They stood to attention in front of the bench seats and sang the verse as quickly as they could. Sometimes they had to start again for it was quite obvious to the teacher on dinner rota that they just wanted to get to their food. Then they sat on command from the teacher at the Formica-topped tables. In small groups they were allowed to collect their first course. Lynn enjoyed her school meals and especially loved the puddings. Her favourite was chocolate-covered cornflakes and she always wanted custard on hers. It was a dish that her mother never made, probably for obvious reasons. Lynn liked the milk pudding as well because the woman behind the serving counter put chocolate bits on the tapioca. Lynn never ate the pig's liver when it was served nor did she like the white cabbage stewed in water; her mother's cabbage was always of the green variety.

She was pleased when it was time to go outside and play but somehow she always felt tired after dinner, preferring to play less boisterously than the other children. Sometimes she would look for one of her favourite "dinner ladies" who kept an eye on the children during their breaks in the playground. Mrs Money was a warm, comfortable-looking lady and Mrs Brooks, though taller and not so cuddly, was very motherly. These ladies would settle children's arguments and patch up grazed knees. They were allowed to cuddle the crying and tell off the troublemakers, sometimes sending them to wait outside Mr Young's office. He was the headmaster. His small office window looked over the playground and no one was encouraged to play noisily underneath it. Many years later Lynn realised that he was a very kind, wise man.

One afternoon Lynn went up to Mrs Money and pulled her sleeve. She looked down at the child and into the tired, hazel eyes.

'Stay with me, Lynn, if you want to, it will soon be time to go inside. What is your lesson this afternoon?'

Lynn told her it was reading.

'If you aren't well, Lynn, tell your teacher and she will arrange for you to go home early.' The lady smiled down at her, giving her a little hug.

But Lynn didn't tell her teacher, not wanting to be different to the others. When her mother came for her at the end of the school day she knew everything would be all right. If only, she thought, this tummy ache would go away.

Lynn was quiet when she got home; she ate little tea but watched her favourite television for a while, though now she had started going to school, she missed her favourite children's programmes. She loved *Watch with Mother*, and *Picture Book* was her all-time favourite. Her mother watched her as she said goodnight to her dad and brother and told her she would be up to read her a story as soon as she called out that she was in bed.

She climbed the stairs and washed her face in the bathroom, but only under the cold tap. She cleaned her teeth and then crossed the landing to her room to put on her winceyette patterned pajamas which she had pulled from under her pillow.

Lynn had a long-scored habit of saying her prayers from the comfort of her bed. She climbed between the sheets turning her favourite ornament at an angle so she could see the pretty figure's face. The little statue of the praying angel had always been by her bedside. Made of moulded plaster the three-inch-high figure was painted in yellow with gold stars across her tunic; her smile was serene, her head slightly bowed. It had been given to Lynn as a baby by her Aunt Tessie and had been blessed by the church as a comfort and prayer for the healing of the child. It was beyond Lynn's recollection but she understood she had been very ill as an infant and had known good health in limited quantities since.

Lynn put her hands together in prayer, kneeling on the eiderdown.

Angels watch around my bed,
At my feet and by my head.
Keep me safe, dear Lord, I pray
Till the dawning of the day.
Amen

She blessed her Mummy and her Daddy and her brother. Then she blessed her favourite uncle Mark and her golly. Lynn kissed the angel, putting her safely back on the bedside cabinet. She snuggled back under the covers to wait for her mother to tuck her in.

The bedtime ritual continued with her mother telling her a short story, usually from her own memory, and setting Lynn's side mirror on her dressing table at an angle so that the child could see on to the landing and partially down the stairs. This light was left on till her parents went to bed. Lynn was frightened of the dark; her night-light glowed till dawn.

As the house was silent and she could hear her father's snoring through the semi-closed doors of her own and her parents' bedroom, she became restless. The nagging pain had woken her and she crossed to the bathroom, trying not to disturb the rhythm of sleep emanating from her father.

Her mother was awake. 'Are you all right, Lynn?' she questioned almost in a whisper. Ever watchful of her daughter she seemed constantly aware of any movement or change in habit. Lynn could never cross the carpeted landing without her mother calling to her, which was a regular occurrence. Lynn answered her mother in an equally whispered tone but this time she wasn't so confident in her reply. She stayed in the bathroom for some time, returning to her bedroom unrelieved. Sleep would not come to the tired child and gradually the pain grew worse. She crossed the landing again, this time waking her brother, whose room she had to pass. She sat for ages on the toilet seat, her feet hardly touching the blue candlewick pedestal mat. She studied the white corded fish design and tried to take her mind off the urgency but resistance to pass water. Her lower tummy now raged with a burning sensation making it doubly hard; it was easier to cry than spend a penny. She reassured her mother's repeated question and returned to bed, pulling her knees up to her tummy tightly. Her mother by natural instinct was not fooled. Lynn looked up through the orange night-light glow to see her standing as an angel in the doorway. She knelt by Lynn's bed and the child turned on her back and reached up for a comforting hug. She told her mother she wanted to spend a penny, but it hurt. In return the warm hug became firmer and Lynn's mother shifted her position to sit beside her daughter on the single bed.

'Shall we go to the bathroom so you can try again?' Her mother pulled back the bed clothes and took Lynn's red dressing gown and put it over the child's shoulders. Fitting her slippers, she took her daughter by the hand to cross the landing, closing the bathroom door discreetly behind them.

On such occasions Lynn's mum would run the bath tap, hoping the sound of running water would stimulate her child. That night it did not help and she was taken back to bed and made as comfortable as possible. She was read to for a while but Lynn's mum knew better than to mention visiting or calling the doctor. Her daughter would be so distressed at the mention of his name that there would then be no consoling her. Eventually she kissed Lynn goodnight and, leaving the door ajar, returned to her own bedroom. Her father's snoring had stopped and Lynn could hear her parents talking in concerned tones, half muffled by the softness of bed clothes. Lynn hugged her golliwog and tried to sleep.

The long night had not turned to dawn before Lynn's parents were disturbed again by the shadow of the little girl by their bed. Usually neither of the children was allowed into the adults' room without knocking but Lynn was distraught, unable to wait for their attention.

'Do you want to come in with us?' her mother asked, lifting the sheeted blanket from her side; pushing her husband over a little to make room. He did not complain and put on the bedside light. His little daughter was pale, her tear-stained face puffy from crying.

She looked at him, 'May I come in the middle?'

'Of course you can.' His tone was mellow. They both shuffled around so Lynn could climb over and lie between them.

Everything was quiet for a while but the child was restless with pain. Firstly her legs thrashed around then she bounced a little on the big mattress, until, in her discomfort and need to spend a penny, she used it as a trampoline. Everyone was awake. Her brother was told to go back to bed when he knocked on the door and her father went downstairs to make a cup of tea. There was no phone in the house and her parents were loath to disturb their elderly widowed neighbour who had a phone line. It would soon be dawn; they would call the doctor then.

Eventually, when it seemed the child could take the pain and stinging no more, she was coerced into trying to go to the toilet one more time. She sat holding her mother's hand; the water running into the bath. She could resist no more and though the scalding pain made her sob, the relief in passing even a small amount was wonderful. Now she cried with relief. Eventually she told her mother she was finished and the exhausted little girl was taken back to her parents' bed for the short time that was left of the night. She was comforted by her mummy's warmth and even her father's snoring.

Now, though, as daylight crept along the window-ledge, Lynn had something more to worry about; she would have to see the doctor at the hospital again; she didn't think her ordeal was over.

Chapter 4

Lynn held her mother's hand, matching her step as best she could as they hurried for the bus. The October day was grey and the autumn breeze heralded the winter chill that was to come. Leaves had already started to twist and dry on the branches of overhanging horse chestnut trees – always the first to thrust out their sticky buds in spring and the first to leave the changing scene at the end of their season. Autumn came early in Dunstable; little Siberia, someone had called it when the full force of winter winds blew across the Chiltern hills, coming up sharply towards Dunstable Downs. Lynn pulled her school raincoat closely around her by tightening the cloth-covered buckle. She knew the cold she was feeling was the freezing dread from within, not the changing weather. Her mother kept the conversation light, unable to amuse her child or distract her from her gloom. She felt her dragging in her hand and urged her on, encouraging her with the later treat, after her hospital visit, of visiting the toy shop Partridge's. Lynn's spirits could not be lifted.

By the time they had reached the bus stop in town the queue was substantial; Lynn hoped there would be no room aboard the green double-decker as it pulled in at the kerb, coughing its smoky fumes as it idled its engine, waiting for its melee of passengers to climb aboard. The platform was high for Lynn's young legs and her mother put her hand under her arm to lift her.

'Plenty of room on top,' called the conductor, accepting that the driver was keen to be on his way, as they were already behind schedule.

Once on the upper deck, Lynn chose a window seat, her mother sitting beside her. At nine-fifteen in the morning the glass of the window was already smudged over with hand prints as the previous passengers had tried to clear the condensation. Lynn peered through as the bus jolted and started the journey between the towns of Dunstable and Luton. Running predominantly in third gear it would take about half an hour to reach the main terminus. From there Lynn and her mum would have to change buses for the shorter journey to the Children's Annex Hospital along the London Road. This was the low-built children's hospital that Lynn had to visit once every few months. The consultant, Dr Fagg, always seemed ready and waiting for her when her mother knocked on his consulting room door. To Lynn it seemed like the end of the world; everything about her would freeze and petrify as she stepped over the threshold and took up the non-smiling invitation of sitting opposite him across the large solid wood desk.

For now Lynn tried to keep her mind off what was to come. She smudged her own hand across the window of the bus and peered down at the pedestrians along the pavements. Women with big prams, the canvas hoods up to protect babies and toddlers against the rising wind, men in overcoats and trilbies, some of them late for work; youngsters dawdling, though the bell must already have rung in the school playgrounds. Lynn didn't really like school but she would have given anything to have been there now, sitting at her school desk, just one of thirty pupils. She wanted to be anywhere but on that big, noisy green bus. She looked up and across the houses; the Luton and Dunstable Hospital loomed large and square-like on the near horizon. The conductor rang the bell downstairs announcing the stop. Lynn knew this was not the hospital she would be attending. The one for which she had an appointment, although annexed to the main hospital, stood in its own grounds on the other side of Luton, and dealt only with sick children. The length of the journey added to Lynn's anxiety. She was unsure whether she wanted the morning over quickly, or wanted something to happen to avoid her having to go to the hospital at all. She rather hoped the lady who had stood up opposite them would take her time and keep everyone waiting. Perhaps she might fall down the stairs and the bus would have to be taken out of service; Lynn would be allowed home having missed her appointment and life could go on as normal. Lynn frowned, she didn't really know what normal was, she only realised that she was different to other children in her class. She let her mind wander, only half listening to what her mother was saying.

'Luton Bus Station – end of the road. Everybody disembark; thank you.' Lynn jolted back to reality at the sound of the conductor's voice. Her mother took her hand again, leading her down the stairs and out into the town air. The next bus was already waiting; Lynn hung back, her feet like lead and her throat dry, so great was her dread. This journey was a short one, only ten minutes, and there was hardly time to sit down.

In no time at all mother and daughter were standing at the entrance to the hospital. Once they were through the doors the smell of disinfectant and the stressful noise of a busy child-filled waiting room became apparent. Lynn was placed on a seat in a row of Rexene-covered chairs and told to wait. Her mother took the appointment card from her handbag and returned to sit by her side. Nothing could describe Lynn's fear of hospitals and, no matter how nice the nurses were, there would only ever be one whom she would come to trust and love.

Lynn's father had worked his printer's trade at the *Luton News* ever since he had moved with his family from the Channel Islands after the birth of their daughter. They had taken advice regarding Lynn's health and his job prospects in Jersey and realised that the move was the only sensible option. The child had been sickly from birth and once they had settled in Dunstable, had been a patient at The Children's Annex hospital under Dr Fagg's care ever since. Too young to remember, Lynn only recalled vague memories of the times prior to her fourth birthday. Now, waiting for her appointment, she looked forward to the one highlight of the day. Sister Canon would be coming down from the ward to say hello. Lynn had been on Sister Canon's ward as a patient. She remembered her kind eyes and warm arms, being pressed into a cuddle of reassurance and comfort when she was too distraught to sleep or lie still. Although her white apron was starched and her lovely silver buckle, shaped as a beautiful butterfly, was sometimes hard against her in a hug, Sister Canon's eyes shone with warmth and her hair, with blonde curls, sat beneath a cap that had a curl to match. Now Lynn waited longingly to see her again; her only consolation of the day.

Over the next half an hour the doors swung open repeatedly. Lynn had almost given up looking for her hospital angel when, like a vision in blue, Sister Canon came into the room. She saw Lynn and her mum straightaway and, instead of standing over the child, she crouched on her haunches in front of the girl and took her hands into her own tender ones. Lynn at once responded, though she knew it was not the place to give the sister a hug; she gripped her hands tightly instead, as if to plead for reassurance. There followed a quiet conversation between her mother and the sister, but the child didn't let go of the sister's hands. Lynn felt stronger for the contact. At the age of five it meant more than words.

Suddenly it was over and a nurse at the high counter called Lynn's name. The three of them stood up at once and Sister Canon patted the child's head, reassuring her that she would be fine and whispering that Dr Fagg was in a good mood. The girl noticed that the sister gave her mother a knowing nod, but she was too young to understand what it meant.

Mother and daughter followed the nurse down the corridor to a door that bore Dr Fagg's name followed by a series of initials. The nurse knocked and then, just as she had imagined on the bus, Lynn was asked to sit next to her mother; across from the consultant. The table was large and of polished oak, and the doctor reached his hands across the seemingly large expanse to take hold of Lynn's pale ones. He held them lightly while asking her mother questions; he must have known Lynn wouldn't have answered them, she was too nervous even to smile.

All the time the questions were being returned with simple answers Lynn stared at the man across the table; she could focus on nothing else but his eyebrows. She had seen men with eyebrows that met in the middle, men whose brows made them look cross even when smiling and men who had one eyebrow raised higher than the other, especially when asking questions. She even knew a man named Mr Philbrow; but she had never seen a pair of eyebrows like those belonging to the doctor! These, Lynn mused, seemed to spin out at the sides of his face like grey springy wings. If he turned his face to look at her case notes below eye level, she could look down on them and see that they were long and course, thick enough to keep the rain out of his eyes should he get caught in a shower. She was fascinated by them, but she didn't like the doctor. She had visited him regularly, but had not allowed herself to respond to his kindly efforts. She recognised him only as the great man with the power to separate her from her family. She didn't know him and certainly didn't want to.

The doctor tried hard to win her confidence; he would hold her hands and move her fingers, she was double-jointed and they held a fascination for him. She did not respond, withdrawing all her energy from her hands and arms as if they didn't belong to her. This made them totally relax, and become pliable; it was a line of least resistance. Somewhere in Lynn's intelligence she had learned that no response was the best response and she carried this through all her medical examinations and investigations, almost, at times pretending not to be in the same room. If she kept her mind under control she could pretend it wasn't happening to her at all but if the point was reached where she was inadvertently hurt or embarrassed she lost her nerve, panicked, lashed out and tried every way to escape. She would then be reprimanded, told off in front of her mother. Yes, thought Lynn, the line of least resistance was best.

Lynn was asked if she minded the doctor examining her. She shook her head. Questions were asked and answered and the consultant felt Lynn's tummy and uttered the sounds of 'Mmm' and 'Ah hah' while directing the cold stethoscope over the middle of her back. Her mother didn't leave her side and it was a relief when Dr Fagg returned to his desk to scribble something down, commenting quietly to the anxious mother who now stood in front of him while Lynn, now dressed again, hovered by the door ready to leave.

'Dr Fagg wants to take a little water specimen from you, my love. It won't take long; we just have to go with the nurse to another room.' Lynn looked fearfully at her mother, knowing full well that her worst nightmare was about to come true.

They went with the nurse down the corridor and the child was asked to change and get on the high bed while the nurse left to prepare a trolley. Lynn was already anxious but dutifully climbed on the bed with the aid of a wooden block. She looked to her mother for emotional support, but she could see by her eyes that she was suffering too. Lynn heard the nurse wheeling the clanking trolley back towards the room in which they waited. The door was pushed open and the nurse came towards her. She asked Lynn to lie still while the nurse lifted the cover off the top level of the trolley to reveal the instruments of Lynn's examination. The child knew as soon as she saw the length of orange rubber tubing that she was to be catheterised. With a muffled sob Lynn's previous resolve of "a line of least resistance" was forgotten. She sat up and jumped from the high bed to the floor, landing and steadying herself before rushing to the door and running down the corridor. The examination gown she wore made her feel vulnerable but she had to escape. Her bare feet were cold on the linoleum and she could hear her mother and nurse behind her. Of course she didn't get far and at the end of the corridor she waited for the adults to catch up with her; there was no escape.

She thought her mother would be very angry but it seemed that both she and the nurse were almost as upset as the child was. She was hugged and reassured and led back to the room, but she did not have to get back on the bed; perhaps, after all, submission wasn't the only answer to her problems. She waited beside her mother while the nurse went to explain to Dr Fagg. Eventually she returned with the doctor and the conversation between the adults was serious and whispered. They turned, as one, back to the scared but resolute patient. Dr Fagg ruffled Lynn's hair and told her she could get dressed. Mother had a strange look of relief and sadness on her face which her daughter couldn't understand, but she was too busy already pushing her feet into her shoes to pay too much attention.

'Say goodbye to the doctor, Lynn.'

Lynn duly obliged, with one hand already on the door handle, in case he changed his mind. 'Goodbye, doctor.' She all but curtseyed in reverence to the mighty consultant. Her mother had to follow her rapidly but caught her up before she reached the main waiting room. She seemed at a loss for words.

'May we go to the toy shop now, Mum?' Her mother remembered her promise and agreed, adding a tone of caution that she couldn't spend too much that day, perhaps a little something for her dolls' house.

Lynn had stopped wanting to vomit as soon as they had left the hospital grounds and her legs had stopped shaking by the time they had climbed aboard the bus back to the centre of town.

Upon entering Partridge's toy shop Lynn was back to being a happy little girl with a shilling in her mother's purse that could be spent on something she needed for her new Georgian dolls' house back at home. She lingered as long as she dared, knowing they had another bus to catch. She trailed her fingers round the wooden cabinet by the counter that held the kitchen utensils. Tiny metal saucepans sat with bread boards with plaster bread and miniature knives. Decorated mirrors reflected droplets of light from the shop window and plates of plaster leeks and potatoes were placed by pots of coloured cloth flowers.

'You have to choose, Lynn, or we will miss the bus home. Remember you have a shilling to spend only.' It seemed the incident at the hospital had been forgotten.

Lynn nodded, engrossed in the colour and detail of all the items set before her. 'Please may I have the plates of vegetables, Mummy? My children are hungry.'

She answered her mother's next question, 'Eleven pence.'

Her mother agreed and she gave her daughter the shiny silver shilling to give to the lady. 'Wait for the change, Lynn.'

Lynn took the penny and handed it to her mother to put in her purse. 'We'll save it for when you come to the hospital next week.'

Lynn stopped, the expression on her pale face changed. 'Next week, Mummy?'

'Yes, dear, we shall add it to another shilling when you come back to the hospital.'

Lynn's bubble burst upon hearing that she would have to return. She took the small bag from the shop assistant but, forgetting her manners, didn't thank the woman. Lynn was only lightly scolded. Realising that too much had been said already, her mother shepherded her daughter to the door and asked what she would like for tea later that day.

That evening, before her own meal, Lynn unhooked the double doors of her dolls' house and lay on the floor of her bedroom so that she could look into the little kitchen. She placed the plaster plate of leeks on the table and placed two pipe-cleaner dolls in their chairs at the table. 'Don't forget to say grace,' she whispered in doll-volume voice. 'I'll bring you the potatoes next time.' She sighed heavily, shut the doors and went downstairs having to admit that pleasure always came at a price.

Chapter 5

Little Lynn attended the out-patients department at the Children's Annex of the Luton and Dunstable Hospital the following week, and after a further series of visits to monitor her kidney condition she was eventually admitted for further investigations. Sister Canon was at the door of the ward to meet her and her mother. The sister bent down to the child to reassure her and then took her by the hand to the bed by the window. Although the ward was vaguely familiar Lynn was filled with trepidation. The ward was long and bright with a glass conservatory at the far end. This led out through French doors to the garden beyond and was to become a joy to Lynn and the other children as they returned to health. She could see the shrubs and trees from the windows and around the grounds there was grass and early daisies in the lawns.

Lynn was to stay on the ward for six weeks, although at the time of admission she didn't know this. The doctor promised it would only be for a short stay. She had been an in-patient many times before, but the memory of a young child is short and she could remember little prior to this admission. She had been a patient in the children's ward as far back as being a toddler but it was her mother's memories she would recall later, not her own.

The story would be related to Lynn, how, as a toddler, she wouldn't sleep or be comforted when under Sister Canon's care. After asking the child's mother, Joan Canon learned that Lynn's baby comforter was a piece of frayed ribbon from a bonnet. The nurse was then able to fray another ribbon and upon giving it to the toddler she became calmer and slept through the night. The habit of needing something to hold stayed with Lynn well into adulthood, though it became a far less obvious comforter. A handkerchief replaced the ribbon though it wasn't until her early fifties that she could settle with just the knowledge that there was one under her pillow! Experiences throughout her childhood had a lasting effect.

Life on the ward settled into a routine; Lynn got to know the other children and was able to play with them when she was well enough. Sister Canon had always been a part of her life and sometimes when she wasn't too busy she would sit by the child and comfort her. Lynn loved the clean, fresh smell about her and was fascinated by the sister's belt buckle. The silver butterfly was ornately cut in filigree and the child would trace the shape and the line of the shiny motif with her little fingers, wondering how the buckle opened and closed. She already had an eye for delicate beauty and loved the sister's starched cap with its frilled edges which seemed to frame her warm, gentle face from which shone sparkling blue eyes. In fact, Lynn loved everything about Sister Canon except the starch of her apron; she could not imagine the world without her.

Sister was a local celebrity before the word was invented. In the 1950s a feature film was made starring the actress Dame Anna Neagle. It was based on the life of a nurse and the film studio, or maybe the actress herself, chose Lynn's Sister Canon as a role model to study for the lead role as an "Angel of Mercy". When she learned about this, Lynn was extraordinarily proud of her dear sister. The bond between them remained throughout her life until the nurse, much loved by many of her young patients, died after retiring, years later. Lynn believed Joan Canon never married and was totally dedicated to her work and her adopted family of children. She kept in touch with many of them, including Lynn, who, as a teenager, went back on to the ward for a few hours on a Saturday to help serve teas for a new generation of sick children.

As Lynn grew up and away from the jurisdiction of The Children's Annex, the communication with Joan Canon continued. In her late teens, having suffered from an intermittent but corrosive bowel disease, Lynn was eventually to undergo surgery. She didn't see much of her Sister through this time, but on one rare occasion they met for afternoon tea; Sister Canon had something to tell her. Lynn's Angel of Mercy confided that she had undergone the same surgery in later life but had been able to continue her career after recuperation. Lynn was fired by the knowledge; it gave her an incentive for her own future. Once again Sister Joan Canon was an inspiration. There would have been many such incidences of her dedication to her many 'children'. Lynn would always be proud to have known and loved her.

However, all this was many years in the future; Lynn's world now only existed within the institution of hospital life. Routine was regulated and orderly, ward life a mixture of control and limited freedom. The boys and girls were allowed to play and if the weather was fine the fitter children would be allowed to visit the gardens just outside the glass conservatory. They were under the supervision of either a nurse or the junior doctor.

It was at this time of her life that Lynn first fell in love. Dr Green was tall enough to lift her in his arms and reach her to the ceiling. He was gentle enough not to frighten her when he spoke to her and his brown eyes were deep enough for her to drown in. He was the only doctor she prayed would visit her and the only adult at the hospital she felt safe with; with the exception of Sister Canon. He made her laugh and forget she was ill. She wanted to grow up quickly – he must have been at least twenty-five and then maybe he would whisk her away to some magic place. But for now she had to be content in sharing him with the other children.

When Dr Green came on to the ward at the end of the afternoon, he would have a word with Sister and gather up the fitter children, open the conservatory doors and allow them outside to go hunting. This was one of the children's favourite games and the doctor played his role well. A relay of young patients over the years had adopted a cat and although it was not allowed over the threshold of the main ward it was friendly and loved to be petted. Dr Green would scout through the bushes looking for it and, much to the delight of the children, he would pretend they were all big-game hunting and call out to it, sharing the children's excitement. Suddenly amidst the joy he would part the undergrowth and stand back, having discovered the ward tortoise chewing dandelions or sleeping in the sun. Dr Green most definitely had a way with animals but more importantly he had a special way with children. Lynn would never forget him and although she never grew fast enough to catch him up and he never took her away to that magic place, he gave her something more valuable; he gave her confidence and reminded her that there was a place in her restricted life for laughter and room in her heart for her to trust him.

Trust was a big word and one that Lynn found difficult to put into practice. She trusted strangers too well but when they let her down or failed to live up to their promises, she withdrew. She was never angry, finding it easier to shrink away, hurt and small. When her parents left her in hospital promising they would be allowed to take her home in a few days, or when the doctor told her he wasn't going to hurt her, she believed them at first, then she doubted them, then she felt deeply let down. Her young experiences coloured her way of reacting. In adult life, if promises were broken or if she was disillusioned she would remove herself to a place deep inside where she could hurt secretly. She wouldn't shout or address the injury but would become small and hidden away. Once she doubted a person, although she would not confront them she would withdraw, eventually becoming small enough not to feel the hurt at all. It was a defence mechanism that lasted through her life, but it was one that did her no favours for the hurt dug slowly within until the core of her being was in pain. Lynn the child would need healing but for now she would find her own way of dealing with that hurt. She decided not to trust.

The lingering smell of lunch wafted away from the long wooden table and empty benches in the middle of the ward. The children were settled to rest on their beds for the hour after their meals, though some were playing quietly, unable to settle. Lynn wasn't tired, but she had become listless. Her father had promised to visit her on his lunch break from the *Luton News*. Sister Canon had given him permission to visit his daughter, bringing his sandwiches to eat by her bedside. It was one of the rare times she ever saw her father at the hospital without her mother by his side and she looked forward to his big, fatherly hug that enveloped her with a smell of chemicals and soft soap. His prematurely whitened hair was well combed, and his man-sized brown shoes were well polished. She remembered her time at home when her father cleaned all the family shoes and even mended his own, turning the rubber heel when one side wore out. He had a shoeing stand of iron called a "last" and Lynn loved to watch him place an inverted shoe upon it and prise the old rubber from the heel. Now in the hospital ward he caught her looking down at his feet but when he asked her what she was thinking she raised her sad eyes no higher than the blanketed bed and shook her head fervently. 'Nothing,' was all she said, but the little injured animal inside her was calling out to him, 'I want to go home.'

Lynn's father, Sydney Joseph, enjoyed games. When he came to visit Lynn, because he wasn't very good at words he would bring a pack of cards. She didn't know the names of the games they played but it was fun and sometimes he would let her win. She thought one of the games was Rummy, but the name wasn't important. She caught on with the more simple games but when one of the senior nurses disapproved of her father teaching her to gamble because they used an incentive system with spent matches, they reverted to Happy

Families or Snap. Lynn liked the grown-up games better but her little hands had a job to hold more than a few cards and it was better when she could lay the tricks down on the bed cover. When she dropped them her father said he hadn't noticed, but they were the games that she lost. Perhaps, after all, Happy Families was better; Lynn liked the characters and the colour and she didn't have to have help from her dad to add up. She liked Mr Bun the Baker for he had a big jolly face. Lynn's father didn't have a jolly face, it was long with a long nose to go with it, but she thought he would have been handsome if he wasn't so old. Her mother had told her that he had had a head of black wavy hair when they had first met, but when he came home from the war it was quite white.

One lunchtime as they were playing cards together, a new nurse came round with her medicine. 'Isn't it nice to have your grandfather to visit you, Lynn?'

Lynn giggled and looked at her father who was quick to reply, 'I'm not her grandfather, I'm her brother!' He kept a very straight face.

The nurse looked embarrassed and hurried about her business. The child thought it funny and her father pretended to be indignant. When the nurse had left he laughed; Lynn liked it when he laughed, but it wasn't often enough. Lynn didn't really mind, she just wished he would hug her more or talk to her more when her mother was with them both. Lynn shrugged. At least I've got him to myself now and playing games is fun, she thought to herself.

Lynn didn't cry when her father left her, folding the grease-proof paper that had held his paste sandwiches and putting it in his pocket. She knew that he would be back and that she would see her mother and father that evening at visiting time. He stood up, pressing the pack of cards into his other pocket. He tied his belt round his rain coat, kissed his daughter, and made his way to the ward doors. They waved to each other and then he was gone. A brief emptiness filled her heart, followed by the joy that he would come at lunchtime the next day and bring the cards with him again.

Lynn missed her own brother coming to see her. However, by seeing her parents most days, she always had something to look forward to and sometimes they would have stopped at Partridge's and bought her a little something for her dolls' house. When the tiny gift had been presented she was allowed to play with it on the bed. Once she was given a model of an electric toaster. It was yellow with Bakelite toast and a black plastic lever so that she could actually put the toast down and pop it up again. The Hoover had a tiny cloth bag with the name of the company on it. She was never allowed to keep the gifts in case they were lost or broken and even when she was given a much bigger cuddly toy it was always taken home, only to be returned for her to cuddle through the next visiting time. Somehow it seemed a double loss; to be given something and have it taken away was hard – to have it returned, on loan so to speak, did not make it any easier.

Gradually, Lynn grew accustomed to her unnatural situation, never realising that most of the little children in the ward were feeling just as deserted and confused. She had such mixed emotions and heartfelt feelings about her parents. One minute she fought her battles on her own and the next she was surrounded by love, tinged with the knowledge that it would be taken away again. She couldn't express herself nor explain it but one Saturday afternoon at the start of visiting and in the middle of her favourite television programme, which in itself was a luxury, her turmoil at being deserted came to a head. The Lone Ranger, riding through the rocky desert on Silver, his white horse, wore a black mask to hide his eyes and identity. He went about doing good deeds with his Indian friend Tonto. Lynn loved the stories. The programme was in black and white as colour television had not been invented and the rocky scenery was in shades of grey. Lynn watched the story unfold and looked up away from the television which was in the centre of the ward, to see her parents open the swing doors and eagerly come towards her. Most of the other children had returned to their beds so there was room for her mum and dad to sit with her. They hugged each other and talked for a while but Lynn was distracted and turned her eyes back to the programme. Perhaps her mother wasn't used to her daughter's indifference, or perhaps she genuinely was trying to consider what her daughter wanted. Eventually Lynn was asked if she wanted to watch the programme or to be with them; it seemed there was a choice, but today she did not know what to choose.

'*The Lone Ranger*,' she whispered, hardly daring to voice her thought and not understanding why she felt that way. It was as if she wanted to punish her parents for never being there when she wanted them. A few minutes passed until they made a move to leave. Lynn continued to watch the television; her mother stood up, her father too, obviously disappointed. They gathered up the bag they had brought with them and kissed their distracted daughter as they said goodbye. It was then Lynn realised how rude she had been and how much she really wanted them to stay; but now it was too late. Her parents had crossed the wide linoleum floor and were about to push the ward doors open, though this time it was to leave.

'Come back,' Lynn wanted to say, but no words came 'Don't leave me, I love you' – but the sentence wasn't uttered, she was too embarrassed to speak out with everybody listening. And then the awful moment came; her parents left her, the doors swung closed and they were gone!

Lynn never knew how her television programme ended; she went back to her bed and sobbed into her pillow. There were so many emotions, so many feelings and experiences that she couldn't comprehend or deal with. The little girl had made a protest but her parents took her literally, denying her the right to be a sulky child, just for once.

This experience of failing to please stayed with Lynn through her childhood and beyond. Upon returning home she would have nightmares about being left and be full of remorse. Years later she would stumble down the stairs while her parents watched evening television to tell them how much she loved them and how sorry she was that she had made them leave her that day. They wondered to what she was referring but comforted her and forgave her just to make her feel better. Lynn hated "*The Lone Ranger*" after that. She could not watch the programme without feeling an extraordinary sense of loss. For some reason she still liked Tonto.

The majority of Lynn's hospital stay was a mixture of illness and new experiences. Children came and left, just like the doctors and nurses, but she remembered very few names. Medical examinations led to investigations often undertaken within a side room off of the main ward and Lynn, although she tried hard to shut out these experiences from her mind, was deeply affected by the trauma of having to submit to these procedures. Nurses and doctors were as kind and as patient as they could afford to be, alternating compassion with sternness when their young patient resisted. Lynn rose from compliancy to panic and dreaded being told she would have to be catheterised in order to have urine samples taken without risk of contamination. Without doubt the vision of the metal trolley wheeled to the bed laden with stainless steel instruments and orange rubber tubing put the fear of God into her. These were not times she wished to remember and when she was later admitted, she was relieved never to have to undergo this procedure again. Any investigations performed at this hospital were carried out under anaesthetic.

Lynn, however, was a resilient child and when eventually she was told she could go home she wept a little to leave Sister Canon. Upon resuming her out-patient appointments she would look forward to seeing her favourite nurse and would always ask after her special doctor. The child never saw the young

Dr Green again but she would never forget the heart-warming man who helped her find an oasis in the desert of hospital life, or the sister who would become her friend through the following years.

Chapter 6

The reality of the dream and the child faded. Lynn was again approaching fifty-nine years old, stirred by the pain in her side. She wondered if very much had changed in her life and then she smiled. Pain is physical, she thought, but life is so much more than that. Perhaps her experiences as a child were helping her come to terms with her life now, making her stronger and less afraid of her own vulnerability. She made a mental note not to use that word again; "sensitivity" was far more positive!

The night was still, velvet, the thickness of it almost palpable; the bedside clock joined hands at three-fifteen. Lynn, now fully awake, snapped on the side light, swung her legs from her bed and pushed her feet into her pink slippers. The oppressive August heat merely served to comfort her. She descended the stairs to the darkened lounge below.

As she waited for the kettle to boil she stood by the unclosed curtains, staring out to the back garden. The street light laid a cover of amber over the patio, glinting on the pebbled path and the leaves of the laurel bush. The short shower earlier had been welcomed. Tomorrow the garden would be replenished by the rain and the worms would come to the surface; the cycle of life would continue. Lynn absentmindedly shrugged and wondered where that thought had come from. Perhaps she was still close to her dream. She realised that she was staring through her own reflection silhouetted against the rain-drizzled glass. As she readjusted her focus she had the instant impression that it was a child who stared back at her. In her twilight state Lynn was not alarmed. The child was familiar to her yet seemed to exist in a different reality. Behind her the boiling kettle clicked off, cutting the current and her train of thought. She returned to the mundane routine of making her hot drink.

She took her tea back to bed with her and in the shadowed light she was already turning back to her childhood and the memory of it all. This time, though, her mood was lighter; perhaps nature was replenishing her spirit as well as her garden. She smiled as her thoughts returned to Dr Green then onward again to the freedom of being home, able with certain restrictions to play in the family garden at their house in Dunstable. Lynn smiled and indulged herself in memories. She awoke the child in her again, this time less reluctantly.

The gravelled tarmac pushed hard into Lynn's bare knees. She leaned back on her heels to relieve the stinging pressure and pull the cotton hem of her summer dress over her skin to protect it, before kneeling again, intent on what she was doing. The morning sun, warm upon her back, filled her with quiet joy; the blackbird above her in the laburnum tree filled the air with song. He paused to watch the girl with birdlike curiosity. Little Lynn did not look up but continued the task she had set herself. She leaned over her mother's flower border deciding on where to dig the first hole and what with. She looked at the small pile of shrivelled earth worms she had gathered from the hot, harsh pathway. There were six of them, dried, petrified, without life or purpose. She counted them all again and reached for another that had adhered to the grey gravel. She was saddened for the worms but had little understanding of death. With the simple wisdom of a child older than her seven years she just wanted to bury them with the respect she felt all living creatures were due. She never reproached the blackbird for pulling a squirming meal from the ground, but to die in the sun on a sharp gravel path was a waste and a shame. She had looked that morning from the bathroom window and seen them, some already lost as they had tried to make their way to the shade of the boundary privet hedge. Encouraged by the damp early dew they had no intelligent idea of the fateful journey they were undertaking. Lynn had closed the window on the scene, her mind formulating a childlike rescue. She would have to hurry if she were to save any of the hapless creatures. It was Sunday and she would need to dress in her best summer frock and eat breakfast at the family table. She doubted she would be allowed out in the garden and would have to avoid her mother if she were to escape at all.

There was nothing pretentious about the garden or the long gravel path leading from the asbestos-roofed garage at the side of the house. The green wrought-iron gates which one day she would loathe, suited the plan of the precisely laid-out garden and the carefully cut golden privet hedge that ran the length of the drive. There was nothing ostentatious about the new 1950s-built semi-detached house that was her home and yet her mother's creative eye had given it a touch of a class. It was a traditional house where she lived happily with her brother and parents. It was a loving home to come back to after hospital stays and holidays. The memories would change and blur in time, but now on that Sunday morning Lynn felt well and well loved. If only time could stand still.

The pair of houses stood together on a hill, on a long, straight, poorly made road that was a continuation of another long straight road of good repair. At the better end of Dunstable the house was positioned within walking distance of the town, but without the convenience of a local store. The seemingly misnamed First Avenue would be the family's address for twenty years but Lynn could not now envisage the many changes to her life and the spread of the town within that time. Now the potholed thoroughfare ended abruptly outside their house as if the men in charge of road-making had run out of both money and will to continue. Her father complained bitterly about the holes that had been scoured deep into the road's rough foundations, making it a hazard for his bicycle and his newly bought motorbike. He would blame the tanks, though this puzzled Lynn for she had never seen a tank coming down the road. She thought it must have been something to do with the war. Lynn's family lived on the boundary of town and country. She was not allowed to go into town without the company of an adult but liked nothing better than to step from the broken-edged concrete on to the dry grassy field and then to fly in freedom to the hilly countryside beyond. Alone or with friends, this is where she belonged.

Today she had a mission. After watching her mother wash the breakfast dishes in the kitchen that overlooked the back garden, she slipped from the house. Kneeling down, she placed the dead worms in a row. Assuming the role of grave-digger she earnestly dug the dry garden soil with the use of a large flat stone. Even in this heat it turned to dust and rolled back into the holes before she had completed her task. By her side lay gathered twiglets from the garden shrubs and twine from bindweed stems. Between her fingers she held the first dead worm before dropping it into the prepared grave. She took another and another until all the worms were within the scratched-out holes. But Lynn had miscounted and had dug one extra grave. There were no more dead worms. She looked around and took a moist, juicy living worm from the flower border as it was about to start its misjudged journey. She knew that living worms belonged in the soil and that it would not die if she placed him by the side of the others.

Indeed, she thought, she may well save him. This one she covered quickly before it escaped. She then proceeded to cover the petrified remains of the seven other worms with finely crumbled soil. She loved the feel of earth between her fingers much more than the flour in the kitchen when she helped her mother to make little cakes. She brushed her hands together and then delicately wound the twine around the twiglets, making seven little crosses. She decided against making an eighth as the last worm wasn't really dead and, besides, she was running out of twine. Leaning back on her heels she admired her handiwork. There was only one thing missing; flowers. She must have flowers and a prayer, of course, she must say a prayer, but which prayer?

She was often taken to church on Sunday by her parents. Her brother was in the choir of the Dunstable Priory, which was an awe-inspiring church, situated within its own well-tended park. Lynn thought it was more like a cathedral than a church, but rarely thought of Jesus when she knelt in the pew, with her family, in deep and solemn prayer. Her head would spin with the smell of incense, the dimness and the monotonous droning of the vicar's voice during the sermon. Eventually Lynn was excused from church service by her parents because of the disruption she caused by fainting during the service and having to be helped out into the fresh air. She tried hard to feel Jesus within the confines of the church, but eventually made up her mind that He couldn't possibly live in such a cold and serious place. Now, standing in the garden, she couldn't think of a single prayer that she had learned in Sunday school that would be appropriate for the burial of her worms. She decided to look for flowers while she thought about it.

She stood, looked around and then crossed the lawn, relieved her father hadn't mown it recently. Little daisy heads quivered in the warm, light breeze. She plucked a few, saying thank you as she did so and returned to the little graveyard she had made. Crouching down she placed each flower head at the side of each home-made cross. The rest she laid at the unmarked grave, the soil of which had already started to turn with the movement of the live worm. Finally she knelt, placing her hands together in prayer, eventually deciding on the shortest prayer she knew.

Now I lay me down to sleep,
I pray the Lord my soul to keep.
If I should die before I wake,
I pray the Lord my soul to take.

She didn't really like that one; it frightened her. A nurse had taught it to her in hospital but it was the only prayer she could remember that day because it rhymed easily and she thought the worms wouldn't mind. She wiped a tendril of blonde hair from her face as she stood up.

'Lynn! What are you doing in the garden?' Her mother was looking out from the side kitchen door. 'You have your best dress on. Come in here now and clean yourself up; they will be here soon.'

Lynn jolted out of her serenity and considered herself scolded. She hated to look up and see disappointment on her mother's face. It was a look she would come to experience more and more as she grew older, not realising until much later that the disappointment was earthed in her mother's life not that of her child.

Lynn clapped the soil from her hands and reluctantly did as her mother asked. She knew this day was an important one. Visitors were coming up from London and as it was such a rare event everything had to be well prepared. Mother had been cooking and cleaning all the day before. It had been worth having to tidy her bedroom just to sit at such a full table, though her brother thought it unfair that he had to clean his room as well as dust his model planes.

Auntie Tessie and Uncle Charles would arrive by car before 12 o'clock and everything had to be ready.

Lynn was tempted to wipe her hands down her dress as she looked down at the little home-made cemetery. She wished she could stay in the garden with grubby hands for she preferred the sunlight and the fresh air. She didn't want to leave Jesus in the garden, alone with the worms; she wanted to stay with him a little longer. Lynn felt even at that early age that this was where she could always find him. He would be to her a bit like Dr Green, always kind and helpful; someone who liked birds and tortoises and worms, but, more importantly, children, especially those with grubby hands!

Chapter 7

Lynn's family didn't have many relatives call on them, certainly not without prior warning or arrangement. Dunstable was a growing town but was about thirty or so miles from London. Her father's family all lived in the London area of South Norwood and the area of Hounslow and even in the 1950s, when fewer people had cars, the traffic was still very busy through the city before joining the less congested roads out to the county of Bedfordshire, north of the capital. Car travel for their relatives was still an adventure or an ordeal, depending on their age and travelling experience. Lynn's aunts and uncles were all older than her father. He was one of six children. He had three brothers and three sisters, though as far as Lynn could remember it was only Auntie Tessie and Uncle Charles who travelled by car to visit them. They were very unlike her aunts and uncle from Jersey, but it was a red-letter day for her father when his sister and brother-in-law made the effort to travel up to Dunstable to visit the family.

Lynn waited for them to arrive that day, wearing the pretty yellow dress that her mother had made her. The skirt blew in the breeze and she felt beautiful, although she was anxious about meeting her relatives. The child was relieved that her aunt and uncle had offered to travel up to Dunstable to see them for Lynn disliked the journey to London. She suffered terribly with travel-sickness and rarely completed the journey without being ill.

When her grandfather lived in Parry Road, South Norwood, Lynn and her family would visit him. Other aunts and uncles lived nearby so it became a real family affair. At this time Lynn's father owned the motorbike and sidecar. Her brother and herself would be wedged in the back seat of the sidecar while Mum in the single adult front seat stared out the Perspex front window at nothing but the road as it zoomed away underneath her. The fumes and noise of the motorbike engine filled the little cabin and Mum could not make herself heard above the noise. Lynn felt ill almost immediately. Firstly she would ask if the journey was almost over, and then she would tap fearfully and then more urgently on her mother's shoulder while holding her hand over her mouth. A ceramic kitchen bowl, used for one purpose only, was stashed in the front, by her mother's feet. It would be handed over and then her mother would bang on the side window and wave at her husband to stop. Father, feeling the wind in his face and the noise of the engine in his head, often failed to look round; completely oblivious to the fact that he wasn't on his own on the open road. Her mother often complained that she felt that one day the motorbike would go in one direction at a junction and the sidecar would go in another and that her husband would not realise it until he arrived at their destination alone. In reality this never happened. Eventually she would catch his eye and he would turn into the next lay-by or field, take off his helmet, goggles and gloves, and unlatch the sidecar roof that hinged open, taking the partially canvas framed top off. Only then could the little half-door be opened. It was a relief to all three of them to get out and allow fresh air to take away the smell of child's vomit! Lynn's dad wiped the bowl out with wayside grass, ready for its reuse, probably on the return journey.

After a brief stop and tidy up the family would be on their way again, heading for Granddad's house with their portions of food in a basket to share for lunch. Lynn didn't really like visiting Granddad, he didn't seem very child-friendly. Secretly, in later years when the programme came on television, he was referred to as 'old man Steptoe'; it was children's humour but their father wasn't very amused.

Not far from Granddad's house there was a public convenience where Lynn's father stopped for them all to smarten up before the visit. Lynn didn't like stopping there; it was all green tiles and disinfectant and the smell reminded her of the hospitals she had been in, only worse. It was a bit like getting off at the bus-stop in Luton, before going on to the Children's Annex hospital; there was an imminent sense of gloom at not being able to turn round and go home. Lynn's memories of these days were not very many for her Granddad, who was a widower, died by the time she was five years old. The family would then visit her father's sister and brother who lived down the road or, more often, her aunt and uncle in Hounslow. These were the people who were coming to visit them in Dunstable the day of the planned get-together.

Bill and Lynn waited for Auntie Tessie and Uncle Charles with anticipation. They both had washed their hands for the third time that morning and were now scrubbed and polished ready for inspection. The sun was still shining and the children were allowed to wait in the drive by the green wrought-iron gates. Bill climbed on to the brick wall and so on to the gatepost. From this commanding position he could see all the way down the road. First Avenue was long and fairly straight and he would be able to see any car come from Friar's Walk. Bull Pond Lane dissected the two roads at the roundabout. Her brother had a boy's interest in cars and knew to look out for the black Ford Popular. Without the common usage of private phones Bill's posting at the gate could be a long one as the family only had an estimated time of arrival. Lynn remembered one year when they were allowed to wear their cowboy and cowgirl outfits and her brother stood for ages on the high gatepost keeping sentry. He raised his new toy bugle when he saw the car coming and set off a fanfare that more alarmed his mother than confirmed their visitor's arrival. Today, however, the children were dressed, as expected, in their Sunday best.

Lynn stood on the driveway wishing she could climb on to the other gatepost. She was not yet big enough, though sometimes her daddy would hold her up there so she could see down the road. Today she waited, gradually becoming bored. She wondered if the live worm in the newly made cemetery was still there or whether he had crawled out of his imagined grave and was even now food for some eager blackbird.

'They are coming; I can see them. Mum, they are here!' her brother called out, shading his eyes in the sunlight. He scrambled off the wall and stood by his sister. Their parents were by them now, a complete family, side by side. Lynn felt her tummy turn over, but it was not with the excitement of seeing loved ones again. She was naturally anxious at meeting people she hadn't seen for a long time; she hung back behind her mother.

Auntie Tessie stepped out of the car and Uncle Charles joined her. Once everyone had said hello and enquired of their journey Lynn dutifully kissed her aunt, while her brother shook her hand. They all went inside. Uncle Charles seemed a kindly man with bushy eyebrows, but Lynn was suspicious of large eyebrows and didn't really want to get to know him very well. They had brought sweets for the children, chocolate drops with hundreds and thousands of coloured balls on them; suddenly Lynn warmed to the couple, they were her favourite sweeties. She asked about Prinny, their Old English sheepdog, with whom she sometimes played in Hounslow, when adult conversation became boring. Lynn wasn't disappointed they hadn't brought him with them because she still remembered the time he had dragged her by the hair round her aunt's garden. She had to have a special injection at the hospital and had been very wary of Prinny ever since. She relaxed visibly when her aunt said they had left him at home.

The car was left in the road; it seemed almost lonely. The concrete road ended outside the semi-detached houses and it looked for the entire world as if the car had stopped because there was nowhere else for it to go – it was the end of the world! Lynn joined everyone in the best front room and, while sitting on the arm of her mother's chair, she let the conversation drift round her. Once it changed back to the mechanics of cars she lost interest and eventually her mother went back to the kitchen, followed by her aunt. Lynn was excluded and her brother had already disappeared; it was her chance to go back into the garden to check on her "cemetery". The daisies had wilted and the live worm had indeed escaped. She asked her mother for some water, pretending it was for the bird bath, and took the small jug back outside to water the flowers. Uncle Charles and her father seemed to be having a very long conversation about the vehicle while burying their heads under the bonnet. She returned the empty jug.

'Call your father in, Lynn, dinner's ready.' Her mother stood by the open oven with a tray of roast potatoes in her oven-gloved hands.

Lynn ran down the drive but dutifully waited until there was a pause in the men's conversation. She knew it was rude to interrupt but she also knew her mother was waiting and would be cross if the dinner got cold.

Everybody loved her mother's cooking. Nothing was ever spoilt or burnt. There was always more than enough although Lynn knew the left-over meat would be eaten cold with salad in the evening and minced on Tuesday for a shepherd's pie. The child knew nothing of rationing or the limitation brought about during the war. Sweet rationing didn't seem to affect the children although, in hindsight, when she was very little she could only remember sweets as a very special treat; perhaps that was why she enjoyed relatives visiting. The vegetables her mother served were always green and well-cooked and the gravy was rich and thick. Sometimes she compared it with the school food, or worse still, the hospital meals; Mother's food came from a different world. Now at her mother's table she would greedily watch the last roast potato being offered to the guests in the hopes that everyone would decline it on its way around the table, until it got to her, the last in line. Of course it never did; Mother's cooking was irresistible.

Lynn could already smell the pudding cooking on the steamer in the kitchen. Today it was syrup sponge which would be covered with Tate & Lyle golden syrup. On a normal Sunday she would have been allowed to lick the spoon, but today she wouldn't be allowed into the kitchen. The pudding would be presented to the table and everyone would show appreciation. The custard would be poured from the jug and everyone would be asked if they wanted seconds. Lynn liked the skin of the yellow custard, but there was little prospect of letting it cool enough to form one when they had visitors. Everyone was offered fruit squash as wine or possibly beer could only be afforded at Christmas.

Lynn had already looked into the large walk-in larder in the kitchen. It seemed cold on the warmest day and this was where her mother kept everything that would spoil in the heat or become contaminated by flies. Milk was kept in a stone pot, still in one of the dairyman Mr Knightly's bottles, while meat had its own storage arrangement in a meat locker or under a mesh hood. Tins were on stacked shelves and while bread was always kept in a bin, vegetables were in their own rack. Today she had discovered a banana-flavoured blancmange made in a mould shaped like a rabbit. This dessert was her favourite and she always tried to gain favour and so be given the head of the wobbly rabbit served on her plate. It tasted no different but, to Lynn, it was the prized portion. Her brother, realising the silliness of his sister, was quite content to be given the rear of the rabbit and always got that bit more. Also in the larder was a strawberry flan which Lynn knew would be served with evaporated milk after their guests had shared a sandwich tea of salmon paste and possibly egg. She forgot about her disappointment of missing out on the last potato and turned her mind to all the lovely food in the larder. She hoped her aunt and uncle would have to have an early tea before starting their journey back to London, in order to arrive home before it got dark.

Everyone said Lynn's eyes were bigger than her tummy.

After dinner Lynn's mum and aunt washed the dishes Lynn and her brother had brought from the table. Uneaten food was saved and put away and when the table was clear the children were allowed to go and play. Their father and uncle shut themselves away in the front room, seemingly to hold an intelligent conversation – however, Lynn listened at the door on her way upstairs and heard her father snoring. She imagined him with his mouth open while her

Uncle Charles tried to read the Sunday paper. Afternoon tea came when the ladies had finished washing up and the children joined them all in the front room for the rest of the day. Lynn sat on the pouffe by the side of her mother, who at last had taken off her apron. Bill sat on the floor leaning against the empty chair; children didn't sit on unoccupied chairs when there were visitors. Lynn watched the hands of the clock on the mantelpiece move slowly round; half past three, half past four. Her mother made a move, enquiring if anyone was ready for tea, and the child was quick to stand and offer to help her mother prepare the sandwiches, or at least to lay the table in the sitting room again. Joyce, realising her child's boredom, ushered her out of the room and sat her on the kitchen stool where she could watch her mother cut the fresh bakery bread and count the slices. Lynn was happy at last; she had spent little time alone with her mother that day and missed her individual attention. Once the meal was prepared Lynn helped carry it to the table and was given the job of calling everyone to tea.

Soon, thought Lynn, I will be able to have the head of the blancmange rabbit!

But when the time came, Lynn was disappointed, visitors had to come first. She saw her brother smirk as she was served with a small piece of the rabbit's tummy, the same as his portion. She kicked him under the table but misjudged it, hitting the gate-legged support instead and making the remnants of the blancmange and Auntie Tessie's strawberry flan wobble in protest. Lynn apologised for the accident and ate her rabbit soulfully.

Eventually the children's aunt and uncle said their goodbyes and kissed Lynn and her mother. Bill avoided the same treatment with a nod of the head and an outstretched hand, copying his father's approach to what he thought of as an embarrassing situation. Their relatives stepped on to the running-boards of their car and climbed into the vehicle, which seemed to Lynn to be very high off the ground. Uncle Charles started the engine first time and made a big turn in the road, thus heading back the way they had come. Bill didn't stand sentinel now, he was relieved to get out of his Sunday best clothes and play on his own while his sister was taken up to get ready for bed.

It was still daylight but it had been a very long day. Soon the light of the falling sun would fade from behind the drawn orange curtains and the little girl would kneel by her bed to say her prayers and climb under the covers to sleep, holding her beloved golliwog tightly to her. Her mother kissed and left her, but did not close the door of her bedroom. Lynn hated to be alone.

Chapter 8

Lynn's very nature was one of natural delight. At an early age she would watch the spider spin a web, patiently waiting for it to be complete. She would be both relieved and disappointed on seeing a fly struggle against the sticky mesh while the spider hurried to capture his prey. She would allow its death and yet be saddened by it, though she could not allow herself to watch a butterfly or bee entangle itself in the spider's larder. If she could rescue it without injury to the creature she would; if she could not, then she would have to turn away and busy herself in another part of the garden.

She would collect rose petals with her friends and try without much success to ferment them into perfume. Somehow, once the petals had been left standing in water for a few days, the smell was more reminiscent of compost. Lynn would dance upon the lawn like a young fairy or slip silently on her mother's lap when she was in need of comfort. When her father reached out to her she would go willingly, but it was not often enough; Lynn loved to be loved. Her parents' touch was the warmest and most comforting she knew and as a child she soon learned to separate it from the hands and touch of doctors and nurses which, though often far more intimate, were cool to the extent of coldness; Lynn needed to be caressed and like a warm puppy she would respond to her parents' love tenfold, offering her heart and loyalty to them. It was because of that she found it hard when promises were broken and distance was put between them.

It seemed that every part of Lynn's mind and heart was sensitive and this would never change. 'Too soft,' they would say in later life but Lynn was just being Lynn and could be no different. A dead sparrow or a fallen tree would have her saddened to tears but, equally, a flying swallow or singing bird would bring her heart to her eyes and she would not and could not change the way she was.

Lynn loved to draw from an early age. She would transfer what she saw and felt into some sketch or picture. She wrote too, though in her early years this was governed by school work. She would become excited when she received a gold star for her early school diary projects and always wanted to improve. Lynn observed, often subconsciously, little mannerisms and expressions she had seen her mother's friends make. Her mind was like a sponge and because her time of illness dictated her exercise, she spent a lot of time in her room or with her dolls. As all children did, she dressed them in fashions and little outfits which often her mother had made for her. However, what she loved the best of all were the rag dolls – floppy, often ugly, but pliable and cuddly. She adopted them into family groups and enacted situations of the life she had already experienced. Golly loved Monkey and Mrs Mop and Lumberjack were a married couple. Most of these toys her mother had made from socks and stockinet without patterns but with lots of love. She could never understand how Golly's woolly hair grew so quickly for she liked to keep it short and often would get her mother's scissors and cut it before she went to bed. It seemed to grow overnight and it took her some time to realise that her loving mother had sewn a new head of hair on her golliwog after Lynn had gone to sleep. Eventually, of course, her mother had to tell her for Lynn thought she could give Golly's hair a trim every night.

Lynn's more expensive rigid-limbed dolls often sat on their own on the toy shelf except when she organised a dolls' tea party in the garden. When she was nine she counted her dolls and found she had nearly twenty. By the time she had reached the age of ten she was organising puppet shows in the family garden, aided by her brother, and inviting friends for the performance. Lynn's imaginary world was one of magic and hours did not drag during times of poor health or school holidays.

The regular out-patient appointments at the Children's Annex hospital continued and these were always a cause of trauma and tears. She had periods of urine infection and pain, but, as children do, she put it to the back of her mind as best she could. Sometimes, however, she would re-enact "Doctors and Nurses" with her toys and Golly had to undergo more than one catheterisation. It was child's role play, innocent and naive, but it stopped short of including her friends! The thought of hospital was never far from Lynn's mind.

Lynn loved the rain and the sunshine equally. She had fond memories of holidays in Scotland, Wales and the Lake District. Though she hated the smell of the Primus stove as her father pumped the fuel into it to light it to boil the kettle, a cup of tea by the side of the road was much nicer than one from a Thermos flask. Lynn and her brother loved to poke stalks of dry grass into the flames, under the watchful eye of their father. On later holidays, when their father had sold the motorbike and sidecar and invested in the family's first car, she would feel safe and content, as she sat next to her brother, on the rear seat of the green Morris Minor. They would be given tinned salmon and lettuce sandwiches to eat. The rain poured down from the skies, hammering on the metal roof, the wipers unable to take the deluge from the windscreen. Though she wanted to feel the sun on her face and play again in the burn with Bill, who would patiently show her how to block the flow of water with rocks, she was content where she was. Yes, Lynn, more than anything else in life, needed to be loved and her intermittent health problems did not stop her from enjoying a wonderful childhood.

Chapter 9

Lynn finished her tea and made herself more comfortable in the big cosy bed. The human mind is a strange thing, she thought to herself, breaking for a moment from the memories of her childhood. Where there is love and contentment the mind seems to feed from it, remembering each episode with an almost healing effect. But where the episode is painful and intrusive, life changing almost, it seems, over the course of years, to fade into a mist of unreality. She deliberated. Although during childhood she had suffered much physical pain, she could not recall it in great detail. The experiences surrounding the pain were still quite vivid, but not the pain itself, while the love she felt was as real as her own beating heart and the excitement of experiencing the touch of a robin, as it perched on her small, upturned palm, would remain in her memory for ever. She realised that perhaps it was the mind's way of coping with life. She pondered on the action of a young mother who swears after the birth of her firstborn that she would never go through the painful ordeal again, only to find after a year or two that her mind has blanked out the pain and the woman is hoping to fall pregnant again. The adult Lynn had forgotten her pain but the memory of having pain remained. Such is the way of natural healing, enabling life as a whole to be tolerated. She found herself once again thinking of young Lynn. The memories of her hospital experiences suffered from a lack of continuity and yet the fragments of this institutional life bound the whole together. These memories wanted to surface, to be brought into a clear adult mind and be healed.

Her mother hugged little Lynn to her, her arms reassuring; the comfort in them all empowering. The child felt safe and protected, nothing could harm her. She trusted every word and snuggled closer, reaching her arms under the heavy fur coat to find her mother's natural warmth. But this time was different; the fear edged back into Lynn's body and did not fade with the warmth; instead she felt her tension and, with a child's instinct, she knew her mother did not have the courage to console her. Mother and daughter clung together, their fear mingled under the beaver lamb coat. Lynn had an overpowering feeling that on this day she would stand alone.

Her mother stepped back, disengaging herself, pulling away from her daughter. In that moment the coat closed around her. That coat which always smelt of her mother's best perfume now embodied the sad spirit of something the child did not fully understand. The sheer bulk of it blocked her love. Too big in shape for the girl to wrap her arms around, it came between them. It smelt of perfume but not the warmth of her mother and that alone was what Lynn needed now. She would grow to hate that coat!

Her mother was saying something but Lynn was not listening. She looked up into her mother's eyes and saw the pain that lay in her own heart. Her mother seemed to be shrinking as if her life's blood was draining away. Whatever was happening she knew she couldn't be helped; worse than that, the growing fear warned the child to mistrust any adult words of comfort about to be spoken.

Lynn was aware of her father in the room – a tall, solitary onlooker, unreachable, untouchable. She couldn't go to him but looked into his eyes and saw a stone wall of sadness. He spoke firmly to his wife. The child could not quite make out what he was saying, but knew, when he called his wife Joyce, that the subject was serious. Something was very wrong.

A voice broke through. 'You can go to the ward with her, settle her down. Visiting times are evenings and weekends. No children allowed.' The nurse's tone was brisk and efficient. Lynn noticed how the belt buckle sparkled against her starched uniform, but it was not the filigree butterfly buckle belonging to Sister Canon. She looked up into the nurse's eyes but was shocked by the dullness of them. Eyes always tell it as it is, the child learned that early in life; trust the eyes not the words.

Eventually Lynn stood by a metal-framed bed on big rubber wheels. It was to become the centre of her world. It was tall and the child felt tiny, but she was vaguely comforted by her mother's presence. Unseen hands wheeled a curtain hung screen across, shielding mother and daughter from the curious eyes of the children in the ward. Her mother untied the laces of Lynn's Start-rite brown school shoes while Lynn gripped her mother's coated shoulder for balance. Her dress was slipped over her head. Joyce gave her daughter the familiar pink fleecy pajamas to put on. They smelt of ironing.

'I want to go home, Mummy. Can I come home now?'

'In a few days, darling,' was the reply, but she could not look her daughter in the eye. She put Lynn's coat and other clothes in the suitcase and tried in vain to close it gently. Lynn felt betrayed and empty. Neither of them could find words; it was as if events had overtaken them both. The child could not appreciate how her mother was feeling, knowing that within minutes she would have to leave her sick child. She could only think of her own loss and her parents' betrayal.

In 1956 Lynn became a patient of The London Hospital, Whitechapel for a total of six weeks. She would not see her brother during that time. There were no exceptions to the rule. The only opportunity for her parents to visit was at weekends, when, even then, visiting-time was limited. The motorbike and sidecar was still their only form of family transport at this time. Although Lynn could not comprehend distance, she understood loneliness. She nurtured a feeling of abandonment – this was like being transported to the other side of the world. Her recent experiences at the local children's hospital were still the subject of her recurrent nightmares and Lynn hadn't had time to settle back at school or feel confident in her life. Now she was thrust again into the alien world of strangers who had control over her; where discipline came before compassion.

'Say goodbye to your mummy, dear.' The nurse smiled, but not with her eyes.

The parting was too traumatic to remember. When she had gone the screen was wheeled away and Lynn looked out from crisp sheets on a rubber-protected mattress into the eyes of curious children. She slid down the bed, wishing the sheets were not tucked in so tightly. She wanted to pull them over her head.

Lynn counted the days. On the first day she looked towards the ward doors, eagerly peering through their circular windows. She knew her mother wouldn't come; but the doctors visited and the nurses and so many other people who were preoccupied in their work. The child hated it when they came towards her; terrified when people in white coats converged on her, gathering in whispers round her bed. She felt as small as a pebble on the sand and wanted to hide.

On the second day she looked towards the door hoping her mother would appear, arms wide to sweep the child up and away, but she didn't. Day three brought disappointment; day four, loneliness and abandonment. On day five,

Lynn repeated the words, 'You promised, Mummy!' On day six, she looked away from the door and into her new small world; Lynn started to reach out.

On Saturday once again families arrived at visiting time. The children were groomed and tidy, tucked between clean sheets ready for the swinging doors to open.

Lynn's mother came, her father followed and the child's sheltered world was full of love and warmth and presents too. But they didn't bring the suitcase, they didn't take her home. At the end of the hour the hand bell on the ward sister's desk rang out constantly and so did the child's sobs; she was inconsolable. Years later Lynn realised how her parents had suffered at the parting, but not now. She was too young to sense anything but loss.

As the weekly visiting routine progressed, Lynn began to separate one life from another. She no longer asked if she could go home; no longer looked into her parents' eyes as they left. Sadly the excitement of their weekly visits was dulled by the dread of their leaving. Part of her became detached from them to protect her from that pain. She learned to become resilient and grew from a needy child into a survivor.

During that period the ward became Lynn's world; the nurses her comfort, the children her friends and tormentors, while the doctors scared her till she was sick. She learned, however, to submit to the treatments and medical procedures, for to be a "good girl" would bring a little praise and that alone was enough reward for her. When the nurses told her if she were good she would go home sooner she believed them and did everything she could to seek approval. Lynn was adapting to hospital life.

Lynn built herself a castle in her head. The barricades were the tightly tucked corners of the bed linen. The perimeter was the rounded metal bed end and the sentry post was of course the hard pillow, guarded by the high bedhead. She had no army but she had a fortress which she could retreat to when life on the ward became too intimidating or children too prying or at times boisterous. When the visiting bell rang and no one came through the swing doors to see her, she would line up the few toys she had been allowed to borrow and pretend to play. She felt left out but knew that each empty visiting day would bring her parents closer, until on the first Saturday afternoon her mother pushed through the swing doors, closely followed by her father. Sadly then Lynn would begin the countdown of minutes before her parents' emotional departure.

It wasn't all bad. She learned to tie her own shoelaces; something her mother had been unable to teach her. Tubby, her favourite nurse, practised with the child and soon achieved success. The kind student nurse realised Lynn was left-handed like herself and taught her the way she tied her own. Proud to tell her mother of her achievement on the next visit, Lynn was dismayed to see that her mother was disappointed. Even at that early age, instead of feeling pleased with herself, she felt she had somehow let her mother down by responding to someone else.

Lynn began to make friends; to share and to play. She was only ever kept in bed if she felt ill or for the regular doctor's rounds. Generally the children were washed and dressed and not allowed on their beds until their afternoon rest.

After the evening visiting, the day staff went off duty to be replaced with limited night staff. Once they had listened to the report around the sister's large desk, a nurse would come round and pull down the big black roller blinds low over each of the long, draughty casement windows behind the children's beds, obscuring the limited view of other hospital blocks and the London pigeons now roosting on the window sills.

Lynn dreaded the nights; they were long and dark. The only light came through the circular windows of the ward doors and the lamp on the sister's desk. The little girl would slide down her bed on the covered rubber-protected draw sheet and spend many sleepless hours watching the duty nurse, her head bent over the paperwork, seriously intent on her writing. Occasionally she raised her head and looked around, or left her station to attend to a child or some other work that took her away from the big desk. From her vantage point she could see all the beds in the full Nightingale ward. To Lynn the darkness seemed heavy and foreboding. Sometimes there was a little cry or sigh but generally it was deathly quiet and this to a small child was quite intimidating; it caused Lynn her biggest anguish. She hated the dark and would do so for many years to come.

When the children were put to bed, Lynn fell asleep quickly, often with the exhaustion of sickness. She willed herself to fall asleep before the main lights were switched off and closed her eyes praying she would sleep till morning. She dreaded waking in the darkness feeling the familiar dampness and the fresh smell of urine on her night clothes. She would then have to face the humiliation of knowing she had wet the bed… again. It was an experience she dreaded. Worse than this experience was to wake up in the dark, dry but with a tummy ache that heralded the urgent need to "spend a penny". Little Lynn would lie there too terrified to call out and hear her own voice echo across the emptiness of the void between herself and the lamp-lit desk. Eventually, she would call out, but the likelihood of her whisper being heard was minimal and when the inevitable happened, she would lie there until her terrible sin was exposed. The light above her bed snapped on, flooding her face with its glare; the bed was changed briskly but without compassion. Nobody was cruel; nobody told her off beyond a minor scolding. Each night it happened the nurse would insist on Lynn telling her why she had not asked the nurse for a bedpan or called more loudly. The ashamed child couldn't tell them that she was too scared and frightened to break the stillness of the dark night with her cry. Now she suffered the ultimate embarrassment of discovery.

One morning, obviously after due professional consideration, one of the nurses called Lynn aside after breakfast and showed her a large terry towelling square. It reminded her of a nappy. She was aghast when the nurse took her into the bathroom and placed it round her waist, pulling it between her legs and pinning it with big safety pins. She was told it would have to stay on for the whole day and though she stood there dutifully until she was clothed she felt deeply ashamed and foolish. Although it was hidden under her clothes she could not hide the bulk of the improvised nappy and felt everybody would know that she wet the bed. She went back into the ward and knew that the other children were looking at her. Eventually one of them came up to her and asked her why she looked 'so different'. Lynn wouldn't say and played on her own by her bed that morning, deeply humiliated and tearful.

Lynn never wet the bed again, nor did she have to keep the nappy on longer than the morning. That night she called loudly for a bedpan, loud enough to avoid the embarrassment of ever having to wear the nappy again. She was still afraid of the dark, but was never again afraid of her own voice.

Chapter 10

The world in which Lynn found herself was alien to her. With no mother to hug or respond to she felt quite alone at first. The child failed to realise that she that wasn't the only one to feel that way. If she could have looked at the other children with adult eyes she would have seen their pain and fear; but children are resilient and Lynn was a child. She soon put the episode of bed-wetting behind her; if she forgot about the embarrassment she could pretend it never happened. With this attitude it wasn't long before the other children had forgotten as well. She never remembered being teased – though of course she made friends with some children more easily than with others.

There was no warmth or character in the décor of the ward. The monotony of the corridor's dark green tiles was broken only by the continuation to the ceiling of equally cold and unimaginative white or cream tiles. The demarcation between the two colours was a single black line some three-and-a-half feet above the polished linoleum floor. The corridor seemed to stretch for ever and Lynn thought of *Alice in Wonderland* every time she had to walk down it. It was like having to walk through the rabbit's tunnel; there seemed no escape. There was nothing homely about the hospital: this was an institution.

Gradually, however, Lynn began to enjoy certain aspects of ward life. Children who had been admitted long before her soon showed her the ropes and little tricks to make ward life more bearable. Every day the laundry man would come into the ward to deliver the large canvas bags of clean bed linen. Lynn had never met a black man before and at first was rather shy of him. But Mr Stanley had a lovely smile and white teeth and the children loved him. He knew many by name and they would plead with him to give them a lift down the corridor to escape the ward just for a little while. He would ask the ward sister, of course, and then turned to the kids as the Pied Piper would turn to the village children. He didn't have pan pipes to play but what tempted the children was much better than that; outside the swing ward doors was a large square trolley, a bit like a children's playpen on castors.

Mr Stanley would tell the children he had room only for five and little hands would go up in the air, children's voices pleading to be chosen as one of the lucky few. One day Lynn hung back till last and watched the smaller children being lifted over the high cot-like sides. One girl giggled and Lynn decided she wanted to join in the fun. Mr Stanley was a kindly man and hoisted Lynn up in the air and into the trolley. The bigger boys climbed the rails themselves and eventually Mr Stanley had to call a halt. 'That's enough now; no more, I won't be able to push.'

Lynn liked the way he talked, his tone was soft and like music. She didn't recognise it as an Afro-Caribbean accent, but she liked him. He was like no one else she had ever met.

The laundryman leaned heavily on the side of the trolley and pushed with all his might until it gained momentum and began to roll down the corridor. The children laughed and begged him to take them further. They wanted him to take them outside but Mr Stanley knew the limits of his authority. Eventually he stopped, and pretended to puff.

'No further children; Sister will give me the sack. Face the other way, and I will push you back to the ward.'

There was a cry of mutual disappointment but they did as they were told and it wasn't many minutes before they were deposited back at the ward doors. Lynn was helped out with the other girls and stood looking at the round windows in the green ward doors. She had looked from the other side so long that she found it strange to see them from the corridor; she didn't want to go back into the ward.

'Thank you,' she said quietly to the man who smiled in approval at her manners.

One of the bigger boys pushed the doors open and the smell of antiseptic and disinfectant struck Lynn's senses and pulled her back to hospital reality. It would soon be dinner time.

Once Lynn had settled down and made an effort to reach out to some of the other children she found her life less lonely. She watched the children play together and began to join in. Some were rough, especially the boys from the Whitechapel area, and some of the girls stayed in little groups. When Lynn sat up in bed she found her eyes were drawn to an older girl in the bed opposite hers. She was mesmerised by the girl's hands but it took Lynn a little while to realise the child was handicapped. Her fingers were longer than they should have been and the shape of her head was unlike her own. Her name was Pauline and she had a lovely smile which warmed Lynn's heart. She wanted the older girl to be her friend and looked forward to the morning when she could pluck up the courage and talk to her. Lynn thought she would wait for breakfast time when they all sat at the long table in the middle of the ward.

That morning, one of the nurses went to Pauline's bed and asked if she would like to join them at the table. The young girl would usually shake her head when the nurse encouraged her to get up, preferring to eat breakfast in her bed, but this day she was feeling better and made an effort.

The nurse left her bedside and fetched a wheelchair. She gently covered her patient with a blanket, tucking it round her waist; Pauline was then lifted into the chair. Lynn watched curiously but it wasn't until the blanket slipped a little and uncovered Pauline's legs that she realised the child didn't have any. It seemed that both Pauline's legs had been amputated. Lynn was both fascinated and shocked and slightly nervous when she was asked to come to the table and sit next to the older girl.

They were destined to be friends. Pauline showed no embarrassment and Lynn warmed to her immediately. Pauline allowed no one to feel sorry for her, but liked Lynn for her gentleness. Once they got to know each other a little more Lynn didn't notice her friend's disability and for the most part neither did the other children. Some of the other visiting parents felt differently and were unable to come to terms with their child playing with a "spastic". Even at that early age Lynn wondered how adults could be so heartless, but she realised not every mother was like her own.

Pauline was made of strong stuff and had quite a high position in the ranks of the children. Not only was she well liked but she also had the added advantage that she had the use of the wheelchair. For some youngsters it was worth appealing to Pauline's good nature. Although there were games for the fitter children to play and a certain amount of mischief they could get away with, the youngsters soon realised that if they played their cards right Pauline might allow them to ride in her wheelchair if she wasn't using it. Ten minutes of fun, wheeling round the ward in turn, laughing and skidding, marking the heavy-duty linoleum with rubber emergency stops, was a highlight for any child and Lynn was no exception. The game, however, would soon be brought to an official halt when the speed got too fast and the laughter too shrill.

Tubby, or one of the other crisp-uniformed nurses, would confiscate the wheelchair, returning it to Pauline's bedside. The guilty children were duly chastised.

Twice a week a duty nurse would come to Pauline's bed with a blanket and a clipboard. She would be helped out of bed and into the wheelchair. The nurse and porter then escorted her from the ward. Lynn didn't know where her friend was being taken to but by the look on her lovely thin face, she was aware that it was to somewhere Pauline didn't want to go. All the children would call to her and wish her well but they didn't know where that awful, unmentioned place could be, or why she always came back to the ward exhausted and crying an hour or so later.

The children tried to be well behaved and quiet on Pauline's return, as instructed by the nurse in charge. Once Pauline felt better, they made a bit of a fuss over her and went back to their old ways.

Looking back on those days Lynn realised that although she had met many children she didn't have a lasting memory of many of their names. Pauline was one child who had left a marked impression on her. She remembered the friendship and the physical curiosity she felt when patting Pauline's stumps as an act of acceptance, comfort and concern.

Two or three years later when Lynn's life had returned to relative normal family life she was to be reminded of her hospital friend in a most amazing way. Her mother came in to her bedroom and told her daughter that she had just seen Pauline on television. She had been watching *This is Your Life*, a programme hosted by Eamonn Andrews in which he related famous people's lives by turning the pages of a big red book.

That evening, at the end of the show, Pauline walked on to the stage in a pretty, fairly long dress and presented Douglas Bader, the Second World War flying ace, with a bouquet. She had been one of the many amputees he had helped and encouraged to walk with the aid of artificial legs, as he had had to do himself. At last the mystery of where Pauline went when leaving the ward of The London Hospital twice weekly was solved. Douglas Bader had helped the little patient to walk again with all the courage and determination it took to use her new legs. Lynn always knew she was special.

Lynn was bitterly disappointed at not seeing her friend walk across the stage in front of a television audience. She harboured regret that her mother had not called her downstairs, even though she was suffering from flu at the time. So many years later she suddenly felt cross with her mother. Was Lynn being unreasonable? She thought perhaps she was. She put the thought out of her head again and returned to the memories of being a patient in The London Hospital.

Lynn didn't often go beyond those ward doors, except when as a treat she was chosen to take a ride in Mr Stanley's trolley or when she was taken to the operating theatre for exploratory investigations. She was fearful when, after waking early, she found the night nurse reaching over her bed, pinning a typed notice upon her headboard: NIL BY MOUTH. Even as a child she dreaded such times and they were more than a few. She wouldn't be able to have breakfast with her friends, but, worse than that, she would have to do everything the doctors told her and go to sleep like a good girl. As the time got nearer she was put into an operation gown and told to stay in bed. The only thing Lynn looked forward to was the fact that she would see her mother on such days and be given her golliwog to hold while she was wheeled to theatre on a tall hospital trolley. She would have to lie flat on her back and keep still, but as she was wheeled along the corridor, she kept her eyes open, focusing them on the ceiling, counting the strip lights as she passed underneath them. She could hear her mother talking as she tried to keep up with the porter's pace and then, when the trolley stopped outside the terrible theatre doors, she would hug her daughter reassuringly before taking away the golliwog so that he wouldn't get lost. Lynn would be alone again with the doctors and nurses. She had mixed emotions about seeing her mother during the week, for it always meant a trip to surgery.

Lynn awoke back in her hospital bed. She looked beneath the sheet but she found she didn't have a scar or bandage and in her small childlike brain she was disappointed. She would not have anything to brag to the other children about and didn't really understand what had happened to her. Her mother never told her but as she grew up she realised that doctors could look inside your body without making a cut. They could investigate when you were given something to make you sleep. Much later she realised that her weeks in The London Hospital had eventually cured the problem and her kidneys were made better. It wasn't until she was an adult that she found out what had been wrong with her, but even then her mother was vague about the details. She wondered if her parents were ever told the full diagnosis.

Lynn found it was hard to understand she was ill. Lynn was just Lynn, just as her new friends were who they were. Everything that happened to her just happened, she didn't know why. She knew she had trouble with her tummy and sometimes couldn't spend a penny and had tummy ache, but didn't everyone? Obviously she was different, but here at least the children around her thought she was the same as them. They cried and laughed together; children are children after all!

Time went on; the daily routine continued and life revolved around the big clock on the wall above the doors, hours, days, weeks and visiting, until it seemed as though Lynn lived there.

Eventually she was told she would be leaving hospital after six weeks on the ward, but she remembered the disappointment when her mother told her she wasn't coming home. Lynn was to go to the seaside, but not with the family. She was being sent to a convalescent home on the east coast of England; a place called Felixstowe where she could get well and strong with other children from The London Hospital. Lynn would be away for another two weeks, but then, her mother promised, she would come home. Lynn was cautious. She looked into her mother's eyes; they were warm and steady; her daughter so wanted to believe her.

Pauline had already gone home by the time Lynn left the hospital. She said goodbye to Tubby and the other friends she had made and was given her suitcase and got dressed. It felt very strange. Lynn couldn't recall her mother being there and felt very alone.

She travelled in an ambulance with other children and hated the motion of the vehicle. Lynn was sick; some things never change. The child was also frightened, for it seemed she was going further and further from the family she loved. She wore a new duffel coat that her parents had given her on their last visit. It felt heavy and stiff and was too big for her. She wore outdoor shoes on previously slipper-shod feet; they rubbed against her ankles in cruel friction. She felt totally alien in her outdoor clothes and was ill prepared for the next adventure in her young life. Her parents promised to see her at Easter, when she would also see her brother again after such a long time apart.

Chapter 11

Lynn's first recollection of the convalescent home was that it was so alien to her that she wanted to run away immediately. It was just like any other hospital; it certainly wasn't a home as she knew a home to be. Having become used to The London Hospital ward and routine, she was once again suddenly alone and without friends, having stepped into another world in which she didn't belong. Lynn tried to stop the tears, realising by experience that to cry meant that she would be marked as a "cry baby" and be scolded for it. Crying got you nowhere, she had learned that much. When she had gone to The London Hospital her parents had come with her, but here she was just one of a little group of poorly, nervous children, fresh from the hospital wards having travelled by ambulance. Lynn straightened up; at least this time she was more prepared for promises to be broken and although she had been told she would see her parents at the weekend, and also her brother, she could gain little comfort from mere words. Lynn would have to see if it came true.

It was lunchtime when they arrived and the new children were taken to the dining room where the others were already seated. It was a big room, like a cafeteria, and they were told to sit down and eat their meal. There were rules here to be obeyed and Lynn sat up straight while the meal was placed in front of her. When she was well Lynn was not a fussy eater, but some foods disagreed with her. The covered dish was placed before her and Lynn's heart sunk as the tin lid was lifted. She almost heaved at the smell of it. Good nutrition was a high priority in the convalescent home but Lynn looked down at her plate in horror and disappointment. Placed under a layer of thick gravy was a slab of cooked pig's liver, the smell of which seemed to fill the whole dining room.

'Eat it all up,' said the assistant as she removed the lid fully and made her way back to the kitchen with her tray.

Lynn looked from left to right at the other children who had already started eating. Some were almost devouring their food while others played around a bit with the accompanying sprouts and mashed potatoes. Lynn decided to do the same and picked up her fork, spearing a sprout to mash in the gravy. She soon found the gravy tasted of liver and had to stop. For the next fifteen minutes Lynn made a brave effort but when she put her knife and fork together and looked at the other children's plates she realised she was the only one on her table who had not finished her meal. She sat and waited.

Eventually the kitchen assistant came to collect the empty plates and stopped behind Lynn's chair. 'What's this, child? You have to eat all your meal or you won't get pudding; it's rice pudding today and it's home-made.' She thought it would tempt Lynn but she hung her head.

The woman left the plate in front of her and went to fetch the nurse. She, in turn, stood behind Lynn and was not so gentle with her. Lynn was made to feel naughty and disobedient. She was told by the nurse in no uncertain terms that she would have to stay with her meal in front of her until she had eaten it. Her plate was not taken with the other empty ones. The gravy went cold and congealed, sticking to the offending meat. Lynn did not pick up her knife and fork and wrung her hands under the table, trying to hold back the tears. The rice pudding was delivered on trays to all the other children, but there was none for Lynn. The girl sitting next to her tried to encourage her but was told off for talking while eating and so she stopped, giving Lynn a lop-sided smile in a show of support. It was the first act of friendship Lynn had experienced. 'I'm Georgie,' the older girl whispered, 'I can't eat swede.' The other children ate their rice pudding while Lynn steadfastly tried another forkful of liver. She choked and placed her fork back on the plate.

Someone somewhere clapped their hands. 'You may leave the table, children,' a voice of authority boomed across the room. The children – there must have been forty of varying ages – were dismissed. They scraped their chairs back and left the hall in silence.

Lynn got up with the children at her table but was told by the nurse who was on the other side of the room to sit down again and finish her meal. Lynn sat but did not eat. When the room was empty Lynn could hear the staff busy in the kitchen. The nurse loitered a while and then joined them in their chatter. The child grew smaller and the passing minutes seemed like hours. Her head dropped low and her tears fell on to the plate of congealed food. She bit her lip. The room sounded hollow and empty. Gradually the noise subsided in the kitchen and the nurse came over to her charge, standing disapprovingly behind her chair. Lynn had rarely been told off at school but expected the nurse to be angry with her now. By not eating her liver she would be marked as a disobedient child. To Lynn's surprise the nurse said nothing, as if having to sit in front of her cold dinner for half an hour was punishment enough.

'You may leave. The nurse in the corridor will show you where to go.' It was a hollow victory as Lynn was both upset and hungry. She had started her convalescent stay badly and didn't think things could get any worse.

The dormitory where the second nurse took her was very like the hospital but brighter and, apart from the obligatory rest after lunch, the children were given more freedom. Lynn climbed on to her allotted bed, curling up on her side, trying to comfort herself. She looked straight at the girl in the bed next to hers. She opened her eyes and smiled at Lynn who felt her friendship for a second time that day. It was the girl named Georgie.

The dormitory took boys and girls of a wide age range and Lynn felt lucky to be given a bed next to the older girl. She had short black curly hair and must have been about ten. She had a nice smile; which reached her eyes. They liked each other straightaway. Georgie felt that the younger girl, pale and skinny and probably frightened, would need a friend. She realised the child did not come from London or the East End and would not be strong enough to fight the childhood battles that would come. Lynn in turn looked on Georgie as her guardian angel and worshipped her. Nobody ever teased or argued with Georgie and once Lynn had been taken under her wing the younger child felt safe.

The children were given a routine of exercise and nourishment and it was a regime that was strictly adhered to. After breakfast they were given their daily teaspoon of cod liver oil which they had to line up for, followed by a sweet. Later the children would be escorted for a brisk walk. They were walked three miles in the morning and two in the afternoon, although it seemed much further to the majority of the children. As Lynn was one of the newest members of the dormitory she was put in the pushchair that first morning. She hated it but it was very doubtful that she could have walked the full distance, as she had just left hospital. The pushchair was a big metal and Rexene model, with large wheels and a handle big enough for two to push. It was cream and ugly but not uncomfortable. That first day Lynn sat in it and was covered with a woollen blanket. It was March, and very cold, but she didn't like being treated differently from the other children. The nurse told her it was a treat to be pushed and that she should consider herself lucky. Soon she would have to walk like the other children. Lynn didn't know why she should be treated to the privilege and couldn't wait to be treated the same as the other children.

The coastal town of Felixstowe was open to the winter gales and cold winds. Lynn needed her duffel coat but the wind still got up the big sleeves and under her hood. The children were all dressed like little parcelled street urchins against the cold and it wasn't long before Lynn was shivering in the pushchair. She thought it would be better if she could walk and move around a bit. Still, her time would come and some other poor, new recruit would have the use of the chair. She hadn't felt fresh air for six weeks and overheard the nurse who was escorting them say to another, 'It will be kill or cure for this one.'

Each day the little Pied Piper column of children went out for their walk. After lunch and their rest they were dressed in their coats again and sent out, in showers or sunshine, for the afternoon. After a couple of walks Lynn was allowed out of the pushchair although she stayed close to the nurse, whom she rather liked. She was allowed to walk some of the way. She started to get her appetite back and was always hungry by teatime, eating her sandwiches as fast as the others.

Bath time was an experience Lynn dreaded and if it were not for Georgie she thought she would have died of humiliation even at that age. She had come from a family who believed intently on privacy and modesty. Bathroom doors stayed firmly closed and the only time the children undressed in front of each other was on the beach. She knew nothing about little boys, and her brother was respectful and painfully shy about his own body. Her mother was not allowed to be seen in her petticoat and if her children undressed in the fire-warmed lounge it would be behind the chair away from their father.

The experience at the convalescent home was quite foreign to Lynn. The boys here had been brought up very differently. Most of them were rough and ready, some born in the Whitechapel area of London just after the war. They were survivors before they came to the home. Lynn had to learn their ways. She was told that on bath night the children should take off their day clothes and underwear and put on their dressing gowns. This was done in the toilets and then they came back to the dormitory, boys and girls alike. The children were then allowed to play unsupervised while the nurses took each child in turn and bathed them in the big tiled bathroom. They would call out the names and the youngsters would queue till the child in front was dry and in pajamas.

There was nothing harmful in their play but the boys were boisterous and mostly bigger. They had energy to burn and played chase with the girls. Lynn ran like the others but was not quick enough and didn't realise it was a game the boys played every bath night. Lynn wasn't caught for she could dip and dive but one night a boy caught the hem of her red Ladybird dressing gown and lifted it as he passed. Lynn died of shame, right there and then, and ran back to her bed. Georgie had seen the tears in the other child's eyes and called her over. She told Lynn to stay near her and from then on little Lynn waited for her bath by Georgie's bed and did not play with the others.

As young and humiliated as she was, Lynn did have the last laugh on the boy who was on his voyage of discovery. After their baths he sheepishly came over to her and handed her a piece of paper. On it was a very rough pencil sketch and the words underneath read, *"Do little girls look like this?"* Lynn went bright red and wanted the floor to swallow her up.

He had seen more than he should have, but instead of tearing it up and running to Georgie, Lynn stared him in the face, as he stood embarrassed, and defiantly said, 'No!' What surprised her was that instead of calling her a liar, which incidentally she was, his mouth dropped open and he went away with a puzzled look on his face. Lynn thought that was the turning point of her experience at the home and it must have put his sex education back some years. It dawned on her that she had to become like the others to survive and so that was what Lynn was going to do.

CHAPTER 12

Easter celebrations took place while Lynn was at the convalescent home. Most of the children were given eggs by their families, though in hindsight Lynn realised that there would have been some who weren't so lucky. The children looked with joy and excitement at their eggs but soon were bitterly disappointed when they were confiscated and broken up in front of everyone and put into the big sweet tin. This tin was only opened after the children had taken their daily teaspoon of cod liver oil. Each mouthful swallowed was rewarded by a florin-sized piece of chocolate egg. Lynn didn't want to share her egg but was more upset to see the eggs smashed into small pieces. How ever would she know which egg she was eating?

Lynn knew her parents were coming to see her at Easter, but she wasn't allowed to wait for them to arrive. She was taken out with the others on their usual morning walk. By now she was walking fairly well and one week after leaving hospital was able to walk in the morning and ride in the pushchair some afternoons.

One blustery March day as the little caravan of kids turned the corner on their way home she saw her parents for the first time in a week. She wanted to let go of the handle of the pushchair she had been holding on to and run to them, but, of course, that would have been frowned upon. Her parents waited until Lynn and the crocodile of youngsters reached them. They hugged their daughter closely to them, but Lynn felt awkward in front of her new playmates.

Lynn's mother wore her beaver lamb coat, her father his trilby. By his side walked her brother; he wore his school cap. Lynn hadn't seen him for seven weeks and they felt like strangers. She hadn't realised till later that on nearly every hospital visit he would travel to The London Hospital with their parents and wait patiently outside in what now was her parents' first car – a Morris Minor. He told Lynn many years later that he had forgotten he had a sister, but she didn't believe him.

For Lynn it was wonderful and yet somehow distressing to see her parents and her brother outside the convalescent home. She had been affected by so many changes in her young world that it was as if she were seeing them for the first time. She wanted to accept the hugs they gave her but deep down she felt somehow let down by being left at the institution in the first place. She was slowly coming to terms with the world in which she now found herself and was unsure if she could go back to the world to which she had once belonged. Her mother's hugs were all enveloping and familiar but Lynn held back a little, knowing with childlike perception that at the end of the Easter weekend her parents would leave her again and she would have to hold back the tears and battle with the disappointment all over again.

She was thrilled to see her brother, though he looked strangely uncomfortable, dressed in his school raincoat and cap while her new friends were wearing a ragamuffin assortment of clothes that had gone through the convalescent home's wash and ringer without care. She wanted to throw her arms around her brother in front of everyone and claim him as her own, but he would have been embarrassed; her heart went out to him and she hoped he felt the same, though he never showed his feelings.

Walking back to the convalescent home Lynn held her mother's hand, while Joyce asked her daughter if she was happy and whether she was getting better and making friends. Lynn wanted to tell her everything but she looked at the love and pain in her eyes and knew then that she would never be able to tell her mother the scary things that frightened her and the times she cried in her loneliness. Even at an early age Lynn was perceptive and knew that she would only be able to tell her mother the funny things that had happened to her. She understood even then that her mother loved her almost too well, and that any pain her daughter felt transferred to her own pain. As Lynn grew up she gradually felt more responsible for her mother's happiness and the edges of loyalty and love became blurred; she would do anything to see her mother smile.

On Easter Saturday afternoon Lynn was excused from the constitutional walk and allowed to go out with her family. Easter was early that year and the afternoon was cold and grey. Her father asked what she would like to do as a special treat and Lynn told them she would like to go to the boating lake. She had passed it on one of the walks and liked the little paddle boats tied up at the side of the pond by the boatman's shed. The wind was chilly and he didn't think it a good choice but when they arrived at the lake Lynn found she wasn't the only one with such an intention. Georgie was by the water's edge with her own parents and Lynn was proud to introduce her new best friend to her mum and dad. She had already told them about her and how she had helped Lynn settle in to dormitory life. The adults chatted while the three children put their fingers in the cold water and splashed a little. Lynn would have liked Georgie to stay but eventually the adults finished their conversation and Georgie was ushered by her father away from the water's edge. When they had waved farewell, Lynn's father said he had thought Georgie was a boy because of her nickname and her short hair. Lynn didn't understand; to her Georgie was Georgie. She was very sad when after the Easter weekend she found that her best friend was well enough to go home and to go back to school at the beginning of the new term; she would miss Georgie a lot.

Brother and sister stood by the side of the pond, looking across to the small paddling boats that bobbed up and down against the stiff breeze. The colourful boats were tethered – like horses, Lynn thought – along the concrete lakeside outside the boating shed. On one shed wall hung a notice advertising the cost of hiring a boat for fifteen minutes or half an hour. Lynn looked along the line and saw one named *Golly*. It was bright yellow and though it was metal and had paddle wheels, it would seat two who could paddle together if they wanted to. Lynn looked eagerly at the boats and her father asked if she would like to ride in one; today was going to be a real treat for her. She nodded her head enthusiastically and looked kindly at her brother. Bill scowled; he knew that if his sister wanted a boat ride then he would have to get in the boat with her. It was too small for grown-ups; he would have to be the one to paddle; he knew his sister wasn't strong enough.

Their father took Bill to one side, telling him to look after his sister. Then, directing his comment to both of them, he said that if they took the boat ride they would have to stay out on the water for the full length of time; he was not going to waste good money. Bill agreed, jamming his cap on his head and tightening his raincoat belt. Lynn could only think of getting into the little *Golly* and being on the water. The man pulled the paddle boat alongside and Bill was given a hand to climb aboard. Once seated, he took the crooked metal bar in both hands. He would have to keep turning it to make the boat move. Then their father lifted Lynn and placed her facing her brother on the cold metal seat. The boat immediately rocked; Lynn wasn't expecting that to happen, and she held the sides of the boat until the man pushed it away from the edge with his boat hook. Their parents waved them off and very soon, with a great effort by her brother, the little boat made its way to the centre of the pond. The cold wind caught it, splashing icy water over the prow and on to their legs. Lynn thought it not so enjoyable now that she was away from the safety of the shore; her parents looked quite small and she felt even smaller. Her brother was working hard to stop the wind pushing the boat the wrong way and she thought he didn't look very happy.

Eventually the far side of the lake looked closer to them than the side they had come from and Lynn gained courage. She felt a little sick, but said nothing to Bill, who was rowing too painfully to inspire any confidence; he had to do all the work himself. Several people were watching the children on the pond and Bill thought he would row closer to the far shore before returning his sister safely to their parents. The wind caught *Golly* again when they were within a few feet of the edge; the boat jarred against the concrete and floated away again. Bill was resting his tired arms and didn't see what his silly sister was about to do. Lynn had had enough; all she wanted was to have her feet on dry land. She stood up in the rocking boat, intent on wanting to get out, and all she could hear was her brother shouting at her! The boat scraped the side again and the child took her chance. She turned sideways, reaching out her arms, her fingers spread to grab the concrete edging. After that she had the idea that she could just step ashore but she had no experience of boats of any sort and the next moment she realised the little boat, paddled frantically by her alarmed brother, was drifting away from the shore. Bill was screaming, she was screaming, and, no doubt, far away by the boat house on the other side her mother would be screaming too! Lynn felt her arms stretch to their full span and yet she could not gain purchase on the flat edge of the pond. Her bare legs were aching and strained but she could not move them from the boat, nor could she jump. Her body was like a bridge and her brother was trying desperately to bring the *Golly* closer while she was inadvertently pushing it away. Just as she thought she was going to fall into the cold water she felt two hands grab her under the arms and lift her out of the boat, high above the water, and set her safely down on to the pathway and dry land. The stranger seemed big and strong, but she only remembered his big overcoat and strong arms; he seemed fatherly.

Within seconds Lynn's mother was by her side comforting her and warming her with a big beaver lamb hug and thanking the man who had seen what was about to happen. It was possible that the child could have drowned, but it would have been more likely that she would have just received a thorough soaking, one that her brother thought she possibly deserved.

Lynn looked down at her discouraged and shocked brother, now bobbing up and down in the little paddle boat that had already started to drift as he had stopped paddling. Their father called out to his son, encouraging him, but also commanding him to continue his paddle for the final five minutes left of the hire charge. Lynn saw him glumly turn the boat around and paddle soulfully back to the choppy water in the middle of the lake. There he waited until the man in charge picked up his megaphone and called out for *Golly* to return to the shore as the hirer's time was up!

Lynn couldn't look at her brother when he came ashore and he said very little to her. She deeply regretted being so impulsive and rocking the boat and knew Bill had tried hard to save them from the danger she had put them in.

In later life, Lynn often looked back and wondered what her brother thought of her when she was a sickly child. She knew he loved her and she certainly loved him, but she wondered how much of his childhood had to revolve around her and how, if at all, he regretted it. The day on the boating lake would often come back to haunt her dreams, but did it come back to haunt his also? She hoped to find out one day.

Chapter 13

The regime of long walks in very fresh air, good basic food and rest and, of course, the cod liver oil began to have a good effect on Lynn. By the end of the first week the child rarely sat in the pushchair and she was confident enough to hate having to walk alongside it unless her favourite nurse was on duty. She would join the crocodile of noisy children who walked along the pavements, trekking down streets and along to the shore. The beach at Felixstowe wasn't sandy, as Lynn had expected it to be. It wasn't like any of the white sandy beaches on Jersey, where Lynn, with her family, spent two weeks of their summer holiday every year visiting her mum's folk. Lynn wouldn't have been able to build sandcastles with her cousins here. Felixstowe beach was stony and grey, just right for boys' games. Now her parents were visiting for Easter, Lynn showed them and her brother where the children played and walked down on to the stones to stand by the sea. It was so noisy. The waves crashed upon the beach in white froth and bubbles and then sucked in retreat, drawing the pebbles back into the water. If she stood too close to the shoreline she could feel the stones move beneath her feet and make her stumble into the surf. It was too cold to take her shoes off to paddle and Lynn was relieved that she had been forbidden to do so for she was rather nervous of the surging waves.

Her brother and father stood near the edge of the tide that particular day and skimmed flat pebbles across the surface of the water. One, two, three; Bill's pebble hopped like a frog and sunk with a plop. Dad went next; one, two, three four, plop! Lynn's brother had another go and beat his father; shouting with joy.

There was no prize but the look on her brother's face was reward enough. His sister had a go but she didn't hold the stone correctly and took three attempts to make it bounce once. Mum laughed. The family hadn't heard her laugh for a long while; she skimmed better than the others.

Once Lynn had learned how to skim the pebbles with her family she would practise when she was down on the beach with the other children during their walks. As she grew more confident she was able to show them how to skim. Lynn had an advantage at last for some of the children had never seen the sea before. They asked her how to make the pebbles bounce over the water and the boys thought it a great game. Her playmates began to look up to Lynn because of her newly acquired skill and she became a valued member of the gang. This was a great feeling, as she was fed up being a mere girl; she wanted to be as strong as her brother. Gradually the dark days of The London Hospital faded; she was no longer fearful of bad dreams or bed wetting. She slept soundly at night, exhausted after the fresh air, and was beginning to enjoy new friendships and the rivalry between the boys and girls. Lynn was getting better.

During their free playtime the children would be allowed to go into the long glass-windowed conservatory room, situated at the end of the ward. There they could play their games; the girls had a dolls' house and the boys a rocking horse. There were wooden building bricks, dolls and all sorts of jigsaws and board games. The children had not been allowed to bring toys from home and Lynn still missed her knitted golliwog, especially to go to bed with. However, it was explained to the parents that something treasured could go missing and then there would be even more to cry about.

One wet morning the unsupervised games got more boisterous than usual. One of the boys decided that the kids should play battles! The boys and girls split into teams; the girls sheltered behind the dolls' house and the boys took the rocking horse to the other side of the room and used it to crouch behind. The children had played this game many times before and the aim was to chuck the building bricks at each other when the nurses were too busy elsewhere. It was great fun for the winning side, but the boys threw harder and longer, usually hitting the wall behind the girls and catching them on their heads and backs as the bricks dropped down. It was quite frightening and it was a wonder no one really got hurt. The game was always stopped by the staff when they realised what the kids were up to.

The first day Lynn played this game she didn't know what to expect but she was becoming a fast learner. This day she got wise for she now liked playing the boys' game for one reason alone, they always won. This was defined by how many hits were made, though they soon lost count as the excitement rose. As the bricks started to fly Lynn decided to change sides and ran across the room ducking behind the boys' rocking horse. She picked up a fallen brick as she did so and threw it back towards the girls' corner, hoping it wouldn't actually hit one of them. The boys gave her a cheer and she got a good few shots in before she heard her mother's voice and that of the staff nurse. The game came to an abrupt halt. Lynn saw her mother before she was seen. Joyce searched the girls' faces behind the dolls' house, looking for her delicate daughter.

'Hello, Mum,' said Lynn, standing clear of the boys and dropping a wooden brick from her left hand. Perhaps this was when they both realised that Lynn was a fighter and, thanks to the tricks her brother had taught her at an early age, she could now hold her own amongst children stronger than herself.

The conservatory emptied of children and Lynn was allowed out with her family one last time before they travelled back to Dunstable. Easter had ended and the visit was over. All the old fears and disappointments flooded back and Lynn's confidence diminished. All she wanted was a cuddle and reassurance that she would soon be home, but the child had another five days before any decision could even be considered. On the last day her mother had the unenviable task of telling her daughter that when she left the Felixstowe convalescent home she would have to go back to The London Hospital. There Lynn would be assessed to see if she needed further treatment. Her mother tried to reassure her that everything would be fine and that she would be home as soon as the doctor had examined her, but Lynn was scared of doctors. She looked into her mother's eyes and saw the pain. The little girl said nothing and wiped her own tears and hugged them all goodbye again.

Once Lynn's family left Felixstowe at the end of the Easter break, amid tears and regret she resumed the routine of institutional life. She wasn't the only child who missed her parents and they played together for emotional support, resuming their gangs and the friendships formed along the way. Lynn didn't realise at the time that she was lucky to have loving parents to miss. Some children were not so fortunate.

Georgie went home with her parents during Easter for she had spent her two weeks convalescing. She would be missed terribly but Lynn was more confident now and her health was returning slowly. Bath time didn't terrorise her and long walks didn't tire her, but she still couldn't eat liver. She knew the convalescent home's routine and tried to help some of the new kids settle in, when they first arrived in the big cream ambulance that disgorged them at the front doors. She remembered what it was like to be afraid and lonely, but she couldn't reach out to them and console them properly; only their parents could do that. Lynn was again missing her own family too badly to be much more than sympathetic. She still held a loathing for the big metal pushchair and looked at the poor child tucked up in it for the first time, recognising their sense of abandonment. She couldn't save them from that experience.

Eventually Lynn's time came to leave Felixstowe. She had already been told that she wouldn't be going straight home and so the thrill of leaving was overshadowed by the fact that she was going back to hospital. It was now eight weeks since she had seen home, and she didn't even know which direction Dunstable was. She was told to pack her case under a nurse's supervision and took the cards she had been sent from the locker drawer. When the time came to leave she said goodbye to her new friends. She felt strangely distant from them as children do when they are ready to move on. She didn't look back; nor did she ever visit Felixstowe again.

Lynn didn't remember the journey back into London, nor the arrival at The London Hospital in Whitechapel, nor the admission to the ward. She remembered overhearing a conversation between the nurse and the ward clerk. Apparently, there were no more children's beds available; the transferred admission would have to be put in a cot. Lynn suddenly felt very small and vulnerable.

She was given hospital pajamas and had to undress though it wasn't bedtime. All the old fear came back to her; it was as if she had never left. Would she ever go home? She did not voice her thought, fearing the imagined truth. She was a long way from home and loving parents.

That night Lynn slept, firstly, with her knees drawn up inside the metal bars of the cot and then, when she was no longer frightened of the dark, she uncurled and tried to sleep with her feet through the bars. As a growing child, she didn't like that very much, for she thought someone might come and grab her feet. She didn't sleep but kept her eyes tightly shut. She dared not think of home, for it was like trying to catch a bubble; bubbles always burst. She had been told the doctor would come the next day and he would decide if she could go home. She didn't know what she feared most, the doctor's visit or Mummy and Daddy not coming to fetch her.

The next morning brought the usual hospital routine. Lynn was relieved to get out of the cot and have breakfast at the big table, but she didn't know any of the children and they looked at her as a strange kid who slept in a cot!

During the morning one of the nurses confirmed that a doctor would examine her that afternoon, and if he was pleased with her, she would be allowed to go home. Lynn didn't think she had done anything wrong; why would he not be pleased with her? She was told that after lunch she would have to rest in a side room until the doctor had seen her. She thought she was being put in a special room because they might do things to her like they used to. She couldn't understand that it was because she didn't have a full-sized bed of her own in the ward. The tears started to come right up from her heart. She was so scared of doctors and had had very little to do with them at the convalescent home, that she barely nodded to the nurse. When she came to fetch the child after lunch, Lynn wanted to run away. She was taken to a side ward and her suitcase was put by the side of the bed. Lynn was then told that she must sleep or the doctor wouldn't come and she wouldn't be able to go home. She climbed on the bed and lay under the blanket. Lynn could see a clock on the wall; it was two o'clock. The nurse left her, closing the door only partially.

Lynn shut her eyes but couldn't sleep. She opened them again; three o'clock; ten past three. She fell into a light sleep; four o'clock. She couldn't sleep any more and tossed and turned; had she been good? Had the doctor called without waking her? She didn't want to be examined; she just wanted to go home. At half past four the nurse came in, but the doctor didn't come in with her. The nervous child looked past her, but the uniformed sister was on her own. She was smiling, even her silver buckle was shining; she stood by the child's bed.

'The doctor says you can go home.'

Lynn didn't know how she felt. She looked into the sister's eyes and saw that she meant what she said; she could always tell by the eyes. She was told her mummy and daddy were coming at five o'clock to take her home and they were bringing clean clothes and shoes. The sister left her young patient, who, she thought, had grown up so much since her admission eight weeks previously. It was on occasions like these that the ward sister felt her career was worthwhile. This was a happy ending to a child's traumatic experience and also the reward of a well-chosen career.

The child stared at the clock on the wall and watched the big hand and the little hand slowly turn. She could only see them move when one or the other covered the numbers. Five o'clock came and went. Lynn was frozen in space and time.

At five-fifteen the doors opened wide and Lynn's mother came in. She wasn't wearing her fur coat and her child could wrap her arms around her and feel her warmth. Joyce helped her daughter take off the hospital pajamas and this time Lynn held her shoulder as she knelt so that she could step into her underwear. Once dressed, she sat on a chair while her mother put new lace-up shoes on the child's feet. Lynn hopped down and stood in front of her, allowing her mother to tie the laces, knowing she was perfectly able to do so herself. It was a simple act of motherly love and was one Lynn accepted readily. The shoes were heavy, her legs were thin.

Lynn didn't remember saying goodbye or leaving the ward and she never did find out if the doctor came to see her; she only knew that she could go home to her family. She held her mother's hand as if she would never let it go and when she saw her father waiting in the corridor he hugged her tightly. He smelt of "Daddy" – something nice and something smoky – and she buried her face in his neck as he stooped to hold her. She knew by that hug that he did love her as much as he did her brother.

The new green Morris Minor was waiting in the hospital car park and Bill was sitting in the back seat, allowing plenty of room for his sister to sit next to him. This was much better than the motorbike and sidecar, although she wasn't sure if she liked the smell of the new leather seats. She was experiencing everything as if it were for the first time and as they drove out of the hospital grounds and away from London, Lynn hoped that life would never be quite the same again.

Chapter 14

Lynn continued listening to the gentle rain, remembering her childhood days, trying with some success to analyse the child within her. She didn't need to do this, it wasn't a therapy exercise, but, long after her original dream had disintegrated, she was left with a compassion for a child she had left behind in her faded memory such a long time ago. She was unrecognisable as the adult who stared back at her from the bedroom mirror. Lynn wanted to pull closer to the child. Although now a stranger to her, she felt an empathy with the little girl. She wanted to stand beside her again, to understand her and the life that had made her what she was today. Somewhere along the line she felt sure that Lynn the adult and Lynn the child would come together at a junction of understanding. Perhaps when they met they would look at each other in recognition and realise the important role the inner child played in the development of Lynn the adult. It was a thought born late at night, in the quiet hours, but as Lynn snuggled under the quilt, easing herself into a more comfortable position to relieve the nagging pain, she thought of the youngster and joined her again on the voyage of memory.

Lynn's heart skipped for joy as she jumped out of bed. Her mother had come in earlier and pulled open the peach cotton curtains. Without turning to her daughter she announced that it was a lovely sunny day. It was the first one of the school summer holidays and her mother wanted to encourage Lynn to get up and enjoy life like any other child.

Lynn had come home from hospital and started to recuperate from her illness. She was given a few weeks away from school and then after the half-term break she went back to class, trying hard to catch up with the learning and the friendships she had missed out on. The doctor was pleased with her progress and it seemed that the diagnosis of deformed kidneys had proved correct. Lynn was coming up for her seventh birthday and since her long spell in hospital and convalescence she had begun to recover. Lynn's mum reminded her daughter that, as long as she didn't get too tired, her progress back to full health should continue; her renal system was strengthening as Lynn was growing. The diagnosis of diseased kidneys had thankfully been set aside, and the condition known as nephritis had subsided.

Her mother carried the little Ladybird elasticated skirt and a top in to Lynn's room for her to wear. Lynn knew clean underwear would be laid in the drawer of her dressing table, freshly ironed and folded neatly, ready to put on. The little girl was thankful that it was summer at last, for all through the winter and spring she was made to wear a "liberty bodice" under her top clothes. In the winter most children were encouraged by their parents to wear these heavy flock undergarment vests to protect their chests from cold and bronchitis, but Lynn was fragile and was made to wear one well in to April. She hated the rubber buttons that showed through her top clothes. Only when the summer weather came could she be free of such encumbrances. Her mother had an old saying, 'Shed not a clout till May be out.' Lynn didn't know whether it meant the month of May or the flowering tree and she was pretty sure her mother didn't either. Just another old wives' tale, Lynn thought.

Her mother turned from the window and looked intently at her daughter. 'We'll wash your hair tonight; it will go another day. Now hurry, your brother wants his breakfast.'

Lynn put her warm feet on the cool linoleum, searching for her slippers.

'Has Dad gone to work already?' she asked though she knew the answer. Her box bedroom was above the kitchen and she had heard him leave by the kitchen door, taking his bicycle from the garage. She hadn't heard any conversation and assumed rightly that as her father cycled the seven miles through the Caddington lanes to Luton he would have left before the family were up. She wouldn't see him till the evening.

When he came home, Syd would hang his working overall in the garage but the smell of chemicals lingered on him. If his daughter was lucky to grab a hug from him she would bury herself in to his side. She loved the smell, but it wasn't until many years later that she realised the chemicals he worked with could have contributed to his death from heart disease and related lung cancer just short of his seventieth birthday.

Lynn's father would wash and take his evening meal separately from his children. They would have already eaten and been banished from the sitting room until he had finished his meal. Lynn was unsure of his mood; although he was a fair father, she felt that his work was perhaps too important for him to be bothered with children when he came home from the *Luton News*. She thought her father's attitude was normal but it was always a delight to be asked to her friend Jane's home to play. When Jane's father came back from work Lynn was not sent away from his table. The children could stay while he ate and even pinch chips off his plate. Lynn would never attempt that at home; she hated to sense her father's disapproval, although he rarely raised his voice to her. Lynn's mother would tell her children to be quiet when he wanted to rest in the front room and the door would be quietly closed behind him as he retired with his paper or book. If the children had been naughty during the day, their mum would threaten to tell their father when he came home from work. Lynn never really understood her father. Sometimes he was serious when he was joking, at other times he was just serious. However hard it was to know her father's ways Lynn and her brother loved him. There was always great joy for the children when on occasions he came home from work, ate his tea then called them to him. He would open his work bag and take out a pencil.

'I'll draw you a bicycle, Lynn, like the one I ride.'

The children stood open-mouthed while their father took the pencil and drew on the wallpaper in the sitting room. They shouted that he couldn't do that because they knew they would be told off if they tried, but their father continued amid lots of children's laughter. Eventually he gave Lynn and Bill a pencil each and said they had an hour to draw anything they wanted on the walls. It was such forbidden fun as both children loved drawing; Lynn used all her imagination.

Suddenly, as quickly as it had started, the fun stopped. Their father told them he was going to start decorating the room that evening and that they must both be in bed early for he was going to work all night if he was to get the job finished. He hated decorating but would indeed work for as long as it was necessary, together with their mother, to get the job finished as quickly as possible. The children were later ushered off to bed and allowed to read for a while. Lynn heard raised voices and lots of banging all through that evening but she never dared to go downstairs to ask for a drink of water.

The next morning Syd went to work tired but, hopefully, satisfied. Bill was impatient to see the new wallpaper and called to his sister to hurry up in the bathroom. She climbed down from the toilet seat which was the perfect viewpoint for the little girl to look out of the window. She ran the water in the sink and washed her face and combed her hair. Her mother would put it into a ponytail with a colourful ribbon when she came downstairs. She jumped down the stairs two at a time, just as her brother had taught her, and joined him at the bottom of the flight. They stood together in the doorway of the sitting room and admired the new wallpaper. It was like walking into a field of bamboo cane. It made the room look cool and new but Lynn was disappointed that not one of their drawings remained. She looked back at her mother who was now standing behind them.

'What do you think then?' their mother asked.

Bill just nodded and sat on his chair at the breakfast table. Lynn, always wanting to say the right thing, told her mother she liked it. She looked more closely at her mum; she looked very tired.

Lynn was excited, the school holidays had begun and she had hoped her friends would want to go out into the fields to play. Usually her mother would give her permission willingly and, judging by her tired expression, Lynn thought it would be easy today to gain her approval just so that she could get her children from under her feet. Joyce put a bowl of cereal before her daughter and having thanked her, Lynn hurried through breakfast to catch up with her brother, who was already on his second piece of toast.

'Mum, I've finished,' she said, long after her brother had wiped the last morsel of toast from his mouth with his hand. 'Can we get down?' they called to the kitchen in unison. Mother gave her permission and Bill kicked Lynn quickly beneath the table to gain the advantage of leaving the table first. She caught his sleeve, delaying him only fractionally. Usually they would be asked to clear the table but as Lynn collected up her dishes she heard a knock on the back door. Her mother answered it. Lynn could hear Janey's voice. She was invited in and Mum put her head round the dining-room door, telling her daughter she could go out and play with her friend.

While Lynn changed from her slippers Janey stood in the kitchen watching her friend's mother prepare for washing day. Joyce had already rolled the top-loading machine from the larder into the middle of the tiled floor. She was relieved to know the children would be out of the way before she took on the mammoth task of the weekly family wash using her new Parnell machine with electric ringer. Lynn was often asked if she wanted to help her mother when the weather was too dull to play outside, but Lynn avoided doing so if she could for she hated the noise it made. Once the centred washing spindle rotated backwards and forwards the machine had the habit of turning on the casters and moving around the floor if the load was unstable. When her mother fed the hot wet washing through the electric mangle Lynn was concerned it would take the wooden pinchers or even her mum's hand as well as the sheet it was squeezing to death. Although Lynn was now seven she had learned early in life to be wary of machines. Anything that made that much noise couldn't be safe.

She went into the kitchen with a hairbrush, ribbon and elastic band and her mother caught her by the shoulders and turned her round, brushing her hair vigorously while Janey watched. Once she was satisfied, her mum released her with the usual command of not going too far over the fields. They were to come back by lunchtime and not to talk to strangers.

The children burst through the doorway together, racing to the garden gates. Joyce heard them laughing freely as one reached the gates before the other. She knew it wouldn't be Lynn, but she was relieved to hear her child laugh freely and without care. She had heard her daughter too often in pain or too tired to play as wildly or for as long as other children. She had become protective of her child and the fear of a return of kidney problems had made her worry for her daughter's health. She wanted a normal life for her child but she was fearful and over-cautious, unable to release her as she had her son. Even today she knew that Bill was going to meet Jimmy, Janey's brother. Though Jimmy and Bill wanted to play boys' games and distance themselves from mere sisters, Bill had been told by his mother to keep an eye on the girls and not to let his sister get too tired. He had groaned at the responsibility and had thought of losing them in the fields, but deep down he knew he had promised his mother. It was fortunate that the four of them got on well and usually enjoyed playing together. Joyce knew she could rely on her son, within reason of course. He thought that it would be better to play locally than face a dressing down if his sister ran off in a flight to freedom and wild flower picking!

There was an uncultivated corner plot next to their house. In November the bonfire for the immediate neighbourhood would be built on it by children and adults alike, ready for the Guy Fawkes celebrations. There was a rough and rutted footpath across this triangular piece of land which was a convenient short cut to Osborne Road and so to school and town via the allotments. It was on this land that Bill and Jimmy had built and disguised a den, hard up against a neighbour's fence but small enough for them to think it would go unnoticed. They were mistaken.

'Is that your den? Can we play in it?' Lynn piped up as soon as they crossed the rough land.

'No; dens are for boys only,' Bill replied, annoyed that she had discovered it.

Eventually, however, with his mother's words ringing in his ears, Bill turned to his friend, shrugged his shoulders, and said to the girls, 'We'll show you, but you can't go in.'

Lynn bent her head to have a look inside. A horrid smell of damp and dirt hit her nose. 'Whew, it's smelly, just like boys. I wouldn't want to go in there, anyway. What have you used? Have you two pinched Mr Knightly's milk crates for the walls? You've used something metal.'

The boys denied pinching anything from the dairyman but admitted finding four milk crates in the undergrowth and to having shoved them in place to use as walls.

'We'll tell the milkman you've got his crates,' Janey and Lynn chorused.

'He won't want them back, they're bent. It was probably him who threw them out,' Janey's brother retorted.

The girls were secretly envious that the boys could make a den at all. Lynn investigated further, 'It needs a garden,' she said. The two girls were good at making gardens.

'No garden,' the boys yelled in unison and then decided to suggest a game of "catch" to distract their sisters' attention; it would be more fun. The den was forgotten and so was the girls' idea of gardening.

The children played well together. Lynn watched Jimmy as he smoothed his sister's hair back when it became tangled in the branches of the scrub bramble; he was gentle with his sister. Bill would never do that for her. He hardly ever touched her except to play knuckle fights or give Chinese burns. She wondered what it would be like to have Jimmy as a brother but dismissed the idea realising very quickly that although they didn't show their affection readily she did love Bill and he loved her. Whom could she fight, whom could she annoy, if it wasn't him? How would she ever grow strong if she had someone to look after her all the time? At least Bill didn't wrap her up in cotton wool and she could always kick him back or tell on him. She decided against swapping Jimmy for her brother, but turned and looked back at the blond boy. *But I wouldn't mind him looking after me if he wasn't my brother.* She let the thought travel in the breeze.

She ran over to Bill, pulling at his jacket, but as she spun away she caught her foot in a hole hidden by a tuft of long grass and twisted her ankle as she fell at his feet. She cried out immediately and sat up where she had fallen, holding her ankle with both hands, and rocking herself backwards and forwards.

Immediately, he professed his innocence. 'I didn't touch you.' He doubted his mother would believe him. They all stood round her. He suddenly realised he would have to get his sister home. 'Can you stand?'

'No,' she wailed, not even trying.

'Come on,' encouraged Jimmy. 'Hold on to me and we'll pull you up.' Lynn stood, leaning heavily on him, but she couldn't put any weight on her left foot.

Bill was starting to panic. It would be up to him to get her home; he took her other arm. She squealed and they sat her back down on the grass. Janey said she would run ahead for help.

Lynn was trying not to cry, but her ankle was throbbing. 'You'll have to carry me.' She suddenly found herself hoisted without ceremony into the air.

The boys started their slow walk home, and the invalid was alternately stretched and concertinaed as the boys walked at different paces. They must have looked a ridiculous sight.

'Put Lynn down; what game do you think you boys are playing?' Joyce did not allow Janey to explain. She berated the boys until she realised her daughter had hurt herself and that it was not Bill's fault; he was, in fact, doing his best to help her.

He would remember the unfairness of such a scolding until his adulthood. He had tried always to help his sister, though sentimentality didn't sit easily on his shoulders. That day confirmed to Lynn that her brother loved her as much as Jimmy loved his sister, but she doubted he would ever tell her so.

Lynn's sprained ankle took a week to heal enough to bear her weight; it had stopped her playing in the fields for a while. She wished with all her heart that she was stronger and tougher. It was bad enough that she had to be called in from play earlier than the other children in the evenings. This accident made her feel even more like a stupid girl. Lynn picked up her pencils and started colouring. Sometimes life just isn't fair!

Chapter 15

By the time the swelling round her ankle had gone down Lynn had nearly filled the small painting book her mother had bought her to keep her amused. She loved drawing and painting and had already spent so much time at home instead of at her school work that she was becoming quite a good little artist. She would copy patterns from her bedroom wallpaper or ornaments from her bedside cabinet, including the little yellow plaster angel. The ornament now had lost a few toes on one of its feet because of a fall. Lynn had cried at the time wishing her angel had working wings so that it could have taken flight before it had hit the floor. Nevertheless, the kneeling angel was still kissed every night after Lynn's prayers and was very much adored.

The nightly routine of prayers and the idea of an angel to protect her seemed to take the place of going to church on Sunday. She resumed attending services when she was confirmed at the age of eleven. But she would always admit to finding her faith and God beyond the confines of a church. The plaster angel became a symbol of God's love, and when Lynn drew the angel, she positioned it so she didn't have to draw the damaged feet.

Lynn had already missed a week of the school summer holiday. She had a lot to catch up on and was quite determined to do so. The day was sunny and the birds seemed to be singing just for her. Janey and some of the gang were coming to call for her today as Lynn's mum had promised to write out a list so that the children could hold a treasure hunt. Her mother was popular; she usually had time for the youngsters and used her imagination to encourage them in their games. It was rare in the fifties for a mother to go out to work and Joyce had a natural way with children. As well as making clothes for Lynn's dolls Joyce could, if the girls were lucky, be coerced into making similar outfits for Janey or Kate's dolls.

Fifty-four First Avenue had a big garden where the children could play if there weren't too many of them or hold puppet shows on the lawn. Summer was heavenly and Lynn was looking forward to joining in with all her friends again though she made a mental note to be now wary of rabbit holes from now on and not to tease her brother into chasing her.

Six young friends came to call after lunch. Her mother had completed the list of things the children had to collect and bring back to the garden for her to judge the competition. Whoever collected the most items on the list would be the winner and receive a prize of a penny or two or sweeties wrapped up to look inviting. This, of course, was an ingenious way to get the children away from the house so that Joyce could get on with all the other things she needed to do or perhaps visit a neighbour for a cup of tea or to sunbathe quietly in the garden.

The lists were given out and the children ran from the gate in a ragged bunch. Lynn was not the last to get away for today Kevin had followed the girls, wanting to join in the game. Kevin was younger than Lynn or her brother and, in the pecking order of the gang, fell last by a couple of years! He was a quiet boy who lived in Osborne Road and would follow the girls and want to join in with their games. This was ideal when the girls were playing Mummies and Daddies and needed a child they could send to school or even put in the pram. Girls can be bossy and they weren't always fair to Kevin, who seemed to put up with an awful lot. Sometimes he wasn't even allowed to play with them. Today was different; Kevin ran with the others, clutching his list of things to collect.

'We've only got one hour and a half; we've got to be back by three!' Lynn called, envious of Janey, who was the only one to have a watch on her wrist. Lynn liked it; it had a picture of Cinderella's Fairy Godmother on the face and the magic wand went up and down with the seconds.

They ran off the broken end of the road outside her house and were immediately in the countryside. They ran to the left of the farmer's field and up the hill of rough pasture grass. It wasn't many minutes before the houses behind them seemed small and insignificant. The gang were more intent on what lay ahead of them in the fields and hedgerows that followed a line to the top of the hill. They trailed along the hedgerow as a group, deciding eventually to split up. An argument ensued when the girls realised the boys were watching which items had been found and where; the boys were told in no uncertain terms to find their own treasures.

'I've found the "egg and bacon",' Kate called, sharing her good fortune with Lynn and Janey. The girls gathered round and put the little flower into the bouquet they had collected. The vetch grew within the pasture blanket. It was a pretty, delicate thing; yellow with red edges to the petals. It was of the low ground-cover variety Lynn remembered from her book. Lynn knew the common names for most of the flowers and the sounds of the birds above their heads. Because she had so often missed out on play and schooling she loved to read about such things, then, when she got better, she would play with the others in the fields and be far more knowledgeable about what she saw.

Now she ran ahead of the others, free and full of life. She reached the summit of the hill, her collection forgotten for a moment; she opened her arms wide and spun on the pivot of her sandalled feet.

'I'm a sky lark; watch me hover in the sky,' she called to no one in particular. The others looked up from examining the hedgerow for some treasure or other, but Lynn had already moved on over the brow of the hill and down the other side. Her spinning made her dizzy; she thumped down in the prickly grass that grew above knee level. First she sat and then lay back in the grass, her eyes staring at the blue sky. Little clouds scratched the heavens, leaving tails of white. She could understand why this type of cloud was called "mare's tails". She shaded her eyes from the brightness and with sensitive ears and eyes she pin-pointed the skylark which was singing its heart out to the right of her. It was so high it was almost a dot. Lynn's heart rose with the continual cascade of sound until the bird stopped singing and dropped beyond her view to some unseen nest. Her mother never condoned the collection of birds' eggs but sometimes she would add the finding of a broken, discarded shell to her list of treasures to find. Perhaps Lynn would be lucky to find one today. She closed her eyes and only opened them when she felt something tickling her outstretched leg. She didn't move immediately; she wasn't afraid of insects. A cricket had hopped on to her bare leg; she let it rest in the warmth.

She heard the other children calling for her and sat up quickly. 'I should have had the jam jar Janey; I nearly caught a cricket!' she responded. The girls gathered round searching the grass, but with all the sudden noise the cricket had hopped away. It would be another ten minutes before Lynn found another and cupped it in her hands, placing it gently in the jar. Janey screwed the lid on; it had air holes spiked through the top to allow any captured creatures to breathe. Once they had handed in their treasures and the winner of the competition had been declared, the jars would be taken back to the fields and emptied, setting all the creatures free. Lynn often wondered if they ever found their ways home; it made her a little sad. The picked flowers if still alive after being held tightly in hot little hands would be presented to Bill and Lynn's mum as a thank-you present for arranging the game.

Kate squealed with delight. Back along the hedgerow, deep in the hawthorn, she had found a "robin's pin cushion". This was a strange thing that grew within the hedge, attached to a small branch or twig. The children thought it was something like mistletoe; though it did indeed have the appearance of a tightly formed pin cushion, as red as a robin's breast. This one was still green with red tinges. They were all springy to the touch and only when they were mature did they change their colour to bright red. The girls came running and held the back of Kate's cardigan while she reached in and snapped the branch of the dog rose on which it was attached. They pulled their friend, who was grasping the treasure, from the bush. Her hand sprung droplets of blood where the dog rose had caught her with its thorns but upon freeing herself she sucked the blood, too excited to bother much about it. Grazed hands and knees were injuries to be cherished when playing in a gang; a wound such as this was an order of merit. If the girls had known then that the robin's pin cushion is, in fact, the home of the living larvae of the gall wasp they, most probably, would have left it alone and asked for it to be taken off the list of collectables.

Janey had already added the dog rose to the bouquet and some of the grasses on the list. They could hear the boys coming over the hill whistling through blades of grass cupped around their enclosed hands. The noise was a bit like the sound they expected a screech owl to make though no one had ever heard one.

'Come on; don't let the boys know we've found the robin's pin cushion.' Lynn took charge and ran with the girls, jumping from view into a deep circular dip. The grass was high here, sheltered from the wind. Someone had told her that it was where a bomb had dropped during the war from a plane on its way back to Germany. Lynn innocently couldn't imagine why anyone would want to drop a bomb in a field but as there was certainly no bomb there now it made a perfect cover to hide from the boys...

'Let's see what we've got.' Janey tipped out the paper bag with some of the treasures inside. The girls lay low.

Lynn took the list and the pencil she had been told not to lose and ticked the items off. 'We've just to find the crab apple and a perfectly rounded stone; we've got the rest.'

'We've got to get another burnet moth, it flew out the jar when I tried to put the green caterpillar in,' said Kate gloomily.

'Not a problem, we're almost sitting on one, it's just come out of its cocoon; it's still sticky.' Lynn snapped the dry grass to which the lovely black and red moth was attached and put it in to the jar complete with obsolete cocoon. 'We might get more points for that.'

The boys came over the rise and now looked down at the girls from the rim of the crater. 'They never found the bomb you know.' Bill grinned at Lynn, who shrugged her shoulders. She had heard the story too many times now. 'We've got everything, what about you?'

His sister was disappointed and lied in front of her brother's success. 'Yes. Have you got the robin's pin cushion?'

'Yes. You've got the crab apple?' The rest of the children gathered around the brother and sister. There seemed to be a battle of wills going on.

'Well,' said Janey, consulting her watch, 'we're running out of time. If you think my watch is right we'd better get back otherwise there will be no prize for anyone.'

Bill and Lynn stared at each other, each trying to work out if the other was lying. There would only be one way now to find out.

The band of happy children played tag as they rose over the hill and down the other side. Lynn didn't feel like running so they gave her the two glass jam jars to carry. She let her friends go ahead; they would reach her mother in time to validate the contest.

Lynn peered into the girls' jar of treasures. Don't worry, caterpillar, she thought, you'll soon be back munching the wild flowers in the field. Thank you for being such a good sport. As she got nearer the dusty edge of the road she glanced down and saw an almost perfectly rounded chalk stone. She picked it up and put it in the jar; it was quite small. 'Now we are only one treasure short,' Lynn said aloud, smiling to herself, her spirits raised enough to get her home with a skip.

Bill and Lynn's mother had put a cloth on the coal bunker and told the teams to lay out their treasures separately. Bill laid out nine of the ten items the boys had collected; the robin's pin cushion wasn't there. Lynn laid out the eight items of treasure the girls had collected, and then added the round stone. The girls were thrilled their team captain had found the ninth treasure, but they had not found their crab apple. Both children had told a lie but it didn't matter now, there was no all-out winner. Brother and sister stared at each other and waited for their mother to make the decision.

'Well done, all of you. Both teams are equal but as the girls found the burnet moth and its cocoon I think the girls have done especially well.' Mrs Zealey's tone was one of authority.

There was a squeal of excitement from the girls and a moan of discontent from the boys. Janey's brother hung his head in disappointment.

'The official result is that the girls have won the prize, but they have to share it equally with the boys.' Everyone was shouting now; their adjudicator handed Lynn the bag of hard marshmallow shrimps which she had bought at four for a penny and went into the house, leaving the children to share them out. Eight shrimps, eight children; Lynn thought her mother had had it planned from the outset.

Chapter 16

School summer holidays seemed always to be full of sunshine and laughter. Lynn shared adventures with young friends and at weekends enjoyed outings with her brother and parents. The new Morris Minor brought freedom and comfort and gradually Lynn was coming to terms with her car sickness.

On her next birthday she was given a two-wheeler bike, learning firstly to reach the pedals and then with confidence to cycle around the perimeter fence of the tennis court in Bennett's Recreational Ground. Her father held the back of the saddle but didn't tell her when he let go. It was quite an achievement when one morning she rode home before her father could catch up! Eventually with her parents' support she had the confidence to cycle with the family along country lanes.

The family had been on a cycling holiday in Jersey two years before. She had been too young to have a bike of her own then but had a most uncomfortable chair on the back of her mother's hired bike. It had still been great fun. Bill had a bike of his own, and the family cycled around the island lanes together. Her mother's family, who still all lived on the island, couldn't really understand Syd enjoying the sport of cycling, but then they never really understood their brother-in-law. He was quite an independent man allowing family life to enter his own life, but not always willing to enter into anything he did not feel comfortable with. For this reason, as she grew older, Lynn loved to go cycling with him along the Bedfordshire lanes. She knew he enjoyed this activity far more than sitting on a beach.

Lynn loved her annual holiday to Jersey and, weeks before their departure, her mother had packed her bags three times in excited preparation. Even at that young age Lynn realised her mum wasn't always the happy mother she made herself out to be. She became a different person when they were in the Channel Islands, enjoying time with her brothers and their families and remembering her own mother who had died when Lynn was only four. She didn't remember much about her grandma but she, too, had a big fur coat; she always wore a hat and had a mole on her face. She died at the young age of fifty-eight but to Lynn she had seemed very old. Lynn's mum somehow took a long, long time to get over her loss.

Now it was holiday time again and the family were well prepared. Lynn's father loved travelling by boat but it soon became apparent that Lynn, like her mother, suffered from sea-sickness! After many family discussions it was settled that Lynn, her mother and her brother would travel by plane from the small local airport at Luton and her father would carry on his working schedule and take the boat train over to the Channel Islands for only part of their two-week holiday. Her father enjoyed the countryside and preferred to take his family once a year to Scotland or to tour Devon or Cornwall; preferring such countryside that included mountains, rivers and wonderful scenery. The freedom of touring meant that they could knock at the door of a bed and breakfast house and be on their way the next day. The children didn't mind a bit for it meant they had two big holidays a year and many Saturday or Sunday outings to interesting places throughout the UK. Not many of her school friends went abroad for their holidays and in those days Jersey was looked upon as a foreign place. Some schoolmates didn't even know where Jersey was, so Lynn and Bill were thought of as being very lucky and a little out of the ordinary.

Lynn loved her Jersey uncles, though she had her favourite from among her mother's four brothers. This year they would be staying with Auntie Joan and Uncle John in Ryburn Road. When Lynn was born at the Dispensary she came home as a baby to this same house; it had been a part of her grandfather's estate after his death. Her aunt and uncle lived in it now and they had two children; Gail was a toddler and Nigel still a baby in arms. Lynn liked Uncle John but her favourite uncle was Mark, the third oldest of the family if she included her mother. Throughout her life she felt infinity with him, though as she was only thirteen when he died of a heart attack, she was never able to tell him. She had such memories though, and treasured them deeply.

The sun was bright, the tide retreating; the sand was white and hot below the sea wall where the family of cousins, aunts and uncles and friends had gathered with Lynn's mum and her children for the picnic on the beach near Green Island, along the St Clements coast road. In one direction, about a mile away, Havre Des Pas, with its outside seawater bathing pool, concluded the bay at the end of the long sandy stretch of beach. The sea directly in front of the little group stretched and sparkled for ever. Somewhere over this horizon lay France. Lynn was unsure in which direction England lay, her sense of direction was poor. All Lynn knew was that she was where she wanted to be. At the other end of the beach, near where the family had laid out their towels and deck-chairs, a grassy island rose from its granite rocky base. The island, which Lynn had been told held the remains of a Neolithic burial ground, would be surrounded by the tide twice a day, but at low water, one could walk out to it, clambering over boulders to eventually climb the eroding rocky sides of the island. The view from the grassy summit was panoramic. It was one of her favourite places, probably because it was her uncle's favourite place too. When Lynn was a child and was upset, lonely or ill she would find herself back at Green Island in her imagination and her Uncle Mark would be by her side. If the truth be known she would spin this dream when she was a young adult as well.

She looked around the family group for her mother. She was talking to her sister-in-law and laughing. Lynn was content and almost a little envious that someone else had made her mother happy. Her father wasn't in the group; he would be coming at the weekend, in time for Lynn's birthday. Behind them, at the top of the sand covered granite steps, stood Green Island Tea Rooms, a flat-roofed building with big, big black lettering that you could read from the sea shore: GREEN ISLAND TEA ROOMS. The big bold letters continued along the sea wall, advertising the available menu. Lynn knew Green Island tearooms had been owned by her grandparents; her grandma had even written a poem about it. It was now part of the estate and Uncle Mark ran it with his wife Helen. Lynn didn't see much of her aunty and thought she was not in Jersey at the time of the family's visit. Lynn thought she was in Canada, but children are never told everything.

Her uncle sold "Velvet Lady" ice cream and homemade crab sandwiches; he caught the crabs himself. There was a juke-box in the corner and ornate glass lamps hung from the ceiling and always, always by eleven o'clock every summer's day, there was sand on the floor and under everybody's sandals.

The sandwiches were finished and so was Bill's and Lynn's sandcastle. They were now busy scraping roads in the sand with their spades, building bridges and brick-like houses, though her brother complained that he would need to make the moat deeper as a precaution against the incoming tide later that afternoon. Lynn stood up, she was getting tired and bored. She looked across to the adults; Uncle Mark was missing from the group. She had not seen him go and scanned the beach for her uncle; she loved nothing more than his attention. Mark had walked away, now a solitary figure losing size as he walked along the beach towards Green Island.

'Leave him alone, Lynn,' her mother called, seeing her daughter stand and start to follow him. She knew her brother had things on his mind and possibly wanted to be on his own. 'He doesn't want company!'

But Lynn was resistant to rejection. He'll want mine, she thought and dropped her spade, setting off at a trot to catch him up. It wasn't very easy for the tide had wrinkled the hard, wet sand into corrugated ridges and each step caught her insteps, hurting her feet, but she would not be put off. Eventually her uncle realised he was being followed and when he saw who it was he waited for his little niece – his favourite niece, Lynn liked to think. He held out a hand and smiled at her and she ran the last distance, oblivious now of her aching feet. He caught her fingers in his hand and could have been in no doubt how much she adored him. His aloofness melted and they trotted on together, making their way to the rocks surrounding Green Island. When he saw that she was stumbling over the ridges, he picked her up and gave her a piggy-back down to the shoreline that would eventually take them round to the back of the island where the low water caressed the warm sand and filled rock pools with shrimp and tiny, darting fish, known locally as cobbos. Lynn was in heaven.

Mark set the child down behind the island. There was no one else around and Lynn felt she at last had her adored uncle to herself. The afternoon sun was warm on her back and Uncle Mark was now in a gentle laughing mood, all cares forgotten. He paddled with her in the shallow water and lay on his tummy, the water coming only up to his ribs. He asked if she wanted to go for a ride on her sea horse and Lynn nodded wildly and stood beside him in the shallows.

'Hop on then.' Lynn had done this before and knew what to do. She climbed on to his broad, brown back as he floated tummy down. She put her little hands on his strong tanned shoulders but had no need for support; she felt perfectly safe with him though she was a little embarrassed to touch his bare skin. She couldn't remember being this close to a male member of the family that she loved this much and it felt delicious but somehow awkward. Uncle Mark was so special she wished she could have been his daughter and that they could have lots of lovely times together. She put the thought away. They laughed together.

Uncle Mark and Auntie Helen didn't have children and Lynn suspected that this was why her uncle was sad. He would have made a good father, she thought.

Uncle Mark floated with the tide until, with his favourite niece still on his back, he submerged his body like a submarine. Lynn squealed as she, too, sunk below the surface till just her shoulders were above water. She laughed and looked below the surface, seeing his hair wave in the current like black seaweed. Now she held on but she wasn't scared. He started blowing bubbles through his mouth, raising his head only occasionally to take in more air to make more bubbles. Lynn thought it was the finest game she had ever played and when he eventually came up for air, swimming back to the shore, she threw her arms round his neck and named him her "Rude Sea Horse", because of the noise he made when blowing bubbles under the water. That nickname stayed with him for ever.

Her uncle was aware of the changing current and tide; it was time to end the magic and return to the family on the beach. This time, without asking he crouched for Lynn to climb on to his back for the ride around the base of the island and across the beach to the others. Their mood was quiet but Lynn had the confidence of a child to feel that her uncle had enjoyed their time together as much as she had.

Until adulthood and beyond Lynn remembered that day and her beloved uncle with overwhelming affection. In January 1963, the year of "the big freeze", when even the sea froze over around Green Island, Joyce received a phone call. Her brother Mark had died of a heart attack after helping repair burst water pipes in the neighbourhood. It was a tragedy for he was well loved and only in his thirties. Joyce's grief took priority over her daughter's sense of loss as Lynn tried to comfort her mother. The most wonderful and unexpected outcome was that it brought Lynn's uncle closer to her, knowing then that she only had to think of him to feel him comfort her. In times of illness and even a "near death" experience her uncle remained close in thought and memory. He would always be her "Rude Sea Horse".

Lynn spent her eighth birthday in Jersey. She couldn't sleep the night she waited for her father to come over the Channel by British Rail mail boat, which arrived very early the next morning. He only came for a long weekend but Lynn and her brother couldn't wait to see him. Happy times always pass quickly, and in no time at all, their father had returned home to Dunstable, having used all his official holiday time earlier in the year. The following week was spent in holiday mood but suddenly it was over. Their mother became withdrawn, without the enthusiasm to repack for the homeward journey. Lynn carefully tucked the sticks of rock down the side of her mother's suitcase; these were for her friends. Bill and his sister had to leave their highly painted tin buckets and spades for another year. There was no room in the luggage for them and somehow, digging in the heavy clay garden soil at home just didn't seem the same. The stones would scratch the red paint from the spades and soon break them. Auntie Joan said she would keep them for the children but invariably when Bill and Lynn returned the following summer there would be new buckets and spades waiting for them.

Uncle Harry took them to the Jersey airport at St Peters in his very smart car, but Lynn continually looked out of the back window to make sure that Uncle Mark's blue lorry was following. She would have much preferred to have sat in the cab with him, high up, seeing the countryside pass by. Even better would have been to sit in the back of the tipper lorry and be bumped around all over the place. It had been one of her many joys and Lynn realised with astonishment that she was never travel sick when she travelled in the lorry with Uncle Mark and her brother.

After hugs and farewells and a few tears from her mum and Lynn their flight was called and mother and children made their way through the departure gate and out on to the tarmac. All the family were out on the roof of the main building waving goodbye.

Lynn climbed up the steps to board the Dakota airplane with her mother's help. They took their seats and Lynn, sitting by the window, looked for her uncle and waved and waved to take her mind off her fear of take-off and flying. Her brother took the barley sugar sweets offered to them by the air hostess and handed them out. He sat behind Lynn and his mother, leaning forward at one point to ask if would be allowed to see the cockpit. Later during the flight his wish was granted and he was taken through the door at the front of the cabin and allowed to see the captain and the flight deck. Lynn was really too terrified to leave her seat in case the plane dropped away from under her, but, when the hostess brought her brother back to his seat she asked their mother if her daughter would like to go forward. Sibling rivalry is a wonderful incentive and Lynn swallowed hard and accepted. It was an amazing experience; she stood behind the captain and co-pilot and looked at all the dials and instruments whizzing round. Everything seemed to vibrate but Lynn lost her fear of flying that day. Now at least she realised someone piloted the plane and they were responsible for everyone's safety. Nevertheless she was relieved to go back to her seat and accept another barley sugar when the light flashed on the indicator board declaring that passengers must fasten their seat belts and extinguish their cigarettes as they would soon be landing.

At the other side of the customs desk, where Lynn, full of groundless guilt, asked if she should declare her golliwog, their father was waiting. He gave her a big bear hug and squeezed his son's shoulder. He took charge of the suitcases, kissed his wife on the cheek and then led the way out of the small terminal and to the car park. Very soon they would be home.

Home life was always so very different from holiday life and for a while Lynn would miss the sand and sea and all her Jersey relatives. She would be sad to see her mother looking wistfully through the kitchen window as she washed the dinner dishes for four. She knew her mother missed her own family just as much as she would miss Bill if he lived so far away from her. Perhaps she would give her mummy one of the sticks of rock she had brought home with her to cheer her up. Then she thought better of it; it would remind her mother of the home and family she had just left behind.

She decided to think of other things and reminded herself that the following week she would be starting a new year at Icknield School. She would be able to tell all her friends of her holiday in Jersey, though she thought that by then she would have lots of other things to talk about. Life through a child's eyes is simple and immediate, leaving little time to ponder on regret. That night she gave her mother a big extra hug and one to her father too, then, having kissed her plaster angel, she told it to look after everyone she loved including her Uncle Mark.

Chapter 17

The memory of a child is fine-tuned to experiences and events, emotions and indignities. Laughter and tears well up easily transferring themselves to memory – stored and often distorted through time. As Lynn lay once again in the large cold double bed as an adult she tried to recall facts about her childhood from an adult point of view. However, the memories were too vivid and she could not remain detached from the child who was drawing close to her again. These memories were so vivid that she could almost feel the Dunstable wind on her face and the aroma of cabbages rotting in the allotments as she ran down the alley on the way to school. Every emotion, every fear associated with the new term and teacher were finely tuned; Lynn was indeed that child. She found it hard to put dates and times to her memory, children find it unimportant; one event or crisis rises from another and life seems one long experience.

Lynn had recovered well from her long spells in hospital and was getting stronger by the month. She played with her friends in the evening now, though she was still called in earlier than other children of her age. She started back at school, and was placed in Mrs Bliss's class but she had struggled hard to catch up and still lacked confidence, seeking approval for the least important venture.

Her favourite time of the week was the last period on a Friday. This involved no structured lesson but was the time when the children were told to finish their work or reading and to put it away inside their wooden desks. Each child had

Lynn entered his class at a slight educational disadvantage but a good teacher was to see potential in the slowest of pupils and what Mr Hurst did, not just for her but for all the children lessons were inventive and exciting, brought to life by the in art, carpentry and creativity. All the skills Lynn en of course of carpentry.

The children loved Mr Hurst's geography bring a big wooden box into the classroom making time and indeed from the box jigsaw. These pieces were large and down the blackboard and put a When the children first saw but when he walked aroun jig-saw, they looked d just as he had show and how it was the pieces a to them how

vision and unknown to Lynn it was decided that instead of remaining in the low school stream that year she would be elevated to 2B. Mr Hurst was to be her class teacher, and indeed he was a visionary in teaching skills himself. It would be a decision that would change Lynn's life not only as a growing child, but as an adult and in what she was later to achieve.

Mr Hurst was a man about her mother's age. He came to school on a bike, taking his cycle clips off as he dismounted at the school gates. He had twinkly eyes and smoked a pipe, often clasped firmly between his teeth as he rode to school. Lynn remembered the tin of Four Square tobacco which he would take out of his jacket pocket when leaving school at the end of the day. Mr Hurst was definitely her favourite; she noticed the way he brushed his hair back from his forehead, making it look as though he had a widow's peak. That was what her mum called it, though Lynn didn't really understand as widows were always women – she knew that much. In hindsight of course his hair line may have been receding.

the gift of
this is exactly
in his charge. His
teacher's other skills
oyed, with the exception

lessons. Occasionally he would
n. The children knew it was map-
heir teacher poured pieces of hand-cut
easy for small hands to manage. He took
framed tray in its place; it was the same size.
it they wondered what they were expected to do
d the classroom giving each child three pieces of the
own at them realising they were all pieces of a country,
n them in the atlas. During the lesson he spoke of the world
made up of land, sea, countries and continents. Lynn looked at
ad thought how many red pieces there were. Her teacher explained
all that this was the colour for the British Commonwealth and asked
many children had red pieces in their hands. From this introduction the
de pieces were fitted in and through the course of the guided lesson each child came forward three times to place their pieces of the world in to the large map. Lynn loved it when she was the child walking down the classroom to place the last piece in position to complete the map of the world. She felt her role was very important. All through the lesson Mr Hurst taught them about the countries they were handling, their neighbours and the importance of the sea. Lynn had never realised quite how much sea there was in the world.

From this lesson their teacher would take the boys and show them the mechanical saw he used to cut the pieces and make the map so that they could see the skills they might like to try when they got a little older. Lynn and the girls weren't interested in such technical details but Lynn loved the shapes and looked at how the land masses must have been joined at one time before they had split apart, just like the jigsaw. She found a whole new interest in geography.

In this educational year the children worked with different teachers for varying subjects. Mr Hurst was their form master and taught the majority of their lessons. His classes were always the favourite of the children who, like Lynn, had an artistic flare. He taught handwriting which was part of the school curriculum. In the first classes the children wrote with pencil, and later they used dipped ink pens but in 2B the accent was on learning to write in italics with an Osmiroid fountain pen during handwriting tuition.

It was here that Lynn encountered her first problem. Her left-handedness was again a disadvantage and she had great difficulty holding the pen and making the correct strokes with a right-handed pen. Also, because she needed to hold the pen at an angle to make the thick-and-thin balance of italic lines, she would have to drape her forearm over her work to produce the angle of a right-handed writer. This left her exercises smudged and her cardigan stained with the wet ink. She was left struggling and disappointed by her poor achievement. Mr Hurst had told the class that when they had mastered the technique they would enter a national competition for handwriting and there would be prizes for first, second and third. Lynn knew she didn't stand a chance and her teacher recognised the problem. He obtained a second version of the nib, especially made for left-handed writers. The angle of the cut-away tip was opposite to the usual nib allowing Lynn and those like her to bring her arm round to a more comfortable and less obstructive angle. This way she was able to maintain the quality of handwriting without smudging her piece of writing. Lynn thought it was magic and her writing immediately improved allowing her to enter the competition. The results were read out during assembly some months later and Lynn nearly screamed with surprise. She had come third in the school and although she didn't win the pen or the box camera she was awarded a certificate with her own name and the award mention on it. She had something to keep for ever. Mr Hurst was very proud of his class and they were proud of him.

Gradually Lynn's confidence grew and much of this was due to her teacher's devotion to the children and his bringing out the best of their talents and skills. Perhaps she was a favourite, she wasn't sure, but she knew that Mr Hurst would take time to help her with work she didn't understand and allow her a little more attention.

One of her favourite subjects was art and drawing and when the weather was nice, later in the school year, Mr Hurst brought inventiveness in to his lessons. He would take his class of children out of school and walk them to Bennett's Recreational Ground. By that summer the allotments had been closed and sheltered housing was being erected on the now vacant site. No longer did the children have to run through the alley holding their noses against the smell of rotting vegetables. Now they walked in crocodile formation past the bungalows to the "Rec".

There was now a general store on the corner and it was a very popular addition to suburban Dunstable. Mr Hurst would leave the children outside on the paved area and go into the shop; he would emerge with a big bag of sweets. The crocodile of children crossed the road and once through the park gates broke free with the energy and exhilaration only they could possess. Mr Hurst let them run for a while before calling them to line, issuing paper and pencils, instructing them to spread out where he could always see them and draw something they saw which they liked. Lynn loved this for it was her favourite subject and one that she found all her confidence in. She didn't have to learn or listen although her teacher would come round to them all in turn and encourage their pencil work, advising them how best to improve. Some of the children of course found it a good excuse to be out of the classroom, but Lynn and some of the others enjoyed every lesson in the park as one in which to shine.

At the end of the lesson Mr Hurst would gather up his young pupils and assess their drawings. The big bag of sweets would come out and he would choose the winners. Lynn was often in the top three. The first prize would be a liquorice Catherine wheel, or the equivalent, the second prize perhaps a Sherbet Dab and the third prize something smaller but an equally tasty chew bar. Once congratulations had been awarded the bag was handed round so each of them had a reward. Sherbet Flying Saucers were popular, made of rice paper that melted in a child's mouth, or pink marshmallow shrimps and sometimes half penny chews. No one was left out. After they had chosen, all the pencils and paper were collected and the little noisy crocodile was duly hushed, ready for the short walk back to school.

Lynn loved it if she could walk beside Mr Hurst and engage him in childish conversation. She was much happier walking with her schoolmates than she ever was walking to the beach with the children from the Felixstowe convalescent home. Those days seemed such a long time ago to her now.

By the time July came round again Lynn was not only much stronger, but she was also more confident and happy. She had loved her teacher and she had responded to the gentle encouragement. She hated exams but when her results came and her school report was handed to her to give to her parents, she was very proud of herself. Lynn had come from near the bottom of her last C-graded class to sixth place in 2B. At last she had achieved!

Lynn was sad to leave her favourite teacher's class at the end of term, but in academic standards and confidence she never looked back. She asked her parents if she could buy her teacher a present at the end of the school year, as a way of a very big thank-you. Tobacco would have to do; it was the only thing she knew he liked – that and teaching, of course.

As she came out of her memories Lynn realised that Mr Hurst had been a cornerstone in her educational and creative life. When, as an adult, she had her first book of illustrated verse published in her own italic handwriting and her original illustrations, she had tried to trace Mr Hurst again to thank him for his encouragement as a child. Alas, she heard that he had passed away; she didn't get the chance to thank him personally. Lynn wished she had tried to contact his widow if she were still alive but she lost the opportunity and life moved on.

She wondered if perhaps he was one of the figures who had climbed the stairs with her that night before her fifty-ninth birthday to wish her well and once again give her encouragement for the days ahead.

She hoped the veil between the worlds we know and fail to understand would be thin enough to allow him to see the reward of all his selfless work with children.

Chapter 18

As little Lynn grew so did her home town of Dunstable. Oblivious in her early childhood years to any change that did not affect her, or her view from bedroom and bathroom window, Lynn was unaware of the social plans feeding their way through council chambers and government bodies. Her father still complained about the state of the road outside their house and yet like she did, he enjoyed the immediate access to the countryside. Some Sunday mornings Lynn and her brother would go for a walk with him while Mother cooked the obligatory Sunday roast dinner with steamed pudding to follow. He would take them up the track across the ploughed field or along Canesworde Road which ran parallel to their own avenue. At the top of that road at the junction with Meadway a new building had been built. Chosen as the site for the new technical school in the mid-fifties, it had now been completed. Lynn was not interested in anything that was urban but understood by her mother's and father's conversations that changes were coming to Dunstable and their way of life would be affected.

'At least we'll get the road repaired,' her father would say.

From the new school site they walked a country rutted lane where hawthorn and buckthorn grew and overhung the path. Chaffinches trilled with crescendo and robins followed their progress as the children laughed and played together ahead of their father. When Lynn grew a little tired she would find an excuse to hold her father's hand, for he rarely offered it spontaneously. She felt so much more comfortable with her dad when they were out in the countryside together.

He seemed to let a stiffness from inside of him go as if someone had loosened his belt. Lynn didn't mind when her brother got older and wanted to go out with his friends, just boys together. She would walk with her father and they were able to share valuable moments together.

One day they passed the farm where horses were kept and riding lessons were given to children whose parents had money. Lynn wasn't one of these children but she wasn't envious. She didn't really enjoy coming this far from home without her father because she knew the gypsies sometimes camped off the lane and gypsies had a bad reputation. She had been told that Mrs Brown's Cairn terrier had been stolen from her front garden and the gypsies had been blamed. This saddened everyone for both dog and lady were inseparable. Of course no one found out the truth, but neither did they find the dog!

When the little group reached the end of the lane they stood looking out over open land. Ahead lay a copse of beech trees tall against the sky line. It ran on by the side of the golf course, which to the young girl was dangerous territory. Lynn never liked to be out of her comfort zone but she trusted her father who would cross the golf course by the official right of way footpath with his children in single line. Halfway along the path there was a big red sign that read, "BEWARE OF LOW-FLYING BALLS". Sometimes someone would call out 'Fore' and they would stop and look to the sky to see if a golf ball was coming their way. Their father would make the children cover their heads with their arms.

Bill's and Lynn's favourite game while out with their father was collecting lost golf balls from the edge of the course. These would have fallen wide or long, out in the rough and the golfers had long given up hope of finding them in the long grass or the edge of the copse. Her father would pop the lost balls in his pocket and take them home as trophies. On one escapade her father found one in the long grass and bent down to pick it up. Suddenly out of the air a shout went up, directed at her dad. He hadn't seen the man on the nearby green, who was by now walking over towards them. Her father bent down, dropping the ball nonchalantly, and pretended to tie his shoe lace. He then straightened up and, without looking at the golfer, gathered his children and continued their walk.

Once they had crossed the greens they were nearly at the top of Dunstable Downs. From here they could cross the Downs road and look out at the view below them. The chalk downs ran as a ridge and although Lynn didn't know the names of the villages spread out below her she thought they looked just like the towns and roads they built out of sand on the beach at Green Island while on holiday. At the bottom of the Downs she could see gliders and bi-planes resting on the green land. Her brother told her they were Tiger Moth planes and that if they waited long enough they would see one take off towing a glider on a long hawser. Lynn was unsure what a hawser was but when a plane took off she could see it was trailing the glider on a long cable, so she guessed that was what he meant. The club-house of the London Gliding Club was situated nearby and Lynn thought it was fun to see the people moving around below. She thought they looked just like ants.

The trouble with long interesting walks is that you always have to turn round and go back, usually the way you have come. Lynn found she tripped frequently, her father telling her to pick her feet up. She had lost interest in looking for balls and was rather concerned that they would come across the golfer who had shouted at her father. She was worried for she knew if the man asked him to empty his pockets, the hoard of golf balls would be found.

'Would you have to go to prison?' she almost whispered in the wind, clutching his hand trying to make him run along the path over the golf course.

'Finders keepers,' he said, smiling, regaining confidence once they had reached the start of the lane that led towards home. 'I'm not a poacher.'

They arrived home a little after the time her father had promised. Her mother was upset that the roast potatoes would burn and none of them got the welcome they would have liked. Her father slipped back into his withdrawn mood but not before the children had raided his pockets and brought out three golf balls, still wet with dew.

The dinner wasn't really spoilt for their mother always knew her husband would never ever come home at the time he was expected. Life was just too much fun in the fields; time didn't really exist and on that Lynn had to agree with him. Father and daughter would share many walks and bird-watching expeditions over Lynn's childhood years. It was from him she learned the skill of identifying birds, coming home elated that she had seen a different species or spied a nest in the reed-bed. She would share his binoculars, though they were heavy and too big for her small hands. The outings to watch heron and grebe along the banks of the Tring Reservoirs were idyllic times, but short-lived. Her father's attitude to space and time caused friction within the home which would bubble up into arguments between her parents. Lynn was torn by loyalty; her mother had worked hard in the kitchen without reward. Even at an early age she could feel the atmosphere between her parents and quite subconsciously started to place herself somewhere between them in an attempt to make things better.

On the afternoon of returning from the walk across the golf course her father dozed behind the closed door of the front room and her mother washed the dishes. Lynn went to find her brother. He was in his bedroom dissecting a golf ball to see how it had been made. He had used his model knife to cut off the white pocked surface and found it to be made of what looked like thousands of elastic bands all woven together with some horrible glue. After the immediate fascination Lynn got bored and went to her own room to play with her dolls. She came downstairs with her brother when her mother called that she had made a cup of tea and that their father was awake.

Weekends were always respected as being a family time. Lynn's friends did not call unless it had been pre-arranged and apart from the exception of inviting a special friend on an outing it was a time for Lynn's parents to plan a family trip out in the sidecar or later on in the Morris Minor. As she grew older Lynn combated her car sickness by distraction. On longer journeys to London or holiday trips the children would take their I-Spy books and pencils. Lynn had to tick the boxes of things she had seen when they arrived home for she still couldn't look down and read at the same time as travelling without feeling sick. She always rivalled her brother in how many sights or places they had been able to identify. When they were bored with that, their mother set them a target to count how many clocks or telephone boxes they had passed. This was, of course, ideal on trips to London, but a little boring when they passed through the countryside. If Bill was preoccupied with his comic and Lynn was feeling off colour she learned the knack of pretending she had a horse. She let the imaginary animal gallop alongside the car, but the trick was to remain alert enough to make it jump over any roadside obstacles or fences and hedges which ran at right angles to the road they were on. This trick worked quite well and seemed to have a better effect than the chain dangling behind the car, as an earth, or the strip of rubber deemed to have the same properties. The worst possible scenario was if either she or her brother accidentally kicked the earthenware bowl under the front seat when getting into the car; it became an omen of what was bound to happen sooner or later.

Saturday was the day of family outings and Lynn and Bill were lucky in the respect that their father loved to get out into the country and, if pushed, even to Welwyn Garden City for Christmas shopping. More fun than that were trips to the Tower of London and famous palaces or historical castles. Lynn loved to watch the soldiers and well remembered the time when she was very little and stood in front of a guard on sentry duty at the Tower and waited patiently for him to notice her. He broke all the rules by winking at her, while still keeping a very straight face. Lynn went off happily then, having got the reaction she wanted. She was only three years old.

All these times were highly documented for their father enjoyed photography as a hobby. Because he knew all about printing he would develop his own film, hanging the negatives in a darkened kitchen once the children had gone to bed. The many photograph albums were full of small two-inch-by-one-inch reminders of happy days and family snaps, each with a caption underlying date and place and some cryptic message to jog the memory. The Zealey family travelled well and the children would come home tired – often sick tired, but with memories and photographs in the camera to record their childhood. Lynn was soon tucked up in bed, her prayers said and her plaster angel kissed. She tried to stay awake till her brother came to bed and then continued to annoy him by repeatedly calling out goodnight and waiting for an answer. Eventually he would get cross with her and complain that she was stopping him from going to sleep.

That was the idea, she thought. She hated to lie awake alone and hoped she would fall asleep before having to call out to him again. Lynn had no idea how annoying she could be.

CHAPTER 19

Lynn was very lucky in her young life; she had a good loving home. Her mother was always there for her when she came home from school or if she were ill. The child's friends were always welcome to play in the garden and she was never locked out, or sent round to friends' parents unless it was with permission to play.

As children, Lynn and her brother had a freedom unparalleled to anything in later modern life. If the weather was inclement during school holidays, or later, when the new estate was being built, Lynn often went to play at Kate's or Janey's house. She liked playing indoors at her friend's house opposite the school but when the sun was hot and they played in the garden the girls had to be careful not to be bitten by the ants; the garden was plagued by them. Mr Dowman had a wonderful greenhouse and although they couldn't play in it, Lynn loved to look at the flowering cacti which were Janey's father's passion. Janey told her that her dad would stay up all night if a rare cactus bloomed, for some only flowered once in a life time. Janey's home was in a terrace block with a covered alley running between the houses. One morning Janey's father found the old Dunstable tramp, nicknamed "Coal Black Charlie", asleep there under some old sacking. If Lynn had to call at the back door of the house she would run down the alley in case the tramp was hiding somewhere close. He never was, of course; he was probably scared of children, especially the local boys. Lynn had only seen him walking round town hoping for hand-outs from the bakery. When she played in Janey's garden she wondered if he might be hiding in the outside toilet. Usually only spiders lived there but they were big and spun big dusty webs that covered the old ceiling. The girls didn't like to play there but used it sometimes for "Hide and See", hoping they would soon be found. It smelt of disinfectant and was too dark to use as a den. Of course, the children used it for what it was intended when they played in the garden.

Lynn's favourite place to play was Kate's garden. Her mother had a part-time job and allowed Kate to play with her friends when she was working. She would leave them drinks and biscuits and remind her daughter to behave herself.

Lynn liked her friend's home in Osborne Road; apart from it being very close to her own, it was also very different. It was one of a series of semi-detached houses, as was her home, but there the similarity ended. Each of these houses belonged to the Police Constabulary and Kate's father was a policeman, but, much better than that, he was a police dog handler. His dog was most definitely a working dog and Kate's friends were not encouraged to pet and play with Julie. She was a lovely animal but Lynn, having already had the horrendous experience of being bitten by her aunt's dog, heeded Kate's parents' instructions and hung back when the dog was free. When children came round, if Julie was not working, she would be put in her kennel in the garden, set away from the house. The children would then be allowed to play but were warned not to excite the animal by peering through the mesh frontage of the kennel. It took a little while to realise that this was not because the dog was dangerous but because she was highly trained and she needed and deserved respect. Lynn had been invited once to watch the dog compete in dog-handler trials and was quite nervous when she saw Julie chase a man until she caught him and wrestled him to a standstill, gripping his protected arm until he had to submit and then be taken in to custody. The family loved Julie and she was well cared for, but Lynn knew that the dog was not your usual family pet.

Kate and Lynn liked it best when the dog was out working with Kate's father and Mrs Wilson had gone to work. The children were not allowed in the house but they enjoyed themselves playing quietly in the garden, knowing they could sit in the big side porch if the summer weather changed.

One afternoon like many before, Lynn went to Kate's house to play.

'Mum's out; she's left us drinks and biscuits,' Kate smiled 'Julie's out too.' The smile broadened and Lynn returned it with a knowing grin.

'It looks like it might rain,' said her friend. The sun was shining quite brightly.

'Definitely,' Kate replied. 'Shall we?'

'Oh yes.' They took their drinks and went about their forbidden and much enjoyed game.

Lynn and her brother had a tent; Kate had a Wendy play-house of which her friend was envious. The problem was that it belonged to Julie the police dog and it was her kennel. It had a resting area where the dog could look out at the world and a sleeping room without windows where the animal could rest undisturbed. Children were not allowed inside but the girls thought that, as everyone was out, no one would realise they had broken the rules and played inside for an hour. They would have to watch for Kate's mother's return but a little time playing families in the kennel would not do any harm and no one would ever know. It was cosy inside and they had great fun; Lynn thought it smelt of dog, but it was clean. They drank their milk and ate their biscuits and had a great time, more so because it was forbidden. When Kate's mother came home she found the two girls sitting in the garden playing unusually quietly.

Lynn could never work out how her mother knew she had been playing in the kennel. At first she thought she had seen her over the three intervening garden fences, but she dismissed the thought. Kate came round the next day and said that her mother had found out they had played in the kennel. Julie gave the game away because when the dog was brought home from the police patrol she sniffed all round inside her kennel and was very restless, sensing that there had been intruders! Kate had been told off and had to vow she would never use the kennel to play in again. The question of how Lynn's mum knew the children had been in the kennel was soon solved.

'Did Mrs Wilson tell you, Mummy?' she asked her mother suspiciously.

'She didn't have to, Lynn, your clothes were covered in dog hairs and you smelt very strongly of Alsatian!'

Lynn was a spirited child, but never wilful. She would sometimes talk back to her mother or refuse to come in earlier than her playmates, and for this she was often scolded. She had been known to run away down the road, rather than lose face with her healthier friends, but it did her no good. She was soon caught, and punished by being sent to her room anyway.

Lynn and Bill both received a slap across the back of their legs if they misbehaved badly, but it caused more pain to their pride than anything else. They knew they were loved, and that discipline was a fact of life.

Bill had suffered only the usual childhood illnesses and yet was tolerant of his little sister and was, no doubt, made aware of her weaknesses. Thankfully he gave her little quarter in their childhood games. From him she learned survival. Their relationship, although never tactile, was strong, enabling her to fight her other battles while growing up and to relate to boys as well as girls. She was glad she was not an only child.

Their mother would often leave them, when they were old enough, of course, to pop to the town for the necessary daily shopping. The household had no freezer or fridge in the mid-fifties and bread would have to be bought daily. Milk was delivered in bottles and fresh fish was supplied weekly from the coast by enterprising fish distributors and sometimes bought by their mother at the front door.

During the school holidays Bill and Lynn would look forward to the times that they would be left alone to play in the house. Bill calculated how long their mother would be away and would suggest forbidden games. Lynn really liked it when he decided to raid the larder and invent a recipe or two. He would climb on the kitchen stool, taking out various packets and a mixing bowl, and the children would spend a happy half-hour spooning in different mixtures and stirring them into a sticky mess. Cocoa powder gave off a lovely smell; she would add currants or other dried fruit while he searched for something runny. Sometimes he didn't tell her what he had added, but would grin wickedly and try to get his sister to taste it. They never broke eggs and they never lit the gas, so everything they made had to be tested uncooked. Lynn was either gullible or too eager to please, and so, more often than not, she was the one who was spoon-fed the ghastly concoction, not realising until it was in her mouth that her brother had added something horrid like mustard and custard powder or cooking oil and tomato sauce. The more inventive he became the more loath she was to play the game. But Lynn had ways of getting her own back and if all else failed she could snitch on her brother, which usually got him a telling-off.

Because their house was at the top of the long avenue they could keep an eye open for their mother's return. They would look from the big bay window in the front room and know that if she was turning the corner at the bottom of First Avenue, pulling her cane basket on wheels, often referred to as her "chariot", the children would have just five minutes to tidy up and appear normal. Of course normality was a dead give-away and aroused their mother's suspicion. For this reason she would sometimes come home the alternative way, turning in from Osborne Road and so not then being seen until she was only one house distant.

Their father had an old heavy hand-held telescope which Bill would use to look down the long road. Sometimes, it was just for fun, other times it was to see if their mother was returning home. One day Lynn was out with her and upon returning, they found Bill upset and full of remorse. He had pulled back the curtain from the side bay window and accidentally let the telescope fall on the crystal vase placed on the window sill. Lynn didn't think that he would ever use the telescope again, certainly not to look down the long road of First Avenue. Although she felt sorry for his dismay she was rather pleased that it hadn't happened when she had held it, which like her brother, she often did.

Bill was inventive; some of his schemes needed testing to his satisfaction. Lynn's small teddy learned to parachute from the bedroom window, ending up often grubby and bruised in the flower bed below when the handkerchief or the plastic chute didn't open. His sister thought all her toys had souls and got really upset when one of her "children" went missing, but all in all Bill was a good brother. In the summer when it was hot they would share bowls of water and float boats or anything else that caught Bill's fancy. It always ended with water fights and screams of joy and excitement. When they were older their parents bought them an inflatable paddling pool; it was great fun but somehow never came up to the enjoyment they had when they had to make do with bowls and buckets. Her brother was getting older then and sometimes on a sunny afternoon he had better things to do than to play with his annoying little sister!

They played many games together; some were educational, others played just to annoy each other. Knuckles was one such game, seeing who was the fastest to rap the other's knuckles while placing them together. Scissors, paper, stone was harmless and less hurtful while Case and Hide and eek took over the whole house and garden.

Generally Lynn admired her big brother. He was skilled at making Airfix model planes and boats and when he was eleven he even invented a pulley system attached to a Lancaster model plane. He suspended it out of the bedroom window and somehow ran the plane on a take-off from garden to upper window sill. Her brother was very clever and secretly she loved it when she could be useful or fetch and carry for him and, although she didn't like him chucking her toys out of the window, she knew he was only experimenting and was secretly very proud of all he did. She was not so pleased with him when he gave her Chinese burns or tried to teach her the Pressure Points of the body when practising what he had learned from Civil Defence classes later in his school years. She didn't know there was an area in her neck which, once pressure was applied, caused you to almost faint; she didn't let him try that again.

On one occasion both the children were relieved that their mum was home, especially Lynn. Their mother was used to being the First Aid post for all the children in the area because theirs was the nearest house when the children came off the fields or building site with scratched faces and grazed knees. She kept a box of plasters and TCP and even bandages; everyone knew where to call.

One day Lynn was playing on the garden wall in the front garden. Bill had climbed up first and walked one foot in front of the other until he reached the gatepost. He climbed upon it and stood as he would do if he had his trumpet and was waiting for visitors. Lynn wanted to do the same. She was about eight years old then and it didn't really take much effort. She sat on the gate post with her feet dangling either side of the closed wrought-iron gate. She didn't know quite what happened but it was presumed that she put her feet on the decorative scrolls of ironwork and suddenly slipped. The pain was indescribable. Lynn sat astride the narrow metal-work having dropped heavily on to it as she fell. Her mother heard her screams and flew from the kitchen and somehow managed to lift her clear of the gate and carry her inside. Lynn suffered heavy bruising and the humiliation of having to be examined by the doctor who came to the house. He reassured Lynn's mum that there was no internal injury and that she would soon be able to walk again. Lynn wasn't trying to eavesdrop on the adult conversation but she overheard the doctor say to her mum that it was a relief it hadn't happened to her son, because the damage could have ruined his chance of fathering children. At the time Lynn didn't know what the doctor meant but she was disappointed that he had more sympathy for Bill than for her. Her brother hadn't even been on the gate and hadn't got hurt – life was so unfair sometimes!

Lynn often thought back on these times. During those growing years she didn't realise her brother's importance in her young life; no doubt he had disregarded her importance in his too. Time alone would prove how much she valued his presence especially when she grew old enough to recognise the raised voices late in the evenings from the rooms below, when both children were tucked up in bed. It was then they both gained comfort by calling out to each other through their open bedroom doors.

'Good night, Bill, are you asleep?'

'Good night, Lynn; no, I'm still awake.'

Chapter 20

Although, to the outside world of friends and family, it seemed that Lynn had put her experiences of hospital life behind her, this was far from the truth. Her physical health had continued to improve and her strength had returned. She played with her friends and was without pain. Her kidney problems abated and to the common eye she was an ordinary child; a little weaker and with less confidence than her peers, but an ordinary child nonetheless. She had taken ballet lessons under the advice of the hospital to help her gain muscle strength and, in honesty, had rather enjoyed the classes of classical ballet and tap dancing. She loved dressing in the costumes her mother had made for her and wearing the little pink ballet shoes and the red tap shoes with big red ribbons. At the time she joined the class her hair was long and she wore it in a ribboned ponytail to match her ballet costumes. She learned to dance with the troupe and took it all very seriously. By nature she was a nervous child when performing in front of an audience and though she was excited at the prospect of showing her parents how well she could dance she was fearful of failure. Lynn left her budding career as a ballet dancer when the nervousness outweighed the pleasure. She had become disillusioned when a classmate continued to be disruptive both off stage and on, culminating with her falling off stage and on to the pianist mid scene! Her parents talked it over and decided that perhaps Brownies would be less physically taxing and more enjoyable for their daughter. Lynn tended to agree with them, resigning herself to the fact that she was happier dancing ballet for her parents in her petticoat around the sitting-room chairs before being ushered off to bed at night; full limelight was not for her.

Lynn continued to have nightmares that were definitely rooted in her hospital experiences. The conscious memories of that time were fading fast but they were relived at night by contorted dreams that left the child stumbling downstairs or into her parents' bedroom to be reassured that she had not been deserted. One reoccurring nightmare, of which there were many, was of being left to go alone into a dark and foreboding public convenience situated underground. She knew her parents would break their promise to wait for her, or that she would find herself locked in. Lynn was never able to break this dream – however, she discovered that if she had sufficient strength of mind, she could change the outcome of the less fearful experiences by reminding herself that she was within a dream. During one recurrent nightmare she would find herself chased by Indians firing arrows from their bows; she knew she would be killed and the arrows were about to hit her. At this point she had to consciously stand still and face the arrow heads while screaming to herself to wake up. Gradually she woke up more often than she "died", until the nightmare held no threat to her. By taking the fear out of her nightmares she defused their power over her. She didn't need therapy or counselling to come to this conclusion, but she did need a great inner strength. Lynn had this in abundance and yet she was still thought of and treated as a weak, sensitive, sickly child. Perhaps she was all these things; but she was oh so much more!

Despite her strength of mind and character Lynn still could not cope with abandonment, or a sense of loss. She needed her family's constant reassurance that she was loved and that she wouldn't be sent away. Her mother, being a very loving and caring person, was able to fill Lynn's needs. Her father was far more uncomfortable and less approachable, although she recognised he loved her. She accepted at an early age that her brother was not demonstrative, but she trusted him and knew he would always be there for her, if he could. Lynn was truly loved and sheltered but there would come a time when she would have to break out of that cocoon of immediate family life.

That time came when her parents were committed to a function that meant a very late evening's return home. It was decided between Janey's parents and her own that Lynn would stay overnight with her friend's family. Jimmy would let Lynn use his room while he bunked down with his sister. It was all very exciting and although Lynn was apprehensive, she was looking forward to the new experience of "sleeping over", a phrase taken from the infiltrating

American culture. Everything went very well until the children finished their supper and went to bed. Lynn heard Jimmy and his sister going upstairs and then later listened to the house being locked up for the night and Mr and Mrs Dowman going to bed. The bedroom was dark, the bed unfamiliar; and what little light there was shone from the gap in the curtains allowing the rising moon to cast a shaft of light on to the wall. There was a big alarm clock on the bedside table; the hands were luminous and the clock ticked loudly. Every second seemed to pound in Lynn's head. It wasn't long before she became nervous of the unfamiliar darkness. She couldn't see a chink of light under the door and wondered what she should do if she wanted to go to the toilet in the night. She had not wet her bed since the episode at the children's hospital, but the fear of doing so stayed with her. Should she wake Mrs Dowman or knock on her friend's door? She thought she might wake Janey's brother by mistake. Lynn drifted off to sleep, only to wake fitfully from a nightmare. She lay still; the clock ticked loudly on. Eventually Lynn convinced herself that she wouldn't sleep again. She snuggled up in a ball and thought of her mother – where was she? She had been told that they wouldn't be away from home all night. Lynn thought perhaps her family would be home already and that her bed in the little box room would be the only one which remained empty. Lynn wanted to go home. She struggled with the feeling for some time, unsure if she wanted to go to the toilet or whether she was just fretting. She heard something in the garden below; Lynn began to cry.

She didn't know how long she cried nor how loudly but eventually Mrs Dowman put the hall light on and came into the room. She could see Lynn's tearstained face and sat on the bed to comfort her, turning the clock so she could see the time. It was two a.m.; the middle of the night. Somehow Lynn had managed to wake the whole house and her misery only worsened when she realised that she had not only made Jimmy give up his bed but also his night's sleep. In failing in such a big way, Lynn thought, he would think his sister's friend was soppy. She liked Jimmy very much and didn't want to lose face by crying like a baby. Lynn must have been at least eight years old and she knew she should behave better than she had.

Eventually her parents were contacted and Lynn was taken home to sleep in her own bed. Her only consolation was that at least she hadn't had to face the embarrassment of wetting the bed. She thought perhaps it was better to sleep in her own bed with her family around her. When her mummy asked her why she didn't want to stay at Jane's house she admitted that she was scared of the dark and of being left. The old fears that were born from hospital life still haunted her and it was a few years before Lynn attempted to "sleep over" again.

Kate ran round to Lynn's house to give her the news. She took her friend by the hand and led her out of earshot of Lynn's mother. She stood on one foot and then the other; eventually she could contain herself no more. 'Dad has told me that the police force is moving us to Kempton.' She stared at her friend waiting for a reaction. They had played together for many years and were best friends. When she saw Lynn drop her eyes to the ground she pulled at her friend's arm, 'You can come and visit. Mum said my friends can come and stay.'

Lynn looked up for the first time. 'Where's Kempton?'

'Near Bedford, I think.'

Lynn wasn't even sure about Bedford but she knew she wouldn't be able to walk home from there. 'When are you moving?' The conversation was monosyllabic.

'Next week.' she said.

Lynn did not know how to react; should she say she was pleased or hug her friend and tell her she didn't want her to go? Eventually she asked Kate if she was pleased and when the child shrugged her shoulders Lynn realised the enormity of parting.

'It will mean a new school.'

And new friends, Lynn thought, deciding to change the subject. 'Race you to the end of the road...!' They turned to playing and backed away from the dilemma of Kate's impending move from Dunstable.

Lynn didn't see much of her friend the following week and when she did, there was a sad remoteness about her, as if she had already left. Children are resilient and Lynn thought her best friend was already planning her new life. However, as she finally drove away in the back of her parents' car she wound down the window to wave at Lynn and her other friends.

'Don't you dare forget me!' she called, and then directing her bright face at Lynn alone, 'Promise you will come and visit!'

Lynn promised.

'Promise you will play with me all weekend!'

Again Lynn promised, but she had no idea how she would keep that promise. She was nine now and still hadn't slept away from home.

Three months after Kate moved to Kempton Lynn received a letter inviting her to go and stay with her. The families arranged it between them and eventually Lynn found herself standing outside Mr and Mrs Wilson's house hugging her best friend. The semi-detached house had a blue door and blue gates, just like the house in Osborne Road, and it was built alongside a series of houses all looking exactly the same. Lynn wondered if all police houses in the country were painted with the same paint pot! After a big welcome Kate showed her friend her room and the room in which Lynn would sleep. Then after lunch she took Lynn out into the nearby fields. Though Lynn didn't think it as exciting as her fields at home she was thrilled when having met Kate's new gang she was invited to catch grasshoppers with them. Mrs Wilson gave the children glass jars just as Lynn's mum would have done, and the happy band headed over the field, which was surrounded by new building work. Lynn was amazed how many different coloured grasshoppers there were; she had only seen green ones at home. These were smaller in various shades of pink and green. Lynn thought perhaps they had mastered the art of camouflage.

Although she was nervous in different company she had long ago mastered the art of getting on with strangers. The best option was to merge and run with the pack and try not to stand out as being different. It worked fairly well though as usual Lynn tired before the other children. The sun was moving towards three o'clock; Lynn rested on a wall and watched her friend. She seemed to have changed, grown up perhaps, and when she ran with the others, she didn't look back to see if Lynn was following. She had found her feet and had already made new friends, but Lynn wasn't jealous, just a little lost and out of her depth.

When Kate's mother let the children into the garden for lemonade Lynn hung behind to talk to her. She liked Kate's mum, though she was very different to her own. Eventually she drifted off to catch up with the others but her heart wasn't in it. Lynn was thinking of the long evening and even longer night and suddenly all she wanted was to go home. If someone had shouted at her at that precise moment she would have cried. Instead she bit her lip and ran after Kate, who was kicking up her heels and showing her petticoat to everyone who followed.

'Come on Lynn, what's the matter?' she called over her shoulder, but Lynn had already stopped running and had turned back towards the house. She vanished through the kitchen door and to the comfort of Kate's mum.

Lynn didn't stay at Kate's house that night. Mrs Wilson sensed the child's distress and knew she would not be happy sleeping in a strange bed in a strange place. She phoned Lynn's parents who came to pick their daughter up within an hour and a half. During that wait Lynn stayed close to the lady who took the child's mind off her impending tears by allowing her to help make sandwiches.

When the Morris Minor pulled up outside the house Kate came to see what was wrong and was told that her friend had a tummy ache and would not be staying the night. Kate, though puzzled, was not perturbed and, having waved her friend goodbye, ran back to her new friends who were by now skipping in the street. Lynn waved back from the open car window.

It was the last time the friends saw each other. Life for Kate had changed and life for Lynn, although she was in the process of changing, was hindered by past fears and memories. She would eventually leave them behind but would never enjoy sleepovers or holidays without her parents until she had become a teenager and then it would be within the familiarity of her mother's family in Jersey.

She joined the Brownies and the Girl Guides but never went to camp, preferring always the security of her own home and family.

Was Lynn marked for life by her experiences as a child? Lynn stood again as an adult, having risen from her bed, to look out of her bedroom window. It would soon be dawn but as she looked along the road opposite her house she counted the number of houses which had lights in the windows. Often a hall or landing light showed and in one house all lights were ablaze.

Perhaps, she thought, there were many children like herself and possibly many adults who had not yet come to terms with the solitude of darkness. It comforted her to think that perhaps little Lynn had not been alone in her fears and that even today there would be adults out there in the night comforted by a solitary glow in the dark.

She stretched. In reaching for the little child she once was she was beginning to realise just how brave and confident the woman standing by the window had become.

She climbed back into bed, snapped off the light. She was comfortable in the total darkness. She had indeed come a long way.

CHAPTER 21

Lynn couldn't remember when she first started noticing them. It seemed that one day she went to school and, when she came home, the field at the end of their unsurfaced road had sprouted white wooden pegs. The stakes were a couple of inches wide and had been firmly driven in to the ground to a height of about nine inches and perfectly spaced.

Lynn looked along the line that ran from the corner of the grass verge right up the field. Nothing had been grown on this land all year but the children had learned about fields lying fallow so that they recovered the nutrients before a new crop was planted. This was different, she now realised, a farmer doesn't peg his land; he must have sold it! Her heart sank a little. She had heard her parents and those of her friends talking about land earmarked for building. The new technical school had been built for older boys and girls and she knew another school would be built somewhere on the land in her immediate neighbourhood. Lynn walked the line of pegs, soon realising that there was a parallel line the other side of the imaginary road. These first site pegs ran in a continued line from First Avenue, over the field in front of her. She ran to tell her friends and when they investigated they found that the marked highway took a right turn to eventually join up with Canesworde Road. In the other direction from the unmade junction, the pegs continued a little way and came to an abrupt stop. The words "phase one" came in to Lynn's mind; she didn't understand it but must have heard someone mention it in adult conversation. The more the children explored the more they found their whole area of play had been mapped out for the developers. The children's world was about to change and they would have to change with it.

Their games continued despite the disruption. First to come were the strangers with clipboards and tape measures, furthering the work already started. Then came the men with diggers and bulldozers, scraping away the field grasses and top soil, exposing the chalk, piling up the earth into small mountains in areas they had cleared. The children played different games now, for the site was too large to be fenced against them. The best times were weekends and light-filled evenings when the men had gone home. Lynn and her brother had been warned about the trenches, which had been covered wherever possible by the workmen before they "knocked off" to go home, but children will be children and everyone knew that the most exciting games were those that were forbidden. Lynn wasn't too interested in the road building, but enjoyed riding her newly acquired bicycle over the new concrete segmented sections. Somehow she felt safe on this unadopted road, for no traffic ever used it while Laing's, the contractors, were building. She was nervous of cycling on adopted roads without her parents to safeguard her and up to that time preferred cycling in the parks; now she and her young friends had a little more freedom to practise their road skills.

They avoided the workmen if they could, often being told to play elsewhere, move along, or go home. Didn't the men know that the children had played there long before the workmen had arrived? Soon, however, Lynn's and Bill's friends found shortcuts through the building site to the fields beyond. They could still climb their hill and the bomb crater was still safely in their domain. From this outpost on the far slope of the hill, the children would gather as a gang, crawling through the grass to the summit where they could look down on all the work that was going on below them. The workmen became the enemy; the children understood that they were best avoided but they would not admit defeat as to whom the land really belonged to. Their games changed and they were pushed further afield to collect grasses and flowers for their summer treasure hunts. Conveniently they were getting older now and were allowed to venture further away from the safety of home. No one could take away everything; could they?

After the road making gave structure to the huge building site, the house building started. The houses, 54 and 56 First Avenue, were no longer to be the last pair in the road and Lynn's neighbour now had a building going up alongside her side boundary fence. The corner site next to the Zealeys' house was developed about the same time and the children were disappointed that they had lost the right to build their yearly bonfire. The bungalow on this land was privately built. The lorries delivered the bricks and all the materials needed to build the new houses and the noise and dust covered the gardens and any vehicle left outside on the old road. The chaos, which the council called "progress", disrupted the harmony of country life. However, the neighbourhood settled down into submission, knowing houses were badly wanted and that the country needed to look forward to the future and not back to the old days of war-torn towns and post war pre-fabricated housing.

The children played on! The great mounds of earth were many, stretching to more distant farmland. The older children had explored the area before but now Lynn and her friends joined them on the new territory. Aware of invisible boundaries, set by other groups of children, Lynn became unsure of herself, preferring things as they used to be. They played in the farmer's weakened haystack, recently discovered by the boys and learned the new skill of communicating between each other with cocoa tins and string held taut between the metal containers. Lynn didn't know if it really worked because when she tried it, her brother was standing only the other side of the haystack and she could hear his voice carry on the wind anyway.

One of the mountains of soil was piled by the boundary fence of another small development. Each sector seemed now to join up with the next construction site. A man who lived in one of the newly constructed houses called out from his garden telling the motley band of children to clear off and find somewhere else to play. It seemed so unfair. Lynn said that the diggers and tractors and earth movers were taking out all the countryside and eventually they would join all the houses together in a huge block of concrete and cement. It would be like removing a piece of Mr Hurst's world jig-saw and replacing it with a singular grey piece, without colour or design.

As she walked home for tea that afternoon with the gang, she commented that at least they still had their hill and no one would dare to build houses around a bomb crater. Her brother plucked a sticky head of grass seeds and threw it like a dart at his sister's back. It stuck on to her cardigan, destined to work its way through to her skin where it would scratch and irritate. It was a favourite game for the children for the grass head acted like a barb and was very difficult to remove. Future generations of children would not be able to annoy each other with such natural missiles. Lynn was right in part; where now the broken grasses blazed their trail, soon only pavements and lampposts would mark the way home.

While the building carried on in its own exordial way, relentless like cancer, the children found other places to play. Lynn's friends would decide which of them would ask their mother if friends could come round and there was usually a choice of Janey's garden, opposite the school they all went to, or Lucy's garden. Lucy was a new friend from Canesworde Road. Of course the building site was an added attraction.

That summer the construction of the Lake District estate continued apace. The nearer properties, those bordering on Lynn's and Bill's home, now took the shape of proper houses and it was the girls' time to be intrigued with what was going on. They forgot about the temptation of playing in the far fields; there were play houses right on their own door step. The earlier properties had roofs and stairs fitted and each floor was partitioned off, making them three-bedroomed houses. The greatest draw to Lynn and her friends was the fact that the builders had not secured the properties by hanging the doors. By climbing on to a well-positioned upturned galvanised bucket or a conveniently placed breeze block, they could overcome the problem of there not being a front door-step. Most of the boys still wanted to play their own games outside but the girls were content to have their own house in which to play. They preferred upstairs as the rooms were smaller and they could not be seen if the workmen looked in through the windows. Everyone was sworn to secrecy as the building site now more than ever was out of bounds to children. Happy Families was always a popular girls' game and sometimes if Kevin wanted to play they would entice him to be the father. Of course he had to go out to work and not come back till the end of the day, so that got rid of him.

The girls would continue playing happily until someone called out that a workman was coming. The game finished abruptly and the children either hid quickly hoping he would not enter the building, or made a hurried exit through what would be the kitchen door. Lynn never felt very comfortable when they played in the houses for no matter how much she enjoyed the games, she was frightened of anyone in authority. Terrified of doing the wrong thing she would try to escape, placing herself between the others so as not to be the first to be caught. The builder would chase them, though he would make it a point never to catch any of them, and he shouted an awful lot. Nobody knew what the punishment would be if they were caught, but they all thought they would be taken to the foreman or, worse still, their parents. The houses, however, were just too much of a temptation and the hide-and-seek routine between the children and authority continued. Eventually, one Saturday morning, they arrived at the site to find all the houses in the road had new front and side doors. Their way was barred and bolted and the fun they had had running through the properties was over. They didn't enter any of the houses in the other new roads, for they were in uncharted territory. The little gang went back to playing on their hill and spying on the encroaching workmen from the bomb crater.

'It won't be long before they take this from us as well,' said her brother one day.

'Never,' said Lynn. However, before many weeks of the new term had passed the forest of white-painted stakes was discovered to be marching up their hill and down the other side. The children had lost their playing ground, but at a convenient time when childhood was losing its fight against early adolescence. The days of running free were over.

Chapter 22

A week or so after her eleventh birthday Lynn started her new school. She had previously passed the Intelligence Test and had gone on with the rest of her year to sit the Eleven-plus. Like most children, she hated exams. She became anxious and suffered the symptoms of tummy upsets and feeling sick. Once the exams were out of the way the worry then became the possibility of losing friends to other schools and having to make new ones. Icknield School was small and friendly but the bigger schools filled their places from large catchment areas. Lynn and her class friends didn't know what awaited them in September; it was the start of a new era.

She had heard her parents talking about which schools were available and Lynn waited anxiously to find out if she had passed the exam which divided friends and siblings. Once children had been allocated a place it was not impossible to retain primary school friendships but it was more difficult; life simply moved on.

Her brother, three years earlier, had passed his Eleven-plus and been given a place at the Dunstable Boys Grammar school. He was a high achiever, and his world revolved around study, organised activities and his friendships with the boys attending the same school.

On the day Lynn discovered she had failed the exam and would be going to a more practical Secondary Modern School she caught up with her friends to find out if they would be joining her at the same school. Lynn's health problems and subsequent poor school attendance had contributed to her failure of the

Eleven-plus. She would be placed at Brewer's Hill Secondary Modern school. Generally considered a less academic institution, these schools placed more emphasis on practical education. Luckily some of her friends would be attending the same school. It had only just been built, though unfortunately it was not situated in the immediate neighbourhood. In fact it was at least a twenty-minute walk away even at a determined pace, along straight, boring roads of indeterminable length. It was decided that Lynn would stay at school for the midday meal, as the return walk home for lunch would be out of the question. She looked forward to the time when she could cycle to school – this would be a much better option.

When Lynn arrived at her new school on the first morning of the new September term a cement mixer was still on site. Less essential buildings were still under construction. It was the second time in her life she heard the word "phase". Luckily "Phase one" was complete and the school year was set.

Lynn thought her school uniform was fine; she loved the colours blue and yellow and the diagonal striped tie suited both the boys and the girls. The only thing Lynn and most of the other children hated was the school motto, "Be Still." Mr Snell, the headmaster, seemed to be a gentle, sincere man and the motto, which the children presumed he had chosen, had been taken from a famous hymn, which was also adopted by the school.

On the first day all the children gathered in the large, cement-dusted playground. Suddenly a voice echoed across the tarmac.

'Be still!'

Every one of the new boys and girls stopped and looked towards the coping on which Mr Snell was standing, raised above the crowd. Having gained the children's attention he proceeded to explain that it was not a reprimand but a foundation on which to base their future lives. 'Be Still'; be still, be calm. Mr Snell was quite an orator; sadly, although some understood what their headmaster was saying, the majority did not and were anxious for him to finish his welcome so that they could get on with the business of making new friends and meeting old ones. The one thing nobody liked was the fact that the motto was emblazoned on their school blazer badge and everyone treated it as a joke. A child from another school would pass a Brewer's Hill pupil in the street and yell out for them to 'be still' and snigger. It probably caused a few fights on the way home from school, but it didn't affect the girls very much. Some of the adults were just as bad, unable to understand why it had been chosen. The school hymn, sung to the tune *Finlandia*, began with the line, "Be still my soul, The Lord is on thy side", was to Lynn, very beautiful and during her later times of illness she would ask her mother to sing it to her to soothe and give her peace.

The verse continued, "Bear patiently thy cross of grief and pain." How true that came to be for Lynn, who would in time hold on to such sentiments until she had battled her way through health problems yet again. On that first term at Brewer's Hill School she was unaware of the illness to come and formed a line with the children as they were dismissed after the headmaster's speech. They were instructed to go to their new classrooms to start their first day of term. Everywhere the buildings were in a state of newness and teachers and pupils alike found it difficult to acclimatise to the change. Lynn's year would be the first to travel through the curriculum from eleven years of age to the final year. They were told as a group that they had to set an example as they would be watched, as one would a barometer, in order to judge the success of the new school's system.

Once Lynn settled at the craft table that was to be her desk she looked out of the window of her second-floor classroom which doubled as a pottery studio. The sun shone and the September breeze shook early leaves from a tree on the school boundary. Lynn shivered; she was unsure if she liked anything at all but she was determined to do her best; it was something that Lynn never failed at. She looked across the room and saw Martin Burridge and smiled at him; he glared back, but coloured up like a carrot. Lynn had had a love-hate relationship with the boy ever since they were both five years old and in the full course of their school life they proved that in strength. On the first week at primary school he pushed her over; she ripped his blazer. He told her her first rude joke and sent her love notes, which she kept in a cardboard box, until her brother found them! This was followed as they grew older by her first Valentine present of a Picnic bar and graduated to a little plastic bracelet with charms on, the following year. Neither of them had any idea how to go about making friends with the opposite sex and in all that time they were too shy to hold a conversation; she didn't even know where he lived. Now in her new classroom which smelt of clay rather than polish, Lynn was pleased to see him and wondered if they would get to know each other better.

Within a few weeks Lynn had cause to doubt this would happen. The boy with red hair and freckles had his head turned. Madeleine was beautiful, with short bobbed blonde hair and a very confident manner. In no time at all Martin only had eyes for her and Lynn's so-called first romance ended in disappointment. After cookery class one day Martin Burridge snatched her Queen of Puddings from Lynn's hands and smashed his fist into the meringue. It was reported and Martin got the cane. By the third year at Brewer's Hill the Tower Block was well established. One day the boy opened the glass door at the entrance of the school block for Lynn to pass through; as she did so he shut it in her face. The only injury was hurt pride but Lynn's retaliation caused injury. Her brother had taught her how to pretend to hit someone on the nose and stop only an inch away from it, causing shock but no damage. Lynn was a poor judge of distance and her fist made contact with Martin's mouth, breaking one of his front teeth. Bearing in mind it was one of his second teeth the damage was irreparable. They never spoke to each other again and the only contact she had with him after she had left school was to see him by the bus stop in Dunstable after she had come out of college. They didn't speak, but he blushed heavily and no doubt she did too. She wished she had courage to speak to him but the moment was gone and they never saw each other again. Perhaps, despite mixing with her brother's friends and those from the East End of London, she still had a lot to learn about boys.

Lynn enjoyed playing with her friends from Icknield School but the children were growing academically as well as physically. By nature this was a time when children formed different groups and gangs away from their home environment. Kate had already moved on to Kempton, and Janey had made new friends and was now physically stronger and faster; she excelled in sports and literally left her friend behind on the race track and classroom. Here, too Lynn was a valuable member of the class but she excelled only in art and English, preferring the subjects where she could use her creative skills or where she could bring the subjects like History and Geography alive with the use of them. Again Lynn thrived under sympathetic teachers only this time with the reverse effect. Her Geography and form master was an inspired and interested man, who in fact was disabled, not having the use of one arm. The children believed it was through polio but it was never discussed. He came to work on a bicycle and was, just like Mr Hurst, very good in encouraging children who were less able than others. When Mr Watling left his post Lynn went from sixth in Geography to near bottom of the class. His replacement was more forthright and academic but without the imagination or patience a youngster like Lynn needed. She had enjoyed drawing maps and learned a lot about the world by using this aid. The new teacher needed to hone the children ready for O-level GCEs and the time for such instruction was limited.

Boys joined gangs; girls gathered in cliques and Lynn soon found new friends in the classroom and playground. Because of the wide catchment area of the school many were unable to play or meet Lynn in the evenings. Instead the little group of friends would walk part of the way home from school with each other or meet at weekends; Lynn's father dropping her at one of her friend's houses on a Saturday morning.

As the first year progressed, Lynn's life developed around school and home, seemingly in separate boxes. This changed when Lynn and Tina met; the friendship brought the two sides of her life together once again and the two girls became firm friends. Tina's father worked for Laings Construction Company, the firm who were continuing to build the Lake District estate and probably one of the very men who had chased the children away from the site prior to Lynn starting her new school. Tina and her family were billeted, as her father would say, on site. They were housed in a caravan on a small settlement just over Lynn's hill. Here Tina and her brother thrived with their parents until, much later, the family was moved to a council house nearer the school.

The two girls got on well together; Tina's mother was unwell and the girl grew up quickly, having to help around the home far more than Lynn ever had to. Nevertheless there was time to play and the children made the most of their proximity to each other. Lynn would knock on the caravan door after having walked through the building site along unmade roads, now bearing names such as Langdale Road, Penrith Avenue and now Lowther Road. After tea the girls walked and played on the ever-developing housing estate. The concrete roads spread like a spider's web across the earmarked fields and all sign of pasture and field were gone. Lynn tried to find the annoying sharp-eared grasses and field flowers but in vain. Occasionally a kidney vetch would seed in a roughly made pathway but pretty soon cultivated flowers would bloom in regimented order where once the wild scabious and cornflower had grown.

Tina closed the caravan door with orders from her father to be home by eight-thirty p.m. sharp! The girls took a tennis ball and bounced it down the road. It was a game they wouldn't have been able to play when the land was still fields. Now smooth and boring there wasn't much else to do. Gone were the days of playing in the houses; some were even occupied. Because Mr Norris was a site foreman he kept a close eye on his daughter. She had learned how dangerous a building site could be, having, no doubt, lived on one before as her father moved the family round the country while he was on contract.

The early evening light was still strong enough to play by and the children, wearing Wellingtons because of recent rain, played catch by the side of the tractor-churned road. They chatted as they played. Lynn wasn't great at catching ball. She reached up for it and as it stubbed her outstretched fingers it bounced from her grasp Tina watched as it dropped in to a huge mud-filled puddle. It wasn't a puddle really; more of a muddy builders' lake that the lorries had churned in to a quagmire! The ball sat, taunting the girls to go and fetch it, some eight feet from the safety of where they stood. Tina knew she couldn't go home without it for it belonged to her brother. After a little thought, and with little idea how deep the lake of mud was, she ventured out to it. The mud slurped and sucked in a very serious manner, unlike normal mud. She made two or three steps but when she paused to call back to Lynn, the mud caught at her boot and allowed her to take no more steps.

'I'm stuck, Lynn! I can't pull my boot out!' At first she laughed and her friend caught her jovial mood. They giggled together, but the more Tina tried to move the heavier the mud became. She nearly lost balance as she stretched for the ball, just out of reach. It was then she realised she was in trouble.

'I'll pull you out,' called Lynn without realising the situation. She stepped out and immediately the mud took her. Her foot came out of her boot and Lynn felt the cold stickiness force itself around her sock and ankle, gradually immobilising her. She caught herself, nearly losing her balance, but now the two girls were in the same predicament.

The shadows were getting longer and it was getting cold. Her father had judged the sunset to the time Tina should be home but now it was eight pm and it seemed unlikely that they would get home at all. They began to panic. Any move they made worsened the situation. It almost seemed as though cement had been poured in to the mud, so great was its hold.

'Will we be here all night?' Lynn shivered.

'I don't think so. One of my father's jobs is to go around the site before it's dark to check everything is all right; eventually he'll find us.' Tina sounded more frightened of her dad than the descending darkness.

'Let's shout then,' encouraged Lynn, cupping her hands to her mouth as a funnel. The two girls called, breaking the eerie silence. They called again and again. The echo came back from the surrounding empty buildings.

Lynn wanted to cry, but she didn't.

As the last grey shadow turned to darkness a man's shape silhouetted against the late evening sky. He stood above them on a pile of earth, staring down; they could tell that his mood, even without his speaking, was as black as descending night. He controlled his temper with stern abruptness, shouting down at the children as they shivered below him. Lynn caught one word in three but she knew him to be very angry.

Tina's father pulled both children from the mud with some effort even for a strong man. He stood them to one side and went back to rescue Lynn's boot; he forgot the ball but the children didn't dare remind him. He gave them a telling off but was relieved to see no harm had come to them. The girls walked submissively by his side as he escorted Lynn to the edge of the estate and to within sight of her house, then turning from her, the father and daughter walked home without a backward glance. Lynn waited for her friend to wave and when she didn't she thought perhaps she wouldn't call for her friend over the week end until perhaps her father was in a better mood. They would meet again on Monday.

Some weeks later as a school project, the class were asked to write an essay on the scariest thing that had ever happened to them. Lynn knew exactly what she was going to write and recounted the episode of the lake of mud and the children's rescue. She thought she would get good marks for the piece for it had remained vividly in her memory. However, upon return of the essay, at the bottom of the piece of writing the teacher had written in red ink… "This could not have possibly happened!"

Lynn was disappointed and indignant, but could never make her teacher change his mind. Lynn, it seemed had been labelled as imaginative and she realised for the first time that the talent she possessed was dismissed as storytelling. Lynn never lied or made up stories to benefit herself; if truth was asked for that was what she gave. Only in her fiction did she let her imagination run away. This, in later years, was to be the making and the saving of her.

Lynn and Tina stayed friends. They would meet at school and in their spare time. Lynn knew her friend had a much harder life than she herself did, because Tina's mother was ill. This didn't stop them enjoying themselves when they could. One day, upon childish impulse, they decided they would each like to own a pet. They put their heads together and decided they could just about afford to buy a mouse each with their saved pocket money. They both knew their parents would condemn the idea, so the girls decided not to tell them. The friends went to the pet shop at the week end. They hadn't really decided where they would keep the mice or what in!

The girls' project was doomed to failure for when they went to the pet shop the assistant told the girls they had no mice for sale, only a hamster. The friends thought about it and decided to put their money together and buy it. Clutching the small box tightly they walked up the high street, but unable to contain their curiosity, opened the box to peep in. The hamster was out in a trice and the two girls, amidst sobs and tears, chased it into the road, only catching it by its back leg as it tried to disappear down a drain. That was the first of its two lives gone! The hamster was deposited with food and bedding in a cardboard box in Tina's shed without her parents' knowledge and the girls arranged to meet the next day and keep the pet a secret. Needless to say, when they opened the shed door the next morning the cardboard box had a big hole chewed in the corner and the seven-and-six-penny hamster was gone. After more tears and recriminations the friends parted company and when she got home Lynn faced an inquisition as to why she had been crying. The story came out and eventually it was decided that as long as she put her pocket money towards a proper tin cage she could have a replacement hamster. The problem was where to keep it. In fact, the nocturnal creature was kept in her brother's bedroom; Lynn's box room being too small. He cursed his sister and her hamster for it kept him awake at night running round and round its squeaky exercise wheel. Lynn could even hear it in her own bedroom! Her brother was not amused and her friendship with Tina suffered because the original hamster was bought with both their combined pocket money. Tina didn't talk to Lynn for days and Lynn didn't know how to heal the rift, for she didn't have any more money to refund her friend. Friendship, however, is resilient and within a week or so she was talking and playing with Lynn, though the subject of the hamster was never mentioned again.

Apart from the nights of lost sleep Bill enjoyed playing with their new pet in his bedroom. The children were meant to take turns in cleaning its cage and once they had kept their bargain Hammy the hamster was allowed to wander around Bill's bedroom as long as the door was closed. Her brother's inventiveness encouraged the children to take their collection of Children's annuals out of the book cupboard and turn them on their edges, making an inverted V-shaped corridor. Bill blocked one end with his sister, of course, and put Hammy in to the other, laying his head on the floor to watch their pet run backwards and forwards. Lynn loved the game and eventually her brother extended the tunnel and made junctions and bends, filling the whole room. Of course this was all very well until the hamster escaped and everyone had to hunt for it in case it made its nest in Bill's mattress. The children were discouraged from this game and eventually the hamster became a sleepy old rodent who was no trouble to anyone except on cage-cleaning day. Both their mother and father insisted that when Hammy went to heaven there would be no replacement to fill his cage!

Tina and her family moved off the building site to a council house not long after the housing estate had been completed. The two girls continued to see each other at school, but Tina rarely spoke about her home life. When her mother died of cancer, Tina's childhood ended abruptly, as she further assumed the responsibilities of caring for her brother and father. The two girls saw less of each other, until, with a class change at the end of the following academic year they, regrettably, drifted apart.

Chapter 23

Lynn knew her mum suffered with her nerves; she was aware of the fact from a young age, although she didn't really know what it meant. To the child, her mother was just that; a loving, understanding mum. Lynn didn't often see her cry, though sometimes she heard her in the afternoons or night time through the partially opened bedroom door. Rarely did she see her cross and it seemed to Lynn that she only got annoyed when there was a genuine reason. Sometimes she was pensive; a word used by her father when underlining a photograph slipped into one of the many albums. As Lynn grew older she would look through the large books, which recorded the children growing up, and the many family outings and holidays. She realised just how many captions read, "Pensive Joyce" or "What's up?" There were pages of photographs where she never smiled although all those taken on the Jersey holidays were full of her smiles and laughter. Lynn just accepted her mother for who she was; she didn't analyse. She was no different from any other child but being a girl and often poorly she remained close to her mother, gaining comfort from the affection and love she was shown. It upset her to think that her mother was not always bright and cheerful and as Lynn's own health improved she noticed a tiredness which overcame her mother and a quietness about her that concerned her. She couldn't remember when she first started noticing the changes although perhaps there were none. Perhaps her mother had always suffered with depression and Lynn had been too young to really notice it.

To the children it was natural for their mother to go to bed and rest on a Sunday afternoon, especially when they were old enough to find their own amusement and didn't need entertaining. Their father would snooze in the front room and their mother would go for a lie-down. She would ask the children to play quietly and to wake her up after an hour. The disappointment came when Lynn knocked on her parents' bedroom door and a sleepy voice would answer, asking for another fifteen minutes' rest; and then perhaps another. Lynn and Bill played well but often their mother didn't rise from her nap until nearly tea time. Lynn thought their mother's day was wasted. Even during the school holidays their mum would go to bed in the afternoons. Lynn was old enough then to make her a cup of tea to wake her up with and, as she grew up, having learned from watching her mother bake, she would spend the time her mother was sleeping making a Victoria sponge. She was thrilled to see her mother smile when she came downstairs later in the afternoon to the surprise treat. Lynn liked to see her mother smile.

Lynn didn't know when it happened but gradually she made her mother's happiness part of her responsibility. Her mother never said she was unhappy but there was often a quietness about her that Lynn didn't understand. A little posy of field flowers sometimes helped or sweets to share from the Kirby Road shop. She worked hard on homemade birthday cards and gifts for Mother's Day from her pocket money and gave her mum lots of cuddles. One day, having saved her pocket money, Lynn took the bus to Luton and bought her mother a large blue glass vase; it was so heavy that she could hardly carry it. The girl decided it would be for her mother's birthday though she knew in her heart that she would have given it to her straight away, just to see her happiness and approval. Little gifts were a favourite show of affection. Lynn understood her mother because in some ways she herself was very much like her. Affection was almost Lynn's life blood, both in giving and receiving and her mother also needed to feel that her love was reciprocated. She rarely went to her dad for a cuddle though she was overjoyed when he held his arms open to her.

Perhaps, thought Lynn, her mother didn't get enough cuddles. She had often sat on her mother's lap on the Parker Knoll high-backed chair and cuddled into her when she was younger and wished she could stay there for ever. As she grew older she found other ways to show her love; moments alone with her mother were precious. It was as if they were both trying to make up for an intangible absence; there was a need in them both. Lynn didn't understand just how much her hospital experiences had affected her; her mother had her own past ghosts to haunt her. The bond between mother and daughter was strong;

their personalities, although not the same, were in sympathy with each other. Although that would change to some degree Lynn always seemed to understand her mother more than other members of the family. She wanted to ease her way, to help others understand, but she was only her mother's daughter and could wave no magic wand.

Every now and again Lynn's mum would clean the house exceptionally well. She would bake and tidy and tell the children that there would be visitors coming around for the evening. Sometimes it would be relatives from London and sometimes it would be friends of their father. Bill and Lynn would be allowed to stay up for a while and sit quietly listening to the adult conversation float around the front room. There would be biscuits and cake with tea or cold drinks and everyone seemed to Lynn to be on their best behaviour. She liked listening to the adults although often it was a little boring. She would look forward to the refreshments and then fidget until she and her brother were sent to bed.

The conversation on most of these evenings often turned to the events of the war and her parents' experiences. Often her father's friends had been in the army with him or the Tourist Cycling club. None of them would have known her mother before her parents married. Her mother was almost a curiosity. She was strikingly good-looking, which put many women on their guard, and a good conversationalist. She had also experienced the German Occupation of Jersey and the Channel Islands and therefore had many interesting stories to add to the evening's conversation. Lynn knew many of the stories that were told at bedtime but somehow when the visitors asked her questions about what it was like things went badly wrong.

The visitors would ask her mother what it was like to be on an occupied island during the war. Her mother would explain a little, trying to keep the conversation light and fair.

The guests would persist, interested in the details. 'Were the Germans very cruel?'

'There is good and bad in everyone,' her mother would reply.

'Was there enough food? Did anyone starve?'

Her mother thought this needed a longer answer and so gave one.

The questions went on and on; the visitors were genuinely interested and each time insisted on further detail which her mother supplied. Then she was telling them heart-rending, fascinating stories without being prompted. Her mother enjoyed centre stage but never bored her guests. Lynn would notice her mother was talking more quickly, becoming agitated.

On one occasion Lynn pulled her father's sleeve; she knew how it would end. 'Stop her, Dad,' she whispered

'She's all right, Lynn, be good.' Her father was equally interested in the story his wife was relating about the Occupation of Jersey.

Her mother carried on, the stories becoming longer and more intense. Why doesn't he stop her? Lynn thought as her mother became pale.

Suddenly it was all over; Joyce stopped, almost in mid-sentence. She was deathly white and breathing too quickly. Lynn knew her mother was about to faint. The visitors were suddenly perturbed and went to help her, embarrassed that such a conversation should have caused the trauma. Her husband brought her a glass of water and it took a few moments to gather herself; Lynn's mum rallied enough to apologise profusely. It spoilt the evening, of course, and even little Lynn realised that it should never had happened. Her mother always reacted in this way if she was made to talk too long about the war.

After the visitors had left and the front room was tidied up and the dishes washed, Lynn's mother was still subdued. It took a long time for her to get over the episode and Lynn felt her father was partly to blame for allowing the conversation to continue until her mother was ill. She got to hate evenings when such friends came round, but eventually they learned, by their own accord, not to ask her mother about her wartime experiences.

Because Lynn and her brother were too young to be fully aware and included in decisions affecting the family, life continued in relative normality. They were aware that their mother was unwell and through overheard conversations they gleaned that perhaps she needed more help and medication than the family GP could give her. Lynn was about ten years old when her mother attended the psychiatric outpatients' department. It had then been decided that a course of electro-shock treatment, a therapy popular at the time, could well help reduce her symptoms of anxiety and depression. It was diagnosed that the mental trauma stemmed from her experiences during the wartime Occupation which began in 1940 when she was an eighteen year old, and in love with an English visitor. The handsome soldier had been on embarkation leave, staying at the family hotel. Lynn had seen the photographs taken of Private Zealey at that time and could well understand the attraction between her father and mother. The war separated the couple. Upon Liberation in 1945 they married and she joined her new husband to start a new life in post-war Luton, trying for a family immediately.

Her mother would tell Lynn how much she had wanted a daughter. Joyce miscarried, but the subsequent pregnancy resulted in the birth of Bill, a healthy son, bringing contentment to the family. Their daughter, Lynn, was born three years later. The family was complete. The birth, however, was premature and fraught with difficulties. Lynn, a perceptive girl, suspected that her struggle for health must have affected her mother's own stamina. She began to feel needlessly responsible for her mother's own well-being.

Outwardly life continued as normal. After Joyce's treatment it was hoped the depression would lift and that the memories of the Occupation would fade and become less distressing, but it was not to be; there was to be no magic wand. Instead of eradicating such memories it stole the happier ones of a family holiday in Scotland. They returned to Oban the following year to try to rekindle the memories of the previous holiday of which Lynn's mother had little recollection. Lynn and her brother had little understanding of their mother's condition and enjoyed both holidays equally.

Lynn remained close to her mother. She had an instinctive feeling that perhaps the memories of wartime Jersey were only a part of her mother's depression. She sensed that, however hard her mother tried with and for the family, she was a very unhappy woman. Lynn never knew her mother without tablets, some for her nerves and others for the early onset of arthritis for which she was soon attending clinic.

Everybody outside the family knew her as the kind, warm-hearted lady who was always cheerful, helping others with her brightness and friendship. Few realised the problems she faced. Only those close in friendship or proximity had any idea.

One day, Mrs Boskett called her mother over the dividing fence of their gardens one day and asked if she was all right.

'Perfectly, thank you, Grace.' Her mother queried why she should ask.

'I heard you crying again,' said the elderly neighbour 'I hate to think you are so unhappy.'

Lynn's mother reassured the kindly lady, but could not reassure herself or her daughter.

Chapter 24

The child stood in the doorway of Lynn's bedroom. She stood as a silhouette against the frame with the backdrop of dawn behind her. She stood patiently as if waiting for Lynn to wake up, eager to be away.

Lynn raised herself on one elbow. As full consciousness returned, the fragile figure of the girl faded without moving out of view. The child diminished, rather than vanished, leaving opaqueness similar to the result of blurred vision. Lynn rubbed her eyes and blinked as her eyesight returned to focus. She turned her head to the open doorway; the child had gone.

At first Lynn didn't remember it was her birthday. The poor night had left a sluggishness which was hard to break free from. It was the sound of the telephone ringing that eventually brought her back to reality. She reached out for it on the bedside table.

'Happy birthday, Gollum.' It could only be one person; he had used one of the more endearing nicknames from childhood. Even from Wollongong in Australia Lynn recognised her brother's voice, the link made across the miles and the years.

'I've timed it right, haven't I? I haven't woken you?'

Lynn answered; the pleasure of hearing his voice obvious by her lightened tone. She remembered Bill, just for a moment, dressed in his Dunstable Grammar school uniform, ready for his new term as a sixth former. He had been a hard-working achiever, going from school to university in Edinburgh, where he met his future wife. Having attained his Bachelor of Science and Doctorate in Astrophysics her brother found married life suited him. His career took them to Australia and Hawaii, returning eventually to Australia with their four children, all having now gained their own university degrees. Bill was awaiting retirement from Wollongong University where he held an established position and was held in high regard. Lynn was proud of her brother though a little hazy as to his career route. Sometimes she didn't pay full attention when he was glib about his working life and most of the time he played down his career success. She loved her brother but knew him little better than when they had been children; their lives were so different. Their "It" and "Thing" nicknames seemed quite appropriate.

She chatted happily now with an over-optimistic view of her near future to quell the anxiety she heard in her brother's questions, 'I'm doing fine, really; going to be great.' There was a pause before she answered his next question. Telephone connections had improved greatly but occasionally there was a delay in the continuity.

'Yes, friends are calling in this morning and later this afternoon. I've been really spoilt, everyone has rallied.' Again a pause. 'Yes, Alan's coming to see me when he gets back from the mainland.'

Alan was still supportive as a friend and as an ex-husband he had done his best; they both had. Having moved to the Isle of Wight five years into their marriage they had settled well. Now after fifteen years apart, they continued a relaxed relationship; it was not intimidating, aggressive or bitter. They had overcome the status of divorce and the difficulties involved without discussing them further; now it seemed they had always been friends more than partners. Lynn didn't know it at the time of their marriage but she had been unable to have children. It was one of the greatest tragedies of her life for she knew in her heart that she would have made a good mother; however it wasn't to be. They tried to find a way round the problem but ended up resigned to the fact that the marriage would remain childless. This, in itself, was not a cause for the breakdown in their marriage. The reasons for divorce were now muddied with time and their friendship was stronger for the separation. At some point, Lynn knew not when, they had both decided that to let go of a marriage was one thing, but to let go of friendship too would be an utter waste of the years spent together.

'You're sixty then?' Bill's voice happily broke her train of thought.

'Fifty-nine; not a pensioner yet!' she retorted indignantly.

'Bus-pass next year though,' he taunted. She heard him chuckle at something his wife said in the background. Lynn liked it when her sister-in-law joined in the conversation.

Brother and sister carried on their sibling banter. The physical play fights had passed with childhood but the sparring continued even over the phone. They understood each other's like-minded humour; it was often sarcastic and sometimes scathing, but always light-hearted. Lynn later used her quick wit when writing comedy sketches for her local hospital radio, at St Mary's hospital on the Isle of Wight. In her personal life she turned her humour to her advantage, as a great way to put down a man who was giving her unwarranted attention. She little realised that some men thought of this as a challenge, having the opposite effect of encouraging them.

'What was the doctor's diagnosis?' The brittle edge of professionalism entered Bill's voice, commanding a sensible answer.

'Adhesions, scar tissue; just as before. It seems my body continues to make the stuff even when the healing of an old wound is complete. After all the surgery over the years and the complications my innards must look as though someone has poured super-glue inside. It was no wonder my small bowel obstructed again.' She laughed with embarrassment; a false humour trying to lighten the situation.

The tone of the conversation was serious now, her brother wanted answers and he was well aware of the miles between them and the inability to get the truth from the doctors himself. 'What are they going to do, send you to the mainland or operate on the Isle of Wight? I don't think that is a good option.'

Lynn had undergone operations at St Mary's Hospital on the island with mixed results but she had never found the surgeons assigned to her case less than skilled. Now she was under the care of the bowel surgeon and had every faith in him. She stood up in his support; her brother backed down.

'The surgeon is going to undertake all my investigations locally, as an out-patient. It will take some months but at the end of it he will know exactly where and what must be done. The bed rest has eased the immediate situation and I'm happy to go along with that. I'll go back to Accident and Emergency if I deteriorate; I know what to do.' Lynn thought back again to the child who had endured so much and who had been so familiar with institutional hospital life that turning up on her own at A & E did not phase her.

Thank God for the bravery of little Lynn, she thought, believing she saw a shadow of the child flit across her peripheral vision. There was a long pause between them; she helped Bill out by changing the subject. 'Thanks for the birthday card; I take it the present is coming later.'

He gave a defensive grunt and told his sister they hadn't found the right gift yet. Rather than buy and send something inappropriate they both often shelved the responsibility until they were struck with guilt or made an impulsive purchase that, at least, had a chance of being appreciated.

'That's OK but no more dried toad skin purses.' She had a dig at him for the last birthday gift that she had recycled.

'It was unique and had been humanely sacrificed,' he said in his defence. 'The culling of the toads was necessary, and the profit from retail goes towards conservation.'

The chat went on a little longer, neither really knowing how to end the conversation.

'Have a great day then,' he concluded, realising that for Lynn this was not going to be the best birthday ever. 'Come out to see us when you are well and let me know if you need me, or anything.' There were goodbyes and the line disconnected leaving Lynn listening to a burring noise; she replaced the receiver and turned over, holding her chocolate-coloured bear to her chest. She corrected her position; the pain in her side had not abated, but it would do; soon everything would improve.

Lynn reached deep inside herself to where the child brought forth strength. It was the strength of spirit born through experience; she had done this all before. When she was a child there was fear and unfamiliarity, now as an adult though tremulous, she was not afraid. She accepted that she was ill but with the old coding of submission she resigned herself to the forthcoming investigations and examinations. Many of the procedures she would have undergone before; it made it no less hard to face but to be forewarned is to be forearmed. Little Lynn had given the adult Lynn courage to move forward. The only fear that she held on to was the worry that she would not be believed; that tests would be inconclusive and the decision would be made not to operate. She knew her body so well that she understood just how serious her problems were. Would others also realise? The answer was no if she continued putting on a brave face to the world. Camouflage did her no favours; this time she would have to be brave enough to admit defeat in her personal battle to be stronger than anyone else in the world around her. Lynn knew deep down that the internal scar tissue was gradually strangling her small bowel; the obstructions were becoming more frequent and lately she had literally been trying to walk away from her problematic pain by sitting on Culver Down, a high outburst of chalk down land that ended with a great drop to the blue sea below. It was one of those places where you could put down your burden and pretend you were in another world. Some people had even tried to prove the point and jumped to their suicide, but these thoughts were far from Lynn's mind. She just wanted to be free of pain and she knew an operation was necessary for this end. Would there come a time when her condition became critical? Certainly it would if a skilful surgeon did not break the hold these internal adhesions had over her health.

'Take a grip on yourself,' Lynn thought out loud. She was standing by the window sill of her bedroom and her eyes rested on the little plaster angel that she had been given as a child; the same angel that she had kissed every night throughout childhood. The yellow tunic had faded, its enamel gloss surface crazy paved with cracks, the broken foot smoothed by years of being held. Come on, Lynn, you have walked down this path so many times, you know the score. You may not have a mother by your side this time, or a man to call your own, but you have the spiritual strength of the child within to see you through. Spiritual strength is all you have, but it is also all you need. Lynn dwelt upon her thoughts; it was almost as if her mother was talking to her again. She accepted it, knowing in her heart that it made sense.

She broke from her ponderous mood, stretched her arms wide, looking out to a brand new day and went to run her bath. She laid out what she needed to change her ileostomy soft-covered bag on the chair beside the bath and added lavender bubble foam to the hot running water. The relaxing essence was her favourite and as she watched it rise as bubbles in the bath she stirred it with her hands, adding then a new block of lavender soap to the soap dish. Lynn removed the dressing from her tummy. Was it possible that she had dealt with the surgeon-made stoma for nearly forty years? She had lived longer wearing a bag than she had lived with a normal bowel; indeed she could not have lived without it.

Lynn sunk beneath the warm soothing water, dwelling more on the sensual luxury of heat and the movement of water over her skin than anything else. At times like this she was glad she had a sensitive body as well as mind. She didn't dwell on the reasons for the operation she had undergone so long ago, though ulcerative colitis was a particularly nasty disease of the large bowel and to undergo such an operation to remove it at the age of nineteen was enough to traumatise any young patient. Lynn insisted then as she still insisted now, that it was necessary to live and proceeded to illustrate the point for the rest of her life.

Lynn had gone on to have further unrelated operations during her marriage, including major corrective surgery when a gynaecological operation went badly wrong. Even in those days the adhesions caused complications that made any surgery difficult. Although not told at the time, her bladder was pressed close to other organs and a hysterectomy would be too difficult to consider. Lynn remained philosophical, preferring to focus on reality rather than what might have been.

She slid under the perfumed water, raising her head to the sound of the phone ringing. The answer machine was on microphone and Lynn listened to the welcome message, disappointed that she could not get to the phone. Her Auntie Joan was phoning from Jersey to wish her happy birthday; she would return the call later. Her aunt and uncle were now the oldest remaining close relatives from her mother's side of the family and she dearly loved them both. Lynn's mind ran back to the beach at Green Island and the summer holidays. Her first holiday alone was spent with the family and Auntie Joan had become a second mum to her; though of course she had dared not admit it to her own mother. As the message finished she sank below the water again and thought of the times with her "rude sea horse", pretending again to be in sea and not bath water.

'Time to get out.' She sighed, rising from the water, snatching a towel to dry herself and emptying the bath of water before renewing her dressing. She sprayed herself with lavender body spray. 'Proper old lady,' she muttered to herself but nobody would have believed her for a moment. Lynn had presence and power; she was becoming stronger in mind by the day and it was during times like these she realised that none of the lessons life had taught her had been wasted.

A little later Lynn phoned her aunt and spoke of birthdays and families and the thought of coming over to visit them when she was really better in health; it would be something to look forward to. She thanked her aunt for the card and gave out as much uplifting news as she could. If anyone had been in the room from which she phoned she would have been heard to say, 'I'm fine, Auntie, absolutely fine; I'm more concerned about you.'

Joan had been seriously ill the year before and had not really picked up in health. John had arthritis in his knees now and was finding his mobility hampered. Lynn remembered him as a brilliant tennis player and a gardener at the Howard Davis Park during the nineteen fifties and sixties before he joined his brothers in their own building contractor firm. She smiled at the thought of Uncles Mark and John and Peter stripped to their waists in the height of a Jersey summer, shovelling cement from the battered mixer. Fit, healthy men; now only John was still alive.

When the goodbyes and promises to visit had been made Lynn put the phone down and went to make a cup of tea. Life wasn't so bad; she was lucky with the family she had and although she knew she had been unlucky with her health all her life she was rather thankful that she never had the opportunity to take good health for granted. Those who first experience poor health in later life find it difficult to adjust and Lynn had great sympathy for the people she knew, who were suffering with this experience. Lynn was ever hopeful that when the next health challenge had been met she would go forward again in her life; although nearly sixty she was optimistic of her future and already had a goal to reach and a new experience to look forward to.

Lynn had applied the previous year to a top cruise line company. She had sent in her art portfolio and CV and eventually had been given an interview in Southampton for the position of an art instructor on one or more of the Mediterranean cruises. She had recently heard that she had been accepted and now was waiting a "wish list" of cruises for which she had to confirm her availability. Although it was not a salaried position it was going to be an exciting experience and a trip of a lifetime. Lynn waited for the e-mail every day and was only thankful that she had not missed its arrival while in hospital. A cruise would be just what she needed and the fact that she had been chosen to teach meant that her talent was appreciated. She really needed the recognition. Her self-esteem had taken a battering and this, she had convinced herself, was just what she needed, when she had sufficiently recovered in health.

It seemed more than coincidental that when Lynn went online later that morning, an e-mail was waiting to be opened. She nearly squealed with excitement realising it had come through from the cruise company. She read the short message and opened the corresponding attachment. In front of her was a table of dates and descriptions of cruise destinations, each one with an empty box for her to tick her availability. Lynn was thrilled; the leaden weight lifted from her heart. Now all she had to do was get well and strong and reach forward again. She was under no illusion; she had found many times before that when something good had been put in front of her it was often snatched away. However, she also recognised that often when the future looked very bleak, something turned to shine in her face and force her to make the effort to reach for a goal previously unknown.

When, as a sixth form school pupil, her brother had been allowed to accompany the younger boys from his school on a Mediterranean cruise aboard M.S. *Devonia* Lynn's school had the same opportunity. Unfortunately because of lack of support her school declined. To avoid disappointment her parents booked a cabin for the three of them to travel as private passengers in the hopes that a sea cruise would bring some colour back in to young Lynn's pale face. She was fourteen and failing again in health. It was her first experience of cruising.

Lynn snapped her attention back to the present, printed off the details and closed the computer screen down. She found the cruise line's brochure and decided to have a very light lunch and browse through the various ship details. She relished the enjoyment of choosing a cruise without having to pay for it, though she understood that she would have to work hard for the experience. As she pulled her atlas from the second shelf of the bookcase, a yellow-covered paper-bound book dropped from beside it; she felt a tingle down her spine. The flimsy A4-formatted booklet was the ship's log and cruise itinerary from 1964. Lynn had kept it as a treasured memento.

Lynn didn't get round to making lunch, nor did she settle down with the 2010 cruise brochure, nor study the '"wish list". She made another cup of tea, curled up on the sofa and opened the pages of the past. Lynn, the child, sat down beside her, she was growing now; the ungainly cygnet upon her lake of life yet still they merged as one.

CHAPTER 25

Lynn was enjoying the cruise. The cold November winds of Dunstable had been left behind. All doubts about her health had been left at home and although she was nervous of sharing the coach outings with her brother's school party she was secretly pleased to be at least on the fringe of some form of society. Her brother would no doubt be embarrassed by his sister's presence, especially because his sister and parents would be no more than a few coach seats away on some of the set excursions. No sixth-form student wants to be with his mates and his family; Lynn quite understood his embarrassment. Apart from these excursions she saw very little of her brother while on the cruise. As he was one of the sixth-form pupils assigned to keep an eye on the younger boys, he had his time mapped out for him.

Lynn waited while her mother and father dressed discreetly in the confines of the shared, claustrophobic cabin. There was an air of style about having to dress for dinner and the girl enjoyed every new experience aboard ship. Each day a news bulletin was set up and delivered to the cabin. The days at sea involved lectures and games and entertainment in the evenings. The passengers could visualise the passage of their vessel and meet the captain and officers over meals and organised events. It was Lynn's first experience as a young adult, for although, she was just fourteen, she was beginning to feel the power of her emotions and the longing to be older than she was. She hated the fact that over recent months she had lost weight rather than filling out at the approach to womanhood. She was of pale complexion and, try as she might, her hair quickly became lank and greasy. She asked her mother if she could wash it more often but her reply was that this would only stimulate the natural oils in her scalp. Lynn wished that, for once in her life, she would be allowed to wash her hair when she wanted to and not under her mother's direction. Common to every youngster she wanted to rebel and be allowed her own choices.

The cruise meals consisted of many courses and always from a complimentary menu card that she could save together with all the other mementos from the fortnight's cruise through the Mediterranean. Each news sheet was gathered to make a diary and at the end of the cruise the Purser stapled them together in a folder. Lynn then plucked up the courage to approach her favourite crew to ask for their autographs. They all dutifully signed, some adding a personal comment which she knew she would treasure for ever. A small caricature drawn freehand by the assistant purser was copied and repeated until Lynn, upon returning home, felt a certain skill in cartooning was surfacing along with her other artistic abilities. She also had fond memories of friendly crew members who encouraged her happiness. She found, however, that many of them knew that the cruise had been undertaken by her parents in the hopes that the sea air would improve their daughter's health. She sensed that her mother received a certain amount of sympathy for having a sickly child. Lynn pushed the thought from her mind. She so wanted to be liked for her own self and not out of pity and she constantly seemed to be trying to prove that she was well and as bright and happy as any other teenager. She wanted to be normal and attractive and although her mother supported her in every possible way, she often undermined her daughter's confidence and optimism, without realising she did so.

The cruise itinerary started from Tilbury. Having then crossed Europe by train, which in itself was a monumental experience, Lynn was entranced. They experienced the changes from the low, grey French scenery through long tunnels to emerge in the bright winter sunlight of mountainous Switzerland. Every tunnel seemed to bring a new delight, a different aspect, and each took Lynn away from everything she wanted to leave behind.

They arrived at the port of Genoa where they joined M.S. *Devonia*. Her father had a hidden agenda in taking the cruise, apart from his wife's gentle art of persuasion. The vessel had been their father's troop ship during the Second World War, carrying soldiers to or from the Middle East. The vessel was named H.M.S. *Devonshire* then and belonged to the Royal Navy's fleet.

Lynn was never sure of the details but her father had fond memories of the ship and was often seen during this voyage, a solitary figure, at the prow or stern of the ship deeply engrossed in memories. Lynn remembered the afternoon her mother mistakenly tried to interrupt these thoughts and a full-blown argument followed. Her mother cried in the cabin and her father, shrouded in a heavy mood, remained on deck. Lynn could not understand the complexity of such emotions. She tried to comfort her mother, deeply disappointed that such storms should blow up on holiday just as they always did at home. Lately there seemed little fair weather in her parents' marriage. The arguments turned Lynn's tummy over and though she tried endlessly to pacify them both, somehow she always found herself on her mother's side. She seemed totally unable to reach out and connect with her father who remained distant for days after such upsets. Sadly the cruise was not exempt from such emotional turmoil and the little cabin they shared was not always filled with a light holiday atmosphere. Lynn wished she had her brother's comfort.

From Genoa M.S. *Devonia* made her passage to the Bay of Naples, docking in the port. This was Lynn's first trip abroad; she thirsted for every experience. Every sight was recorded in her diary and memory. She would recall the details many times in later life.

Lynn was shocked by the poverty of Naples and her father was shocked by the forwardness of the Latin men. Her mother was attractive and one of them thought nothing of giving her bottom a playful pinch as she passed by. Her father had to be restrained!

The half-day excursion to the ancient ruin of Pompeii was an experience Lynn would not forget. Her brother's group joined the other schools while Lynn and her parents joined the tour for cabin-class passengers. The whole experience of Pompeii left Lynn with a feeling of sadness, as if she were caught in a time warp. She saw the encrusted fossilised bodies of the city's population contorted and entombed as they lay sheltering. Pebbles of pumice and later ash first fell from the erupting Vesuvius to a depth of up to ten feet. It was obvious by the attitude of the fallen figures that it had happened in an alarmingly short space of time. Many were suffocated by the clouds and flames of sulphuric ash; she could feel their fear. Following an earthquake in AD 63, the well-documented eruption of Italy's most famous volcano in AD 79 killed over two thousand of the twenty thousand inhabitants in the fall-out. Some sheltered, some had run; a dog lay in submission to his death. Yet under the ash their world was stilled as an English village under a snowfall.

After the excavations, paved roads were freed of their ashy blanket and the city returned to a ghostly facsimile of its former self. The paved roads were uncovered and so too were the stepping-stones to allow the pedestrians to cross the streets. Alleyways led to villa gardens where statues and ponds stood as if waiting for their builders and sculptors to return. Time hung as heavy as the perfume from the now blossoming bougainvilleas; murals lovingly and accurately depicted the family life of those who had died where they lived. Lynn wanted everyone to go; she wanted to be alone. She was sensitive to atmosphere and felt that, if she stood alone for long enough, the world which had been tragically stilled would have come to life again. She knew she would hear the laughter of children and the clatter of horses on the paved roads; she would hear a mother sing a lullaby. She also knew that she would hear the mood of the city change; anxious calls, heart-wrenching sobs, chaos and screams and finally the slow submission of life overcome by death.

'Lynn,' her mother called, 'we're falling behind the group. As much as we both want to stay we have only a limited amount of time.' Lynn had inherited her sensitivity from her mother. They had a similar understanding of life but, all the same, Lynn wondered why she couldn't just stay there alone and let the whole world move on.

From Naples M.S. *Devonia* sailed south through the Straits of Messina and north again through the Gulf of Athens. She docked at the industrial port of Piraeus and in warm sunshine; the tourists, schools and cabin passengers alike were ferried by coach to the city of Athens.

Lynn saw Athens and the Parthenon. A cloud of fume-laden smog had settled upon the city giving the rising hill on which the Parthenon had been built an ethereal air as it rose above the yellowness; other ancient sites stood below, peaking through the morning pollution.

The tourists could walk freely around the ancient sites with little restriction. Her father even picked up a small piece of fallen marble and brought it home. Lynn remembered it being on the mantelpiece for years until one day her father's guilty conscience got the better of him. He swore that it was diminishing in size and that it had brought the family no luck. When a member of his printing firm announced he was going to Athens on holiday one year in the seventies, he was asked if he would return the marble to its original site. Her father's co-worker did not realise how difficult it would be for, by that time, security of the ancient site was strictly controlled and it was difficult to get close to the columns and temples. He would have been at risk of prosecution for it was doubtful that anyone would have believed he was returning the marble and not taking the small piece, which measured about five inches by three, out of its country of origin. When he returned from holiday he told her father that it was a most worrying episode. Lynn felt sympathy with the man but her father was relieved that the relic had been returned to its rightful home.

Lynn didn't mix with any of the young people aboard ship. There was a definite social line drawn between the fare-paying passengers and the school parties. Lynn had a certain amount of freedom aboard ship and was able to wander on her own, attending the lectures and film shows that she chose and yet have the adult company of her parents and the passengers they interacted with. Joyce was a very sociable lady, she was both gregarious and intelligent and male passengers and crew members found her easy to talk to. In attracting their company the family's circle of shipboard friends expanded. She got on well with women as well, unless their husbands paid too much attention to the attractive lady, who was concerned for the health of her daughter.

Lynn's underlying personality was enough like her mother's to want to shine in her own right and she was gaining the ability to do so. However, the brighter the sun that was her mother, the greater the shadow that fell on her daughter, at this time of her life.

From Athens the ship sailed south on through the Elaphonisos channel, round Cape Matapan and on to the harbour of Itea. Lynn couldn't explain her feelings but she was completely in love with Greece. She hadn't felt it in Athens, for she was never a city girl, but the cerulean skies and the turquoise-blue seas that they were now experiencing warmed her heart to a point of calmness and inner health. As M.S. *Devonia* dropped anchor in the mirror-like water and the lifeboats dropped from their davits ready for debarkation Lynn felt as though she was coming home. She instantly knew she would not want to leave. The boats ferried the passengers to the harbour shore where they waited to board the coaches. Lynn, the teenager, had lost her childhood; she did not belong in the past, nor did she eagerly reach out for her future. She stood in the "here and now", caressed by the warm breeze and the Greek winter sunshine; she wanted to be nowhere else but where she stood. That feeling was never far from her for the rest of her life. Lynn was attracted to Greece, it was here she discovered a part of herself that she could only identify as her life's spirit.

The day continued to be one of unexpected delight. She loved the temples and the oracle but once again, if she had had the choice, Lynn would have stood away from everyone. Her heart was both heavy and light as if she had drunk wine of the purest sort. Even her spirit was warmed by the sun. The very atmosphere of the high cliffs and deep inspiring gorge unsteadied her yet calmed her also. Was it the power of Greek history or, perhaps, the spirit of the gods? She leaned back into nothing, shading her eyes from the sun, hoping to catch a sight of the eagle she could hear high above. She saw it, just a circling dot in the blue, blue sky. Her eyes caught a flash of red and then a harsh cry attracted her attention.

'Wall creepers; look,' she called out in her excitement, pointing to the deep cleft above her that dropped past them into the gorge below. Lynn had never seen such a bird; they were not native to England. In her darker days she had, however, studied her book of world birds and picked the small rock-climbing bird out by its striking plumage and cry.

'Could there ever be a day more perfect?' Lynn knew the answer to her whispered question. 'Yes, of course, but that too would have to be God-made.'

She remembered little about her parents that day apart from occasionally standing with them or sharing refreshments at the small purpose-built taverna before they made their way back to the coach. Delphi was her time and place. She would never return to it, fearing that with the shifting of time and so-called progress the enchantment would vanish and the gods would secrete themselves in dark corners that the tourists couldn't reach. That day in November 1964 Lynn thought she walked amongst them.

The cruise continued and Lynn became alive, though those around her did not register the fact. Outwardly she was the same but inwardly she was growing. She reached into her soul and would not deny her right to independence. She enjoyed the ship's events alone or with her parents and when the second engineer asked them for drinks in his cabin after sharing a table with them at supper she hoped it was because he liked her and not just her mother. Several of the engineering officers joined the little party and Lynn, it seemed, became a guest of honour. The young fifth engineer, a junior rating, grinned at her with boyish charm. Lynn smiled back, trying, in earnest, to find something intelligent to say, and so keep his attention. The men included her in every conversation and at the end of the evening the family's host took two leather figures from the porthole shelf. They were about nine inches high and dressed in Tangier costume. They were skilfully made and had obviously been part of the cabin décor for some time. These figures were presented to Lynn who was so surprised and thrilled that she almost cried.

Someone liked her enough, she thought, to give her something that was precious to them. Her cruise was complete – in her mind anyway! Lynn, it seemed was destined to be a romantic!

The next day the family were offered a private trip around the engine room of *Devonia*. Lynn saw the fifth engineer in his overalls and remembered his cheeky grin during the weeks that followed. A schoolgirl crush, they would call it, but to Lynn it meant more; for a while at least.

Upon returning home Lynn was disappointed when her mother recounted the episode of the gift of the costumed dolls, for she added that her daughter had been given them by the crew because they had felt sorry for her poorly daughter. Her mother's remark seemed brutal and undermined Lynn's illusion that someone could see her as an attractive and intelligent teenager. Her confidence dipped, but not her spirit. It was only years later that Lynn looked back at the photos to find she was looking at an emaciated, pale girl-child, who seemed more anorexic than the blooming teenager of her imagination.

Corfu was the next port of call. The weather was changing, becoming wetter. Somehow Lynn had seen the best of Greece; her heart remained in Delphi and her dreams in the hands of the engineer whom she never kissed and would never see again.

By the time the ship sailed up the Adriatic coast to Venice, their last port of call and disembarkation point, winter had placed its cold fingers around the heart of the Mediterranean heat. St Mark's square was partially flooded; the gondolas were black and bobbing against their mooring poles like stallions preparing to bolt from the cold. The crowds were melting away and the pigeons were sparsely fed by the remaining tourists. Duck-boards were in place allowing access to the cathedral's entrance above the rising water level and Lynn's mother had diarrhoea!

The *Devonia* was moored next to her sister ship *Dunera*. Bow to bow, they disgorged the full complement of passengers and crew the following day. Heating had been reduced and the holiday atmosphere had ended. Lynn didn't mind, she had seen all and experienced all she had come for and a little more besides. It would have been nice if her mother had felt well and had been in good spirits for the return journey across Europe by train, but all good things come to an end.

Lynn's life, she felt sure, was not coming to an end. The cruise was just the beginning of a life of happiness, travel and romance. She would weave these dreams into her reality and in truth they would give her the backbone of strength she would need in years to come. Her experience of Delphi opened up her spirit, allowing her to thrive and grow. Lynn was becoming a very special person, but it would take many years and perhaps the writing of her story to convince herself of her qualities. Only when the woman looked back at the child would she recognise herself.

Chapter 26

The inspired freedom Lynn found while travelling across the Mediterranean during the cruise lifted her spirits but, alas, made no difference to her problems of health and home. The girl knew what it was like to feel her heart beat fast with the exhilaration of the experience of salt wind in her hair; alas, her hair remained lank and in poor condition. The warmth of the sun upon her upturned face did not bring a lasting colour and the good food upon her plate did not add inches or ounces to her thin frame. She wished her hair was long and blonde as it once was when she was healthy. She wanted the energy to run along golden beaches and not just dream of it; but, more than all this, she wanted to stand away from her parents and their problems which ran like storms across the horizon. She wanted to know what it was like to be admired and even loved for herself and not pitied for her condition and illness as yet undiagnosed and yet she could rise above it. She could only dream.

Bill was growing up fast. Once he reached the sixth form, decisions were being made regarding his chosen career and steps towards university. Lynn looked up to her brother who continued to try and help her when he could. She struggled constantly with mathematics and an hour of such homework would extend painfully to two. He would sit beside her and painstakingly try to explain an easier solution to the problems set before her. He would guide her through each stage, checking that she was following.

'You get that, Lynn?'

'Yes, Bill.' She squirmed a little on the settee they were sharing.

'Well, good, now do you understand this next part?'

'Yes, Bill.' Lynn was lost and yet she so wanted to understand and to take in everything her brother was explaining to her. When it came to figures her mind just froze. Some part of her just withdrew, just as it had when the doctors visited her in hospital; a compartment seemed to shut down. Numbers turned round in her head and made no logical sense. She wasn't dumb, she understood letters and words; she could paint pictures with words. Somehow she never saw the reality of numbers and Lynn always struggled; she guessed she always would.

Her brother was at an age of exploration. He enjoyed the freedom with his pals and, like his father, cycling was a great escape and release. Even in this he was an achiever, cycling the length of the British Isles from John O'Groats to Land's End and back again to Dunstable with his two of his friends. Lynn saw him almost fall off his bike as he turned through the gateway at the end of his long journey; he was exhausted. Their mother asked him to go back a few yards to the gates so that she could take a photograph of his return for the family album. His eyes were glazed and staring from the long journey on the road and he had the start of a beard; he was skinny and exhausted. Although he posed for the photo, he did so reluctantly. It was taken as a witness to just how hard and far he had cycled and the photograph was a brilliant record of his exhaustive journey, but at what price? Bill was not amused.

In those years of early and mid-teens, the youngsters never discussed family life, preferring to ignore what was happening within their otherwise loving home. They were both loyal to their parents, even in their unhappiness, and preferred to enjoy their time with friends and each other or make the most of the happy times they still experienced as a family. Life continued with a certain amount of normality for, indeed, they had nothing else to compare it with. It was only when voices were raised and tears were shed that their parents' unhappiness spread to their world.

Lynn turned on her new radio, tuning it to an Indian station she had discovered on short waveband. She could not of course understand the language, but escaped into the rhythm of the music. She turned up the volume to drown out the background noise and weaved her hands in front of her mirror, copying the movements of the Indian dancers, a world away from her own. The movements suited the subtlety of her slim wrists and fingers. The music ended abruptly – the silence being broken only by the sound of her parents arguing downstairs. Lynn stopped her hand dancing and wrung her hands, digging her nails into her palms. Gradually the voices below become raised and continuous. The conversation became forceful, each voice rising in competition with the other. Lynn closed her bedroom door quietly, but it mattered little. Her hearing was acute and her parents were too intent on their argument to be aware of their children, who by that time of night should have been asleep. Lynn retuned her radio, but it was to no avail; she could hear her parents above the distraction of the music. She turned the radio off, yet now she had the guilty feeling of eavesdropping. She toyed with the idea of going downstairs to fetch a drink of water. She thought her interruption would make her parents aware that their argument had disturbed her. She stepped out of bed and knocked on her brother's door. He didn't hear above the sound of Radio Luxemburg; Lynn pushed his door open.

'Go back to bed, Lynn,' he said in the gentlest tone he could muster; but there was a tension in his voice that he couldn't hide.

Lynn did what she was told; even at fourteen she respected her brother's common sense.

The argument went on until their mother's voice was high-pitched and insistent. Their father seemed to be shouting now, claiming ground. Lynn heard a bang of a fist on the table. There was never any physical violence, the child never thought there would be, for she knew her parents loved each other; they were a complete family. She tucked her head under the bed covers; all she could do was wait until it was over.

Eventually she heard the sitting-room door bang as her father left the room and, later, the definite closing of the front door behind him as he left the house. The stillness was not that of relief at the breaking of a storm for the tension was still in the air. Lynn heard her mother weep and yet she was unable to comfort her. The youngster's legs were weak with exhaustion; she didn't know what to do, feeling the need to comfort or help her mother in some way, yet feeling inadequate.

Her brother called out across the landing. 'Good night, Lynn; go to sleep now.'

Lynn didn't sleep. She listened to her mother cry quietly downstairs until, eventually, she heard her tidying up the sitting room and washing the last cups and saucers. She came upstairs and went to bed, without calling out to her children. The light in her parents' bedroom stayed on for a long time. Much later Lynn heard her father turn his key in the door; he must have been out for hours.

At least he is home, thought Lynn. She remembered the night her father didn't come home until early morning, having slept under a hedge until the local constabulary moved him on. She couldn't remember how she had heard about it but supposed it was from her brother. Their dad always told his children that he had wanted to be a tramp on the open road. Later, of course, she realised it was partly because of the great unhappiness in her parents' relationship. This night her father climbed the stairs and entered the bedroom. He left the door ajar, as was the habit in their household. Lynn listened for any conversation between her parents but there wasn't any. She heard the bed creak as he got in beside his wife, but not a word was spoken. Lynn held her breath till she could hold it no more. The silence was tense and without comfort. She waited for a while and when she thought one of them at least had fallen asleep she thought it safe to let her guard down and turn her head to her pillow and close her eyes; it was over. She was so tired. She had wrapped her fingers around her little plaster angel but did not say her prayers.

When she awoke the following morning she was still clasping the treasured ornament, her fingers stiff from lack of movement, her tummy cramped with tension. She heard her father leave the house for work and listened to the receding rhythm of turning wheels and gears changing as he cycled down the path. Only then did her mother rise, go down stairs and start the day's routine as if nothing had happened. Lynn lay there hoping her father would have forgotten the argument by the time he cycled home. Sometimes this was the case; sometimes the atmosphere lasted for days.

Bill and Lynn never discussed their parents' outbursts, and rarely admitted, even to themselves, that there was anything wrong within the family. They were not used to confiding in each other, fearing it was disloyal or out of the reach of their understanding, although as brother and sister they were both deeply affected by the disharmony.

Life was changing for the whole family. Syd had left the *Luton News* and formed a partnership with three other printers, setting up their own firm of commercial printers in Luton. It had been hoped that the partners' sons would have wanted to join the firm and carry on their ideals, but it was not to be. The days of fathers handing down a solid business and future to children who wanted the same ideals had long ago disappeared. It had always been obvious to the family that Bill was destined for, and attracted to, brighter stars – quite literally – and the sons of the other three partners were not so inclined to follow in their fathers' footsteps. Lynn's father worked hard; he was a skilled process engraver and though he didn't involve himself with the "front of house" business he was reliable and competent in his work.

Lynn used to love to go shopping in Luton, by bus, with her mother, and pop in to see her father at the process-engraving premises along the Old Bedford

Road. The building had been fully converted from its old usage as a hat factory. Lynn wondered how the men had got the huge cameras and machinery up the rickety stairs and on to their rails. It didn't dawn on her that they had taken out the windows, but Lynn, while logical on many subjects, did not have a practical mind when it came to machinery of any kind. The larger and noisier it was the more intimidated she felt.

Once her father had greeted her he would continue his work. Her mother had gone down to the office to talk to the lady who worked there; she was also one of the partners' wives. Lynn was pleased to have her father to herself though she stood quietly to one side. He set up plates and worked the arc lights and camera distances. The huge camera trundled on its rail like a big X-ray machine, humming and processing. His daughter pretended to watch the procedure at a safe distance, but Lynn wasn't "learning the trade"; Lynn was watching her father. Some part of her loved to look at him when he wasn't aware of her. She breathed in the pungent smell of the acids he used and watched his face as he stood intent on his work. It was strange what things attracted her. She liked the line of his face when he stood silhouetted against the light, especially the shape between his strong nose and upper lip; she didn't know why. She looked at his working overall and wondered why brown didn't suit him; she thought he looked tired and not at all like an owner of a business. She was more than a little in awe of him and yet in moments like this adored him. He looked up and caught her staring; he winked; she blushed. She wanted to put her arms round him but the big machine was in the way. She would wait patiently until the process plate was ready to be developed in her father's darkroom, but then, of course, she wouldn't have the opportunity and he was not a demonstrative man. Lynn's father couldn't be more different from her Uncle Mark and yet she loved them both.

'Do you want to see the picture come to life on the paper, Lynn?' She nodded her head, unable to take her eyes from him. Her father pushed open the darkroom door and followed her in.

'You will have to stand very still when I turn the light off and there will only be a red glow. If you put the electric light on, all my work will be wasted!' He pretended to be stern. She nodded, only wanting a few more minutes with her dad.

Lynn had done this before and had always been good, standing just where her father positioned her; close enough to see the tray of developing fluid in which he would swill the processed photographic paper, but not to be in the way. On the first occasion she had watched him she had to go up on tiptoes but now, a year or so later, she only had to stretch her neck a little.

Lynn used to think her father could work magic. Now, a little older and after many visits, she understood the process of developing. She watched as he proceeded, dipping and submerging the paper into the shallow tray of fluid and allowing it to run backwards and forwards over the surface. Gradually, something started to happen. A picture began to appear upon the wet paper; an image of a motor car started to materialise in black and white. A few more seconds and Lynn could make out the driver and the advertisement written across the bottom of the image. Thousands of closely formatted dots toned the picture from light grey to shades of black just like a photograph – which of course it was. The process was complete and Lynn stood fascinated as her father took it from the tray with big tweezers and rinsed it off before hanging it like washing on a line above the sink.

'I can put the ordinary light on now; we can't ruin the photograph as it's been fully developed.' Her father reached across her for the light. She smelt his perspiration mixed with the chemicals and wanted to hold it to her, for in her mind this was how she would remember her dad. She thought it strange that she could love her mum and she could love her dad but that when it came to loving her mother and father together she couldn't seem to conjure up an image. Her dad could only give out affection when she shared time alone with him. Strangely, when her parents were in a position to show her affection together, her mother always came forward and her father backed away.

This is why, thought Lynn, time alone with my dad is so important.

They laughed together at the image hanging above them and he opened the door, allowing natural light and air to enter the box-like room.

'Lynn, we'd better leave now otherwise we'll miss the bus,' her mother called as she climbed the old wooden stairs and came over to them. Lynn was disappointed; she wanted more time with her father. She looked at him but he was already withdrawing the affection he had shown her, letting her mother take centre stage. He smiled, though just at Lynn, and returned to his work, measuring his next project.

Mother and father kissed each other lightly on the cheek and though the child was dissuaded from hugging her father she reached on tiptoe and gave him a farewell kiss as he bent towards her.

Chapter 27

Bill was working towards the end of the sixth form and preparing to embark on a new life at university; Lynn was working towards a goal of her own. She had not achieved all that she was capable of at school and was now about to leave Brewer's Hill Secondary Modern to attend the local College of Further Education. She would never achieve academic distinction and it was felt that her O-level grades in GCE examinations would not do her justice. By this time Lynn had decided that she wanted to be a trained Nursery Nurse, and for the best possibility of gaining entrance to the course she had been advised to enrol in a "pre-nursing" course at the Dunstable College. It was thought that she would learn the necessary skills and be appreciated for the talent she had, not the academic skills she had not. Lynn was thrilled with the idea of leaving the school one year earlier than her friends and launching into a career that was much closer to the humanitarian side of her nature. Because Lynn was looking forward to her own freedom and future she did not regret her brother's plan to leave home the following year to make his own mark on life. Achievement was important to both youngsters and his sister was thrilled for his academic success and was very proud of him. She was excited at the prospect of being able to brag about her brother and was happy that going to university, even if it were in Edinburgh, was not entirely leaving home. Bill would return for long holidays and she would probably see far more of him during that time than she expected. For now she put it out of her mind; she had another year of his company and comfort before he would pack his suitcase and prepare to meet his own challenges.

Lynn enjoyed the adult concept of college; the discipline was less formal. Although regulated it was up to the student how hard they worked and what they achieved. Lynn was no longer a pupil but a student and, for the first time, she found that she was treated as a young adult with intelligence. She knew from the beginning that if she wanted to be chosen for enrolment into the N.N.E.B. course for Nursery Nursing the following year she would have to show her worth and her practicality. If she attained a place as one of only eighteen positions, she would be enrolled in the course which, upon completing and passing the N.N.E.B. examination after two years' hard work, would allow her the freedom of travelling the world if she so preferred as an employed nanny. The qualifications were necessary and as highly regarded as the S.R.N. in general nursing. Lynn wanted to become a nanny and look after other people's children. It was a career once thought of in Victorian England as being on the higher grade of servitude; now it was a highly regarded profession. Even to be admitted to the course would mean undergoing an examination and interview to whittle down the number of applicants; Lynn was desperate to be one of them and once she set her mind on anything she fought to succeed.

The pre-nursing course would be valuable to her. Even the mathematics was based on feeding and drug ratios and, because they held meaning to young Lynn, although she still hated figures she persevered and won through. General subjects such as English and even Spoken English were on the curriculum as well as the more specialised topics that would aid the "would be" nurse in her future career. On the completion of this course the students would be ready to train for their specific form of nursing. The majority of them wanted to be General Nurses; only a handful, including Lynn, were waiting to go forward to the N.N.E.B.

This should have been a time of Lynn's blossoming and, in many ways, it was. She met new friends, leaving many of her old ones still at school, moving forward in their own educational direction. She hardly saw any of them now, not out of choice but because of the inconvenience of travel and lack of time. Friendships blossomed and waned during childhood but no one seemed to hold a grudge and some friendships would rekindle in adulthood should circumstances present themselves. Lynn made new friends and though she tired more easily and rarely got together with them after college, she enjoyed their company and also appreciated the different level of relationship between students and lecturers. She could talk with many of them and learnt much from her one to one conversations. She even discovered through her mother that the deputy Head of Department had been the clinic nurse of her babyhood. Miss Williams held a commanding presence as a lecturer but was in fact an approachable woman who was sympathetic towards Lynn and indeed her mother when her student's illness was first diagnosed.

Lynn involved herself in everything she could. She started to enjoy college life and enthusiastically joined in with the planning of forthcoming College Rag week. It was her first great experience in student life and she entered into the spirit of things. She found herself allocated to a float in the procession as a "Flapper/student". The idea was hardly inspirational and it was easy to alter a dress and make a headdress for her costume. She decided on the role of decadent Flapper and made herself a garter to complete the effect. She met different students, boys and girls, and was able to feel, for a short while at least, "one of the gang." The lorries used were mostly flat loaders and were dressed in relatively simple decoration. The main idea in those days was to get as many of the students involved as possible. Lynn was pleased to be one of them and made the most of every minute, rattling her tin and riding on the float, jumping off at odd times to collect for the college's chosen charity.

Of course Lynn was still Lynn. Somehow in her enthusiasm after a great morning in the procession Lynn fell off the float! In reality she jumped and landed heavily, falling on a twisted ankle and breaking the skin on her knees. She was swept up by one of the engineering students and carried away from the lorry wheels, where, unceremoniously, she was dumped on the grass verge. Her day in the "Student Rag" was over, but Lynn finally had the excited thrill of being "one of the crowd". One of the student organisers was old enough to drive and he decided he should take Lynn home by car. Everyone climbed in to his V.W. Beetle and with the tannoy blaring they made their way out of town, along Friars Walk and on to First Avenue. The continued message over the loudspeaker referred to the "coming home of Lynn" and warning Mrs Zealey of her arrival. The car pulled up outside number fifty-four to find Lynn's mother by the front door wondering what all the noise was about. Once again Lynn's mum had the shock of seeing her daughter carried up the drive! She flew at the boys for alarming her and the neighbourhood with their loudspeaker announcement and Lynn felt so totally embarrassed that she couldn't see the funny side. Lynn's spirits dropped for the first time that day; her knees and ankle began to hurt terribly!

Lynn really enjoyed that first year at college. Unfortunately, she was battling bouts of diarrhoea and exhaustion. For a lot of the time she tried to keep the problem away from her mother but Joyce was attuned to any problem in her daughter's health and witnessed the slide into more serious complications. Lynn's condition was finally diagnosed as ulcerative colitis but the extent of the illness did not become apparent until the end of that college year.

Fortunately Lynn had an understanding head of department, Miss Neal. Any time lost was made up for with Lynn's willingness to complete home studies and she continued that first year at college with as little disruption as possible. She enjoyed the lectures designed to prepare the girls for the nursing of patients. Her own hospital experiences had given her an insight and advantage, though the nursing profession and the N.H.S. had changed considerably since she was a child. She watched the educational films with trepidation and was surprised just how poignant her own memories still were. One afternoon Miss Williams set the projector and fed in the reel of one of two fifteen-minute films. The thick curtains were closed and the students watched the flickering start. The title came up on the white screen: *A Two-Year-Old Goes to Hospital*. A subtitle explained that her admission was without her mother being accommodated at the hospital to comfort and help with the daily routine of her child. The word abandonment came into Lynn's mind.

At first she was intrigued but as the film moved on she became more uncomfortable. The child's eyes stared into the lens of the camera, swimming with hurt and loneliness; Lynn sympathised. She expected to be able to relate to the tiny patient's situation but not feel the same heart-rending temporary loss of its parents. The vision on the screen knotted her stomach and pulled her heart-strings. Lynn had not forgotten her own experiences, they had remained in her sub-conscious waiting for a trigger to bring them flooding to the surface. Lynn didn't know how she kept control but eventually had to leave the classroom under the pretext of using the toilet. She returned only when she knew the film had ended.

The second reel was of a similar subject, but this time, filmed a few years later, it was titled: *A Two-Year-Old Goes to Hospital with her Mother*. Lynn sat through this film without a problem; the child was confident and safe from the loneliness of feeling neglected by her parents. At the end of the film show it was discussed by the film presenter how the lives of these two children had been affected by their differing experiences. Lynn well understood how the first child had been denied a confident approach to growing up. She wanted to stand in front of the class and shout, 'That's me; I understand.' But even then she never had the confidence to do so.

At first Lynn's lapses of health were infrequent and she continued to enjoy not only the further education but also the social side of her teenage life. She would meet some of the boys from the nearby grammar school at lunchtime with the friends from her class. She was comfortable in a group and because she was used to her brother's friends coming to call on him Lynn was able to interact quite easily. It resulted in Paul asking Lynn out one lunch time after a kick around with a football. Lynn said yes and spent the next few days worrying that she wouldn't know what to do and say on their first date and even more worryingly, wouldn't know what he would do and say. For all Lynn's friendliness she was very unsure of herself and wished the whole episode had not arisen. But Lynn could not stay a child for ever and so she was launched into the most uncomfortable aspect of growing up; dating!

It was not a very satisfactory episode in her life although Lynn went to the pictures with the young man; he must have been almost seventeen. He also invited her to see *The Son of Oblimov* with Spike Milligan in London's theatreland. It was her first trip to the capital with anyone other than her family and the innocent couple spent the wet, cold November day walking the streets of London waiting for the early evening performance. Some of the time was spent in the darkness of a cartoon cinema, just to keep warm, Paul said, but Lynn thought he had other ideas in mind; she could be very dissuasive if she put her mind to it. By the time they had had a pizza and reached the theatre they were both cold and disillusioned. Paul handed the tickets to the usherette who promptly guided them through two separate doors. Lynn wondered if they would even sit together, but eventually they met again in the middle of the auditorium, a good position for centre stage. Lynn had never understood Spike Milligan though her brother seemed to thrive on his comedy. She realised at that early age that all boys had a similar sense of humour and perhaps girls were not meant to understand them at all. In some aspects she never changed her way of thinking. Thankfully the theatre was not a good place for a boy to practise his seduction technique; Paul behaved like a perfect gentleman. They returned home by train, thankful to be picked up from the Luton train station by her father some hours later.

Paul persevered and Lynn agreed to go to afternoon tea at his house. Paul was the youngest of four children. It seemed it was his family's aim to see him settled, and once Lynn had met his parents the young couple were ushered in to the front room. The door closed silently behind them – they were alone together. The settee loomed large and vacant; Paul patted it as an invitation for Lynn to sit, while he put some music on. He chose a vinyl long-playing record of romantic music which Lynn was rather uncomfortable about; it was only four o'clock in the afternoon. Paul made himself comfortable leaning towards her, pulling her in for a proper kiss. Lynn was not a prude but she was uneducated in such things. She responded a little but when she felt things – or rather his hands – were moving far too fast for her, she sat up abruptly.

'Have you got any different music?' she asked coolly, adjusting the collar of her blue rayon blouse.

Paul responded by bragging about his record collection and duly got up and chose another record, equally as long. This one was by Frank Sinatra. The singer crooned his way through the first few songs before Lynn realised she would have to distract Paul from the top buttons of her blouse. This time, instead of choosing an inappropriate artist, he asked if she would like to look through his collection. She jumped at the chance and seeing a pile of 45 r.p.m discs of The Shadows and Searchers, she chose one of these. There was a method in her madness for 45 r.p.m. discs only had a playing time of three to four minutes. It would leave Paul no time to even kiss his new-found girlfriend let alone discover how to undo her buttons. Lynn was amazed at his patience and he played her selection of discs, jumping from the settee each time a song ended. She was relieved that he didn't seem to have an automatic stacking system on his record player that would have allowed him to play five or six short playing records in one session!

Even then Lynn was relieved when his mother knocked tentatively on the door and whispered that the tea was on the table in the next room. Paul became the perfect son and gentleman and the light meal was spent asking Lynn what she wanted and passing plates of paste sandwiches round the table. His mother went to great pains to tell her visitor that Paul was the youngest son and that his brothers were all settled in good relationships. Lynn was relieved when her father collected her. Paul gave her a polite kiss but she could tell that her tactics and coolness had not put him off at all.

Lynn didn't go to tea or go out with Paul again. She did not feel comfortable and was not ready to be anyone's special girlfriend. Without confidence and with a little motherly guidance Lynn was dropped off at Paul's front door some days later and after a lot of stammering and waffling she eventually got the rehearsed words out of her mouth. She told him that she didn't want to get serious or go out with him again. The look on the boy's face made her feel that she had just kicked a puppy and she fled back to her father's car as he started the engine.

Weeks later the two mothers met by chance in town. Mrs Welland told Mrs Zealey that she thought she had interfered with her son's romance and that he was so upset that they had promised to buy him a car to relieve his disappointment. Her mother tried to explain that her daughter wasn't really well enough at that time to enjoy an intense friendship with any boy. Lynn secretly thought it had been a very close shave and that perhaps Paul had just wanted to be settled in a relationship like his brothers. She disliked men in leather trousers after that; they reminded her of young Paul's squeaky clothing on the black leather settee! She also decided she wasn't ready for romance because she really, really didn't know how to handle it.

Chapter 28

Lynn's first academic year at the College of Further Education was coming to a close. Her first written examinations had taken place. She had sat and passed her various O-level requirements and had taken her course entrance examination. The results of this would put her forward to an interview board and from this it would be decided if she were to be accepted for the N.N.E.B. course, due to start that following September. Lynn would then be sixteen and eligible for training; she had improved greatly with the aim of achieving a placing in her chosen career. Throughout her life Lynn had needed an aim to meet her highest potential. She worked harder and tried her best if she knew it was for a good reason. The negative side of this was that if there were no goal to reach or if there was no aim which someone else had set her, she thought there was no point in reaching her potential; Lynn needed a reason to achieve. Towards the end of the summer term she heard by letter that she had passed the required exam and a date had been set for her to attend an interview at Luton Town Hall. She found out later that eighty candidates had been chosen and only eighteen would be successful; Lynn prayed she would be one of them.

Lynn was gradually losing ground against her battle for health. Her symptoms of diarrhoea, nausea and stomach pain were handled as quietly and secretly as she possibly could but her mother was watching closely and the GP was observing the decline. Now she was losing blood and any anxiety added to her problems. Her condition worsened and improved in episodes so referral to a hospital consultant was deferred several times. Unknown to her parents Lynn would walk or cycle home from college and collapse on the hall floor once she had put her key in the door. This of course only happened when her mother was not at home. Lynn would lie there with her head on the lower stair waiting for the strength to pick herself up and make herself a drink before her mother came home.

The exciting occasion of her brother being awarded The Duke of Edinburgh's Gold Award and being presented to receive his medal and certificate at the Buckingham Palace Garden party award ceremony took place that summer. Lynn watched as her parents and brother left for London in the morning of the event. Invitations were not extended to siblings, but Lynn, although slightly envious, was happy for her brother and preferred to stay at home anyway. She decided to bake a celebration cake and decorate it for the occasion and set about the project as soon as her family had left home. The sponge rose well in the oven and the Victoria sandwich came out of its tin perfectly. Having filled it with strawberry jam Lynn then rested a while over a sandwich lunch before starting to make the icing; Lynn was tiring. She was annoyed that her energy was now almost completely depleted and her stomach ached badly. The tiredness was making her job harder and the lumps of icing sugar, despite being sieved, were not blending with the added water. Each stir of the spoon should have smoothed the mixture but Lynn's heavy hand only made the icing into something solid and immovable. She added more water and sat on the floor of the kitchen, too tired to climb on to the stool and hold the mixing bowl in her arms. She began to cry out of sheer frustration and eventually she gave up. The final addition of water had turned the icing in to a run-away flow which she poured over the cake hoping that it would set even if it didn't have the professional finish she had hoped for. She left the cake on the unit and lay down on the settee in the front room, now no longer out of bounds as she was no longer a child. Lynn roused herself after an hour and looked at the ticking clock.

'They will be home soon,' she said out loud. She went back in to the kitchen and made a little tent immortalising the camping expedition Bill had gone on as one of the targets it took to secure the award. She made it with paper and a broken matchstick and decorated the cake with a few words of congratulations. This in itself was a chore for new icing had to be made to complete the decoration. Lynn stood back, but found it hard to admire her work.

'Could do better,' she murmured to herself, hoping her brother would be pleased with the effort she had gone to, if not with the cake itself. She tidied the kitchen, tidied herself and waited for her family to return.

Lynn's cake had the desired effect upon their homecoming. She was pleased that her effort had not gone in vain and that Bill had enjoyed his day and her cake. His proud mother would be able to tell the neighbours of her meeting with royalty and show a photograph of herself in a cream suit and the obligatory hat, standing next to her rather bored-looking son. Her brother always hated having his photo taken. Her father, it seemed, was only too pleased to get out of his suit and into his slippers. Although he was proud of his only son, Lynn wondered if he had ever told Bill so. Her father liked the cake too; he had taken the biggest slice.

That night Lynn went to bed wondering just how long she could continue, feeling the way she did. She looked deathly pale despite smiling cheerfully back at the image of herself in her bedroom mirror. Her mother seemed to be aware that things would take a further turn and hoped then, eventually, someone would listen to her when she told them that her daughter needed medical intervention other than that which their GP could offer.

The morning of her course interview came. Lynn dressed smartly, preparing to travel by bus with her mother to the Luton town hall. The time was set for eleven o'clock and Lynn, though confident that she would do her best, for at the end of the day that was all anyone could do, was ill at ease with herself. Her stomach ached badly and she had spent more time that morning in the toilet than preparing herself for the inquisition. Worse than that was the fact that she was bleeding from the bowel again, only this time it was worse. The colitis had returned with a vengeance but Lynn felt that as long as she got through the interview she would start to recover.

'Nerves are a powerful force; just get through the day.' If only Lynn believed what she was saying.

The bus journey was a bit of a trial though her mother distracted her with light conversation. Now that she had grown up it was a rarity to travel by bus with her mother, and the journey bore a marked resemblance to her trips to the Children's Annex hospital as a child. Certainly she felt the same nervousness and tightening of the stomach, with no joy of a visit to the toy shop at the end of the ordeal. Lynn grimaced at the memory and chatted to her mum instead of dwelling on the past.

Both mother and daughter were nervous of missing the appointment but they need not have worried; they arrived in plenty of time and mounted the stone Town Hall steps, entering through the solid dark wooden doors. They were directed to the correct floor and saw before them a seated row of other likely applicants and their mothers. Some of the girls were standing confidently, others shifting their feet nervously. Many sat looking at their hands, while others were more interested in their surroundings and the other girls than their own predicament.

'Hello, Lynn,' Linda Delmar whispered loudly down the line, not daring to break the spell of tension that wound round them as wickedly as a snake.

Lynn was pleased to see someone she knew from her own class. She waved politely in acknowledgement mouthing the word 'hello' in return. None of the mothers knew each other; they stood by their offspring, as nervous for their girls as if the interview was intended for them. These had already started. Someone came out of the room at the end of the corridor with an official-looking clipboard; Lynn didn't recognise the woman who called a girl's name loudly, returning with her to the room she had just appeared from. Despite the sun shafting through the intermittently spaced windows, the corridor where the applicants were seated seemed ill-ventilated and gloomy. The tension racked up a level; Lynn looked around. Eventually she had to make the choice of asking someone where the toilet was and risk missing her slot or holding herself together and fluffing the interview through lack of concentration. Lynn chose the former and told her mother where she would be. She turned back the way they had come and asked the concierge for the directions. She reassured her anxious mother as best she could that she was OK and she told her not to worry. It had little effect; her daughter, pale with dark rings under her eyes, was her greatest concern these days and this morning was no exception. She tried hard to release her from the stranglehold of caring but lately she knew her daughter was keeping aspects of her health from her. She waited in the corridor, listening in case Lynn's name was called. Lynn stayed in the toilet for a long time.

The interview went well enough although nothing could be perceived from the panel of prominent and qualified persons. Lynn couldn't remember much about it except that she did her best, tried to appear confident and talk above the noises her stomach was making. She did remember, however, just how glad she was to get home. Her mother put the kettle on while Lynn ran upstairs to the most familiar room of the house. She felt safe to be home again but wished for the tenth time that morning that she didn't always have to run to the toilet. Perhaps a cup of tea would soothe her nerves and calm her stomach. Sadly it had the opposite effect.

A week or so later, during the summer holidays, Bill was preparing for a cycling tour with his two mates. Lynn liked one of his friends, a blond boy named Peter. He was more laid back than her brother and the other lad and perhaps a little slower, but, argued Lynn, he joined the two other friends on all the cycling trips including the previous tour of the length of Britain and was probably the lad who made three a good working combination.

On the morning of their departure Lynn saw her brother off. She always missed him when he was away and looked forward to the stories, should he care to divulge them, on his return. Once his rucksack was packed and his cycle prepared, she waved him off, not realising that the next time she would see him it would be from her hospital bed in ward 10 of the Luton and Dunstable hospital.

Lynn couldn't remember much about that weekend. She started to bleed heavily, going to the toilet ten or more times in quick succession. She was sent to bed, which was just as well for she was almost too weak to stand. She eventually confided in her mother that she also had an abscess that was weeping badly; Lynn couldn't take any more.

Dr Jackson was called out and serious decisions had to be made. He decided that his patient's prognosis was worsening and the periods of recovery were lessening. Lynn's condition had become an emergency. An ambulance was called, a bag packed and Lynn, attended by her very concerned mother, was taken to the Accident and Emergency department of the hospital they used to pass on the way to the Children's Annex hospital ten years previously. Lynn was unsure if life was repeating itself. She held her stomach to ease the cramps and turned her head away from her mother's anxious gaze as she vomited into the stainless steel bowl. There was only one thing she was certain of; for the first time in her life she actually wanted to be in hospital. She was wheeled into a cubicle to await assessment. A diagnosis of an acute attack of the condition chronic ulcerative colitis was made and she was eventually admitted on to the ward.

Her mother walked beside the trolley as the porter and nurse wheeled Lynn along the corridor. She bent towards her daughter and with words meant only for her she quietly but forcefully said, 'For goodness' sake, Lynn, stop smiling at everyone we pass – you are half dead, but no one would believe it to see you put on such an act!'

Lynn didn't want to be a nuisance and did not close her eyes until she had been lifted on to the ward bed and curtained off from the three other women patients in the four-bedded bay; then and only then could Lynn stop fighting.

Chapter 29

Lynn seemed to think she had done all the hard work. She had fought to stay at college, fought to be like other teenagers, and even fought to be well, or at least appear to be. Now, in familiar surroundings, albeit in a different hospital, she knew she could let go of the reins that drove her life on. She had no more strength and at last didn't have to pretend that she did. She was in pain, serious pain, and the symptoms of ulcerative colitis were both distressing and anti-social. She was not allowed out of bed even to use a commode, and cold metal bed pans were the only choice. If the doctor could have told her not to move he would have. So severe was the risk of her bowel haemorrhaging that Lynn was ordered to complete bed rest for a month and for much of that time she remained seriously ill. The consultant wished to save her from a major life-altering operation which in the 1960s was rarely performed on a person so young. The words "ileostomy" or total colectomy were never uttered and removal of the large bowel was outside Lynn's comprehension. As Lynn's consultant was a doctor of medicine and not surgery it was understood that Lynn's proposed recovery would be by drugs and not operation.

Lynn lay back against her pillows and submitted, as only she knew how, to being a patient. Her life for now was out of her control and in the hands of others. It was strangely comforting and though Lynn never gave up her fight for life she did submit to being too ill to worry about life at all. At first it took all her strength to help with her own bed-bath, though her remaining cheerfulness made her a good and willing patient. She took the twice-daily steroid injections as her treatment without objection or fuss despite the drug being thick and difficult to take in the form of intra-muscular injection. Her bottom became a bruised pin cushion and the nurses disliked having to administer the injections; however, Lynn had learned many years before that submission was the best course of action. The "line of least resistance" had usually been her policy when it came to being hurt!

Lynn needed blood. Her weight plummeted to six and a half stone as dehydration and anaemia kicked in. She was light-headed and very weak and relieved when the decision had been made to halt the downward swing. They started the intravenous drip in the night giving Lynn three pints of cross-matched blood. Lynn went to sleep as best she could, the needle in her arm causing discomfort, but she was tired, so very tired. She began to dream and the heat in her arm radiated throughout her body, filling her head, pulsing through her veins. She was unsure if she was dreaming and was only aware of a swimming sensation. She thought of nothing at all; it seemed she couldn't. The heat grew stronger, confining her as if in a box without ventilation. She wanted to call to be let out but only then realised there was no restriction, it was her body itself that was the confining influence; perhaps if she relaxed she would be free. Her mind was confused; where were the nurses? She suddenly felt a different sensation, an upward pull like suction, which in itself was terrifying. She felt she was in a vertical tunnel or tube, or at the bottom of a well travelling very fast towards the surface. With some semblance of understanding she wondered what death was like. She had heard of experiences similar to this and had the sense to look up as she travelled, but she saw no "light at the end of the tunnel". For her there was no floating peace, no resignation of her mind; she knew she had to fight. The imagery of the tunnel was dark and long; she felt so helpless that it was as if the tunnel was moving and not her. She became alarmed, fearing that she would actually reach another place without the comfort of light to guide her. She could not stop the journey; she knew she needed help and called out loudly and continually, 'Markie, Markie!' She needed the support of someone she loved and trusted with her life, or death. She called again, understanding the need for her uncle. She recognised that he would have travelled the same path and was aware of her suffering. She called again and her world at last began to slow. The frightening speed of her journey slackened and stopped, though she was unaware of the exact moment the experience ended. She didn't reach the end of the tunnel, if there ever was one; she eventually slept.

The following morning Lynn awoke; she did not mention her experience to anyone and it would have remained an episode likened to a vivid dream if a neighbouring patient hadn't told Lynn's mother at visiting time that her daughter had been taken very poorly in the night and had called out for her. Lynn knew it had not been her mummy she had called out for but her uncle Markie. As if in confirmation the following night, Lynn awoke to hear a nurse talking to that same patient. In whispered tones the nurse told the concerned woman that they nearly lost the girl the previous night and hadn't expected her to recover. Lynn listened, eventually realising that the two women were talking about her. Had she nearly died? She would never know for sure, for no one spoke of it to her, but she was in no doubt the episode could be classed as a "near death experience".

The blood transfusion and the steroid treatment gradually pulled Lynn back from the brink. She was soon allowed to wash herself and eat a light diet though she was extremely disappointed when she asked her consultant three weeks after her admission if she could get out of bed.

'You could get up, Lynn,' he said sternly, 'but only if your bowel remains in bed.'

She didn't know if it was said with humour but it was another two weeks before Lynn was allowed to sit in a chair, and a week later, take the first tottering steps to recovery. She was patient, relying on her old skills learned in another hospital so long ago. She began to draw cartoon animals using pencil and crayon, filling up book after book with Walt Disney-type characters. She worked the cross-stitch designs of embroidery her mother brought her and watched and listened to the women patients who were admitted and discharged from the beds around her. Lynn absorbed their lives and their stories, unaware that her schooling, far from being curtailed, was becoming an education unfound in the classroom yet more important to her future life than she could ever realise. She understood her own pain, but, more than that, she understood the pain and distress of others.

Lynn was a month short of her sixteenth birthday on her admission and during her six weeks' stay in the hospital was to see summer almost come and go. Patients who shared the four-bedded bay were mostly short-stay patients and the ladies were generally friendly and motherly, adopting Lynn and reporting the day's events when her mother visited. Her father came at weekends and some evenings and her brother as much as he could, sending cartoons and messages to his sister when he didn't visit her. Lynn knew by the drawings he produced that he cared and thought of her daily.

The ward was of a mixed sex design, the women's bays separated from the men's accommodation by a day and television room. Side wards for either sex were situated opposite these bays, along the length of the ward corridor. This meant that Lynn didn't get to meet many of the other patients until she was mobile. She heard the men and the odd joke or laughter shared by those fitter than she was and looked forward to the time when she could use the bathroom and shower and explore a little further. The only men she met during those first restricted weeks were those who had volunteered to bring round the early morning cups of tea.

Most of the ladies looked forward to their early morning cuppa brought to them on the trolley by two or three of the fitter male patients. Morale was raised by this dawn event and Lynn would smile when Mrs Bates combed her hair and put on lipstick at six-thirty in the morning in time to smile at Mr Cooper as he wheeled the squeaky trolley in to the ward with two shy companions. Lynn chuckled, noting that the middle-aged patient suffering with gallstones, never wore lipstick when her husband visited in the afternoon.

'Morning, ladies; who's for tea?' Fred had obviously washed and had brushed his hair, giving a toothpaste-enhanced smile around the ward. His eyes darted to and from Molly Davis's cleavage. It was quite obvious even to Lynn that Mr Cooper's recovery was greatly improved by such a social event. 'How are you today, Lynn? The boys are asking after you. Terry says he'll be on the trolley again tomorrow; he's nil by mouth today so he's still in bed.'

Lynn raised herself on one elbow and smiled back. Terry was a twenty-one-year-old lad about town and she was secretly keen on him and desperate for any attention shown her. Despite her weight improving to seven and a half stone she knew she still looked emaciated and very poorly; inside, though, she was just a teenager wanting to be let out. The group of men in Terry's bay of four were very considerate to young Lynn and she shared hours in the television room in the evenings enjoying their often jovial company with other patients. As her health improved the nurses would push her bed down the corridor to watch television in the Day Room next to Terry, when he, too, was immobile. Social etiquette went out of the window but Lynn improved in humour and health in the company of such people.

Lynn celebrated her sixteenth birthday while on the ward and Fred had asked her mother what she would like as a present. On the tea round on the morning of the 30th August he presented her with a hastily wrapped package from the four men. Inside Lynn found her favourite record by her favourite artist – *Born Free*, by Matt Monro.

Lynn was almost disappointed when Terry popped in to see her some days later to tell her he was being discharged. He wore a blue suit and drainpipe trousers and looked very smart. However, she had to admit to preferring him in hospital pajamas and a corded dressing gown. Lynn's mother, realising her daughter had a crush on the young man, seriously hoped he would not get in touch with her once he had left hospital. In fact he visited the ward and Lynn once and sported a hairstyle to suit his Teddy boy wardrobe. Lynn knew they probably wouldn't have looked twice at each other on the street but she treasured the imagined hospital romance and the parting hug he had given her. They never saw each other again.

On the day England won the world cup Lynn was still on official bed rest and not even allowed to watch television that day. The ward sister was standing by Lynn's bed when the cheer went up from the men in the day room; she stormed down to them to remind them that they were in hospital. Lynn wondered if the men had taken any notice of her at all. She was thought to be a bit of a dragon but Lynn doubted she could hold her authority over the winning of such a world sporting event.

On the positive side morale was high because of the introduction of mixed wards. Men's beds were never set beside the women and there were separate facilities for both sexes. As Lynn recovered her appetite she also began to recognise the disadvantages. The food trolley came up from the kitchen and the meals were served by the nurses. Lynn's appetite was returning with the influence of steroids and meal times eventually became an important event in an otherwise dull routine. The food trolley passed through the women's section after the men were served and by the time it reached them their meals were often of smaller portions. On one particular day food was minimal and the sister had to calm a situation similar to the "five loaves and two fishes" parable, only in this case it was half a dozen pilchards and two lumps of mash between four. The kitchen was called but as it had closed, bread and butter was prepared on the ward kitchen as a "stomach filler" before the next scheduled meal. After that the food trolley started its journey alternating between the male and female ends of the ward. The food was rarely hot as the ward corridor was long and serving it took time. Morning tea was definitely the highlight of the day.

As the steroid treatment started to kick in Lynn found her appetite rise to gargantuan levels. She wasn't able to succumb to such desires and she was on a special diet but she was always hungry. Her mother made treats for her sometimes and when visiting one afternoon she brought Lynn four little cakes that she could share with the other ladies in her bay. Lynn whispered to her mother to put the other three in her locker. She made the excuse that she didn't get enough to eat, which was untrue.

'It's so unlike you, Lynn,' her mother commented, almost insisting that she share.

'Please, Mum; just give one to Jane in the bed next door; please leave me the others!'

Her mother did as she was asked but in subsequent conversations Lynn realised that she would never live her act of gluttony down.

Lynn was well liked by patients and staff. She knew that if she did everything the doctors and nurses told her, the journey through her illness would be smoother; it had always been that way. Gradually the cortisone steroids were having an effect on her illness. The symptoms declined and her strength to a certain degree improved. However, as with any drug, there were side effects and Lynn discovered this to her dismay. Her weight improved and then carried on ballooning. She became "moon faced", the shape of her face mirroring the description. She had regular migraine attacks and though by now she was out of bed and relatively mobile she often felt very unwell. The consultant told her mother that steroids would continue to be prescribed and the dosage would only be reduced when the colitis was held in check. Eventually it was hoped that Lynn would maintain good health without the steroid drugs.

Lynn got to know and like the house doctor and his regular visits, even when he hadn't been called, were a highlight to her day. Although she often felt like a piece of meat, to be examined and investigated as a regular procedure, she was a spirited teenager with all the feelings and emotions relating to her early womanhood. To have a man, albeit her doctor, show an interest in her as a person and not as a body was a joy to her. Dr Whitman would chat to her, or call in on passing the ward. Perhaps he filled the role that Dr Green had had during her hospitalisation as a child. It didn't matter what the reason was, but when this young doctor told her mother that Lynn was a wonderful patient and a wonderful girl – truly wonderful – Lynn glowed and once again wished that she was older and not a patient of his. Later she heard that Dr Whitman had got engaged to a country girl he had met on a farm holiday and she was thrilled for him but hoped one day she would be able to meet a man such as he; someone to love and cherish her for who she really was.

Eventually her health improved enough for Lynn to be discharged. The injections had been stopped and steroid tablets were prescribed, in readiness for going home. Her mother had to buy her new clothes three sizes larger as she had a weight gain of three stone and it was still rising as much as five pounds a week now. She was told it was an accumulated effect of the drug but she was unhappy with the explanation, suffering now with indigestion as well as migraine. She knew her father had suffered from ulcerative colitis when his daughter was a child and had been treated with a sulphonamide drug, which kept the symptoms at bay. By a cruel twist of fate, Lynn proved to have an allergic reaction to this drug and so had no choice but to uphold the steroid regime, despite the debilitating side-effects.

The long summer was ending when Lynn put her new clothes on for the first time. She slipped into new sandals though even these were tight around her swollen ankles. She found herself to be unattractive before her illness, and now she hated the mirror image before her. Her tummy was swelling and the tightness around her waist was uncomfortable. She had to be very firm with herself. On the day of her discharge, having said goodbye to some of her new friends and the hospital staff and received a hug from her favourite doctor, she took the first steps to her new life. As so many times before her parents took her home from hospital in the family car. She felt quite alien to her new surroundings and after spending five and a half weeks in an open hospital ward her bedroom was claustrophobic and as silent as the grave she had so narrowly escaped. She sat on her low single bed, alone for the first time, and stared into the dressing-table mirror.

You are alive, Lynn; heaven doesn't want you yet. Now you must get better and get on with your life. Perhaps you are here for a purpose, but for whatever reason, you must not waste the time you have been given. She thought of her Uncle Mark and decided that only the good died young. He seemed to smile back through the mirror at her in reassurance. She knew she would be safe if she remembered how he had loved her.

Lynn smoothed the plaster angel on her bedside table as her mother came into her room and sat beside her daughter. She drew her into her arms and Lynn became the child again. A tear trickled down her cheek and on to her mother's blouse and then she began to sob – deep heartfelt cries from the heart. She sobbed from her soul.

'Let it out, Lynn, let it all out.' Her mother knew that her girl would need to heal from the inside as well as in her body and until the trauma of all she had endured surfaced the spiritual healing could not begin. She would be there to help her as she always was. She pulled a large handkerchief from her pocket, wiped her child's eyes and gave it to her. 'You're safe now, Lynn, welcome home.' She spoke with confidence but secretly she feared for her child's future as she looked at her swollen body, thinning hair and stretch-marked arms. She prayed for healing but knew in her heart that Lynn's trials were not over yet.

Chapter 30

During the last week Lynn was in hospital a letter arrived at the house for her. Her mother brought it in at visiting time and Lynn opened it to find that she had been successful in her interview for enrolment on the N.N.E.B. course at college. Out of eighty candidates she had been one of the eighteen chosen to go forward on the two-year course. Lynn was both elated and saddened for now there was no possibility of her being well enough to join the course in September at the start of the first term which was only two weeks away. The course involved two days only at college studying theory and the other three week days on secondment at one of the local children's nurseries. Lynn would not be fit enough. It was decided that her mother would talk to the Head of Department who was aware of the problems; she was sympathetic. Upon her arrival home, Lynn heard that the college would hold her placing open for her for when she was well enough to commence training. Nobody realised it then but Lynn would never take up such a position and eventually after leaving it open for two years, the college were in agreement that the place should be filled by another student. For Lynn, the pressure was removed, but she was able to return to college the following year to continue general studies including further GCEs. The challenge to return spurred her on and at the end of the first college year she received a special award for the "The Best Endeavour in the Face of Adversity". With the received book tokens she bought three books on doll making and went on to excel in the craft. During further times of ill health the skill was a blessing and Lynn became adept at the fine work and character-making of the dolls, some of which she sold. When her strength failed periodically her mother firmly stuffed the finished toys her daughter had made, enabling her then to bring the characters to life. Lynn never gave up; she never looked at herself and asked why it should have happened to her. Her glass was always half full and it was this perseverance that saw her through adulthood and on to her fifty-ninth birthday!

Even her illness and slow recuperation did not deter Peter, her brother's friend, from cycling to visit her. He now worked in Norwich, but came down most weekends to see his family and visit Lynn. Bill was away at university but Peter continued to keep in touch with the family and when Lynn felt well enough he would take her out or invite her round to his family's home in Luton. Lynn felt comfortable with Peter but unfortunately for the young man held no notions of romance in her head. She loved him as a friend and the families accepted that Lynn was still not well enough to consider anything more.

Recovery was not straightforward. Bill had left for Edinburgh University to study Astrophysics. Lynn and her mother were alone during the day and it seemed to Lynn that her father did not play a big part in nurturing his daughter. However, this was something her mother always had the lion's share of and so life settled down to one that seemed to be without future. Lynn's weight gain was rapid and destructive. It continued to balloon despite a restrictive diet and soon she had reached twelve and a half stone. The steroid side effects roughened her skin, thinned her hair and enlarged her stomach to the extent that the following summer her mother regretfully had to buy her second-size maternity clothes and even these she filled.

'The material is very pretty,' she would encourage her daughter.

'But will it ever end? When will I stop growing in to someone I am not?' was Lynn's reply. Her mother had become Lynn's tower of emotional strength, but this question was one she could not answer.

After a couple of months she attended an out-patient appointment at the hospital. The consultant said she was doing well and that he would reduce the prednisolone steroid gradually over the following interval. Slowly her weight reduced and the headaches became less crippling. At their height they would last half a week and during that time Lynn could do nothing but lie in a darkened room vomiting. She had no social life outside her family and missed out on most of her sixteenth year, though filled it with creative hobbies that would stand her in good stead later in life. Once the tablet dosage was reduced things looked up for her and although she was still wearing maternity clothes she was able to walk holding her mother's arm and go out with the family, sometimes being joined by a friend from college.

Susan had had a form of polyneuritis a few years before. She had recovered well, but her legs remained weak and one needed the support to enable her to walk with confidence. She understood how Lynn was feeling and they were great company for each other. Susan was an expert seamstress and studied tailoring. Together they would make dolls and enjoy each other's humour and attend college part-time.

One day while on an outing with the family Susan walked ahead and though she limped the calliper she wore helped her considerably. Lynn followed on, holding her mother's arm. The little group were laughing and enjoying their day when a passer-by said something to Lynn's mum. She went rigid and started to shake with anger. Susan turned back and asked what was wrong. Mrs Zealey could not keep the insult to herself and blurted out the stranger's comment.

'That woman wanted to know why I wasn't holding your arm as you are disabled.' Joyce directed her comment at her daughter's friend, wearing the calliper. 'She had looked at Lynn and thought her pregnant and shameless, wearing no ring and had the cheek to infer as much.' Joyce looked, in turn, at the two girls and realised she had added further damage to the stranger's insult. Lynn felt ashamed and angry and Susan, far from feeling hurt, wanted to go after the woman and 'bop her one'. The girls were determined not to let the conversation ruin their day, and laughed it off; however Lynn never forgot the episode. She wondered why her mother had had to repeat the woman's comment, as it was so hurtful. Later she realised her mother's outburst had been spontaneous, without understanding the further hurt it had caused, but, unfortunately, the damage had been done.

Lynn was pleased that her hair had stopped falling out and that the definite hump of flesh at the top of her spine was disappearing. She counted out her pills every morning and when the dosage was reduced yet again she thought there was hope for a future. She had a lot of time to make up and just wanted to get on with her life.

One morning after she had weighed herself with a pleasing result she had to return to the bathroom. After a while she came down the stairs for breakfast and was strangely silent. A while later she went upstairs again but upon her return to the kitchen where her mother was washing the dishes Lynn had to tell her that she had started to bleed again. The old symptoms of ulcerative colitis had returned, and along with it the pain and discomfort; she cried. And so began another long spell of appointments and drugs to balance up the effect of the illness. The headaches returned, she gained weight and life was pretty miserable.

Her brother came home from university for the Christmas break but by then Lynn was back in hospital. She had deteriorated and on top of that her parents were rowing again and it seemed to her that it was because they were not receiving support and love from each other. This had always been a feature of their marriage and once her brother had left home it seemed the only time they stopped arguing or hurting each other was when she, their daughter, was ill. It wasn't a very comfortable position to be in and she never told anyone how she felt. Sometimes the hospital doctor would ask if anything was worrying her, but she would deny anything was wrong because it seemed to her a betrayal of the family and her loving parents. Lynn suffered the tension and the disturbances and then when the stress was too great and it coincided with her drug reduction the pain returned and the vicious circle began all over again.

During this hospital stay Bill and her parents visited her on Christmas Day and it was decided she could go home for Boxing Day, to return to the ward in the evening: Lynn couldn't wait to get back to her hospital bed. She wanted a happy family but this time it seemed something was missing, even at Christmas. She felt she must have spoilt her brother's vacation for Lynn now suffered depression as well as illness and the darkness didn't seem able to lift. Bill went back to university and Lynn came home to a cheerless life. She felt totally trapped within her own skin as well as family life. It seemed to her that she was in a dilemma. Her loving mother gave her great strength and comfort through her illness, she could not fault her, nor would she want to, and yet the stress within the marriage weakened Lynn's strength. It was as if the very power of love gave with one hand and yet, inevitably, took with the other. There were many times when Lynn tried to help her parents, interrupting their breakfast discussions that eventually led to arguments and long moody silences. She would sit with them at the table trying to be the go-between or arbitrator but rarely with any success. Sometimes it was Lynn who ended up in tears of frustration and unhappiness. Only then did her parents' disagreement end.

'Now you see what you have done.' Her mother flung the words at her father, who said nothing in reply but left the table silently. Minutes later the back door slammed and Lynn looked from the window to see her father start work on some undetectable fault under the bonnet of his Austin 1100. The beloved Morris Minor had been sold years earlier and the whole family still held it in nostalgic regard. The story was often told of the time, while motoring on a dual-carriageway, that a chrome hub-cab, from a car travelling in the opposite direction, spun across the road towards the family car. Syd told everyone to get down, as the hub-cab bounced on the road and up on to the bonnet of the Morris. They were still motoring. The only thing that saved the family was the chrome centre strut that divided the front windscreen, which, it was discovered later, had been badly dented. The Zealey family had a lot to thank the little green car for. The Austin 1100 had a lot to live up to, and Lynn's father never gained the same satisfaction, either in maintaining or driving it. Looking out of the window at her father now, Lynn could see by the slouch of his shoulders that another morning was spoilt by argument and the weekend still loomed ahead.

Sometimes if the atmosphere was too thick between them Lynn's mother suggested to her daughter that they go out visiting, just to get out of the house. Lynn would agree but the unplanned visitation was a mixed blessing to her. Often because she was upset by the recent argument, Lynn's mum would pour the details out to the neighbour and the whole incident would be gone over and digested all over again. However, Lynn was able to be a bystander in this and tried to disassociate her mind from the conversation. The neighbourly visit was only in part successful.

Lynn often sat in the rocking chair in the front room. It was a modern piece of furniture, something her mother had always wanted to own, and was positioned in the bay window enabling the occupant a view of the long road of First Avenue. Lynn liked to shut herself in the room when it was dark; the only light coming into the room was from the street lights. She would rock herself backwards and forwards, faster and faster, as if travelling somewhere. Gradually, as her mood calmed, she rocked at a gentler rhythm to soothe herself and wondered if she would ever be well enough to live her own life, enjoying the freedom she knew other friends of her age enjoyed.

The chair rocked, "one day soon; one day soon; one day soon". It was as if, by chanting the words, perhaps they would come true. Lynn knew her health would not allow her to escape her enclosed environment. Her one aim was to get well but the intermittent colitis and repeated medication continued to hold her back and the problems at home held her down; would there ever be an escape?

During these two years Lynn thought she was standing still in her life. Unbeknown to her she was growing strong in a much deeper way. Her mind strengthened and her compassion and understanding of her mother grew. She regretted many times that she could not show her father the love she gave to her mother and also regretted that her father rarely approached her with the show of affection she desperately needed from him.

That is what made it hard; through all this time she loved them both and knew they loved her. Lynn still sought approval from both parents and yet she found peace away from them, when she was ill. Her attitude shocked her into thinking there was something wrong with her to feel this way. She seemed to realise that avoidance of confrontation was the only way to maintain some control over her own life. It was a practised childhood response. It was not her fault.

Through this time Lynn's spiritual awareness strengthened. It was as if during her lowest times she was more in tune with God. She never defined who God was, she had no need to, but during this time He really became like a father to her. The plaster angel still watched over her at night and Uncle Mark drew close in times of trouble and joy. She would sit in some quiet corner or even in the stillness of a hospital ward at night and believe that her uncle's spirit comforted her. It was easier for her to believe this after her experience of the "long dark tunnel" as she called her near-death experience; the thin veil of life and death had been broken. She asked God for comfort, nothing more, and this was what she always received.

Her mother had a large part to play in her awareness, often sitting on her daughter's bed at night singing softly to her and thumbing through the hymn book until Lynn chose one she wanted to hear. Her mother had a melodic voice and could soothe all pain and stress by just singing one or two verses to her daughter. Sometimes her voice would become strong and forceful, especially when she sang songs that she had composed herself. Lynn would sit up in bed or snuggle down while her mum, sitting awkwardly by her side, closed her eyes and sung as if she were praying for her daughter's return to health; willing it, almost. The tears would fall from her face and Lynn would be moved and uplifted to a place of harmony and love. These were very important experiences for them both and when she had finished singing her mother would talk to her of strength and love and all positive subjects between heaven and earth. The wisdom of understanding was powerful and Lynn found that these times were some of the most important in her life. Her mother would write strengthening pieces of poetry and text in a most powerful hand. These words reassured the girl, and she kept what had been written in some corner of a drawer or dressing gown, to be brought out and read when she was alone or in hospital. Lynn was unsure if she believed in fate or destiny but she did believe that some things in life were ordained and although she hated every moment of crippling ill health she held a resignation that perhaps it was meant to be. Having decided to think this way she knew she could glean the best from her life. Eventually she hoped she would be able to help others; this way her experiences would not be in vain. This was most important to her; life must not be wasted. Her mother encouraged her in this belief thus turning a negative time of her life in to a positive one, from which healing could flow. Not only did mother and daughter have a special relationship with each other but also each had their own loving relationship with God; He was never doubted.

Chapter 31

The vicious circle had a wide circumference; Lynn lived her life day by day under the restrictions of her health. Her eighteenth birthday was a duplication of the one before and it was sad for her to realise her sixteenth birthday in hospital had, in fact, held more optimism for the future than the one she now celebrated. This could not go on!

A few weeks later Lynn was back in hospital and the drug regime was prescribed in higher doses just as it had been during other relapses. Lynn's mother was not amused. Having watched her daughter suffer enough without hope of well-being she asked the ward sister if she could see the doctor. After being patronised her mother's attitude changed. She became as a vixen defending her cub in desperation. The sister walked away, returning ruffled and contrite; an appointment had been made for Joyce to see the consultant with her husband the following morning.

They met the doctor at ten o'clock; the atmosphere was frosty. It was quite obvious that Mrs Zealey would hold the lion's share of the conversation, with her husband's support. She looked the consultant in the face.

'How long will you continue dosing my daughter with steroids?'

'Every occasion the disease returns,' he commented.

'Then I think she will have no life at all.'

He looked at his patient's parents across the table. 'There are side effects with any drug.' He tried to pacify the mother to no avail.

'Then it is time we sought a second opinion for my daughter's well-being.'

At this he looked up. His professional pride had been hurt but he was not prepared to let it show.

'If you wish I could send her to another hospital.'

'Which one?'

'Perhaps Watford.'

Lynn's mother was not reassured, 'I was thinking of London.'

Because Lynn had not been included in the consultation she was not privy to the details of the conversation, apart from what her parents related to her on their return to the ward. Lynn was aware that something had dramatically changed.

'We are going to have a second opinion at St Bartholomew's hospital. It's going to be arranged as soon as you are well enough to travel.' Her father was the first to speak, he seemed confident, as if a weight had been lifted from his shoulders.

'We'll get you well, Lynn, you have a life to lead; it's been long enough coming.' Her mother seemed fired by her despair and Lynn thought that if she could have, her mum would have moved mountains.

The sister and doctor had thought Joyce an overprotective mother through most of her daughter's hospital admissions. Lynn's parents knew the Luton and Dunstable hospital and medical staff had done all they could but now Lynn's mother could remain passive no longer. She had defended her case for a second opinion. She didn't care what the medical staff thought; she was going to see her daughter well again, and her husband backed her up this time.

Some six weeks later a letter arrived for Lynn at home with an arranged appointment to see Mr Ian Todd, consultant surgeon at St Bart's. She travelled with her parents by car and her first impression of the hospital was eye-opening. The old hospital originated in 1123 and stood on its original site. Surrounded by a high stone wall and archway entrance it was in close proximity to Smithfield's famous meat market. At the time they arrived the butchers in their heavily blooded overalls were taking their coffee break. Some sat on the benches against the hospital's boundary wall. Lynn smiled for the first time that morning and jokingly said she didn't much like the look of the surgeons!

The hospital was impressive, not because of the décor of the interior or the potted plants but for the pure industry of internal functioning. The reception hall was much like one of the London main railway stations and as busy as any rush hour. Areas were being updated and redecorated and everywhere there were bustling nurses and streams of young doctors rushing to get to where they should be. Lynn and her parents queued at the reception desk to be directed to the correct floor of consulting clinics. They took the old caged lift to the second floor and entered the large clinic, already full of patients. Lynn thought back to her time in The London Hospital at Whitechapel; although it was a childhood memory she was aware that the green and cream tiles and linoleum did not differ very much between one hospital to another. Nor had the decade improved the severity of the décor. She felt she was stepping back in time, but now, in 1969, she was hopeful and unafraid. She was pinning her future on the success of this appointment and when her name was eventually called, she stood up with hope and a little trepidation. She breathed in deeply and caught the familiar smell of disinfectant in her nostrils.

Mr Todd was an approachable doctor from the start. He introduced himself and his team of surgeons and students and asked her permission for the latter to observe her examination. Lynn withdrew within herself, the habit of submission reaffirming itself; she agreed. First though he spoke to her on her own and put her mind at rest. Her medical notes had not accompanied her so it was of benefit that the surgeon review her case thoroughly. After the examination he stated to his students that errors of judgement had perhaps been made and warned them not to become complacent just because they were being trained at such a prestigious hospital. The surgeon then invited Lynn's parents into the consulting room where he told them of his decision. Their daughter would be admitted within a few weeks purely to reduce the drugs in her body. He realised the colitis would return and then the decision would be made whether or not to perform a total colectomy and ileostomy, enabling her, once she had come to terms with her new "plumbing arrangements", to lead a normal life and catch up with all she had missed. His grey eyes sparkled as he told her he wanted her to lose weight so that he didn't have to go in up to his elbows. Lynn took the humour in good heart; she liked the man and had every confidence in him. He was honest.

Lynn went home with her parents and from then on her mood lifted. She was cautiously optimistic though afraid. Despite her many weeks in hospital during and since childhood and trips to the hospital theatre she had never actually had an operation; this one would be major. Mr Todd had explained that a total colectomy was the removal of the whole of the large bowel. The end of the small bowel would protrude on to her abdomen as a stoma. Lynn would have to wear a bag on her tummy, possibly for the rest of her life. The surgeon would try to leave the last few inches of large bowel in the hope that at a later time the operation could be reversed and the stoma returned inside the abdomen and joined to what is known as the rectum, thereby returning her plumbing to normal. It all seemed complicated to Lynn who was just relieved to know that someone in their skill and wisdom was going to do something to make her life and health better.

The letter for her admission to Harmsworth Ward came within a few weeks. Her weight had ballooned again to twelve and a half stone and she could understand the reasoning for getting her off the steroids under hospital supervision. She would also be put on a diet but she knew from past efforts that that would make little difference.

Lynn entered the Nightingale-styled ward; she was introduced to the nurses and the regime, and as so many times before, said goodbye to her parents and climbed on to her bed to wait for the admission procedure; Lynn felt at home.

Over the course of the next month she was allowed out of the ward for exercise and occupational therapy. She was not ill but under observation and as she made friends easily was allowed with one or two of the other women out of the claustrophobic ward and into the fresh air. The dressing-gowned ladies strolled arm in fragile arm into the lovely tree-shaded square which was the focal point of the hospital buildings. A beautiful circular stone fountain gushed with cool fresh water, the presence of which cooled the face and calmed the mind. The cascade blew with the breeze and splashed those who stood too close. On clear early autumn days Lynn saw some patients' beds encircled round the fountain allowing a number of occupants to escape the wards and enjoy the fresh air like herself. Lynn loved it here and would often find her way through the corridors and down in the lift and sit in the dappled sunlight alone, listening to the light chatter of patients and staff and the cooing of the London pigeons.

When allowed, she would take the smaller lift to the upper floor and with two of her fellow patients discovered that they could push the door open to the roof top. Here it was magic; the low-walled perimeter was meshed for safety but the view across London was amazing. From this height Lynn could look down on St Paul's Cathedral and many of the famous sights along the river Thames. The light reflected clear from heaven, reflecting pink and gold upon the buildings. The smell of the air was clean and autumn-fresh yet just below their bird-roosting position the city traffic droned continually, pierced occasionally by the sirens of the emergency services. The odour and pollution of city life hung at street level; the pedestrians oblivious to the perfection above. Lynn came up to the roof as many times as she was able during those first two weeks of her stay but autumn came quickly and the warmth was lost from the sun; permission was no longer granted

Lynn didn't like occupational therapy, preferring to sew or complete jigsaws with the other ladies. "O.T." was like being back at school and she saw no reason to bake or perform tasks just to prove she was busy. She understood that it was healthy to get away from the ward but eventually, when the sister saw she was well adjusted, she didn't try to persuade the girl to take part.

The month went by quickly enough. Once again Lynn continued her education of life and met many interesting people, some of whom she kept in touch with after her discharge. She was gradually weaned off of the steroid drug and her weight dropped to eleven stone, though it left her with further stretch marks on her arms, legs and tummy. These red wheals faded over the years but marked her for life. Later, those who didn't know her past would enquire if she had had children. At first she thought it a casual question, only later realising they had wrongly surmised this because the marks they had noticed were to an unprofessional mind only a result of pregnancy.

Lynn was discharged from hospital in the sure knowledge that the ulcerative colitis would return now the drugs had been withdrawn. She was to keep an out-patient appointment where her weight and illness would be monitored. Then, Mr Todd had explained, Lynn would be called back to London for her operation. He squeezed her shoulder as he left her bedside and told her she had done exceedingly well. From there the usual procedure for discharge home was adhered to and the young woman found herself looking forward to the next few months with trepidation.

That night she unpacked her small luggage bag in her room. Her mother sat on her bed watching her daughter who seemed at last to have light in her eyes and a confidence she hadn't had before. She mentioned it.

'I see a future, Mum; for the first time in nearly three years someone in the medical world has given me hope. Whatever happens next I will always remember Bart's hospital fondly and if I need to feel calmness I will think of the fountain in the hospital square.' She reached in to a pocket of her suitcase and gave a folded written sheet of A4 paper to her mother to read, saying nothing as she did so. It was one of the first pieces of inspired writing she had conceived. It began…

The square was bathed in dappled sunlight while the plane trees above whispered their prayers to the sky. They whispered peace and hope filled the patients with a calmness that only nature can provide.

I was one of those patients and I looked up at the cooing London pigeons which perched oblivious on the trees. Down below, upon the head of the fountain, they cooed also and I shut my eyes and just listened to the sigh of this world – a world that seemed detached from the city traffic and the terrible happenings of our times. It seemed to me that this square was ageless and detached and I wanted only to belong to this world, where people smiled or just sat around the fountain, peacefully gazing at the water and the upsurge of the fountain's flow. It was the perfect focal point of healing.

Coins glinted, lying so still in the shallow waters and each coin seemed to hold a story of its own; one of hope, not the usual shallow wish of coins tossed in to lucky wishing wells. These coins seemed of solemn intent; the earnest wish for health lay beneath the surface. The goldfish lazed, occasionally tossing their tails or darting for small morsels of food. They knew nothing outside their small world and somehow, just at that moment I felt the same.

People dwindled, now seemingly unnoticed they disappeared in straggling groups or silently, singularly. Evening made shadows so tall they reached out to each other and merged into the coolness that comes only with evening. Beds were moved inside and now the peace became thick and full and silently the square was left in the gentle light of evening.

I was almost alone and sighed. No one nor any thought could disturb that peace for it had grown as the trees had, with time and events. It was watched over by majestic buildings on all sides, with only a small archway to the outside world. I shivered, almost feeling the ghost of the past haunting me and the whispering trees seemed now to change their prayer and share their secrets which no human could conceive.

I stood now breathing deeply the soft air, trying to hold it as if so doing would make me belong. Then I sighed again and some deep feeling within me stirred, 'Remember me,' I whispered, as if to this quiet world, 'and let me not forget.' I then left peacefully and slowly as if not to disturb the atmosphere and disappeared as the others had, swallowed up by the imposing buildings. But the peace stayed with me and with God's help I will not forget!

Lynn had signed the sheet of writing and had dated it September 1969. She looked sideways at her mother and could see a softness in her expression as she handed the writing back to its author. Her mother had recognised her daughter's inner strength and from that moment knew that her experiences had brought her wisdom beyond her years. Lynn, no longer a child, had the simplicity of innocent understanding. It would be that "child within" who would see her through the experiences ahead.

CHAPTER 32

Autumn had passed to winter when the postman trudged up the long cold road of First Avenue. Lynn was sitting in the rocking chair reading quietly. The late November winds were blowing against the bay window and the garden trees were bare. It seemed to her that the whole world had gone into hibernation, preparing itself for rest and rebirth in the promised spring; but that was a long way off. Lynn sympathised, for her feelings were in tune as they always were with nature and the changing seasons. She felt her body and soul were entering a different season; a winter of their own. She was waiting, like the puffed-up robin and blackbird, for things to get worse before they got better. As prophesied, her medical condition had deteriorated once the prop of ugly drugs had been taken from her. She had waited for the letter a long time, half hoping for and half dreading its arrival. She heard the latch of the gate knock, metal against metal, and looked up to see the postie walk up the driveway pulling letters from his bag. He mounted the front steps and pushed a letter through. Lynn felt a flutter of intrusion into her expectant world and it took all her will not to run in to the hall and to snatch the letter from the jaws of the letter box. She acted out the week-long routine and pretended to ignore the arrival of post. She heard her mother's footsteps along the hall and then the snap as the letter box let go of its prize. This time, though, instead of her mother calling out that the postman had brought nothing for her, there was a pregnant pause. Lynn waited; her mother entered the room holding out a brown envelope.

'It's for you, Lynn, from London.' She put the letter in her daughter's hand and waited for her to resign herself to open it.

Lynn said nothing, looked at the post mark and tore the envelope open without regard. 'It is from Bart's; I have to go in at the end of November – just two weeks away.' She handed it back and looked to her mother for reassurance and confirmation that it was the right and only thing to do.

'You have no choice, Lynn, you've told me that yourself. At least now we know. It will all be over by Christmas.'

Lynn and her mum realised it wouldn't be over but, in reality, just beginning. It was just that neither of them knew exactly what would be beginning and what was ending. Life wasn't really like that; it just continued through experiences and episodes until it eventually ended. Lynn's life wasn't about to end, she had decided that a few years back.

'Do you fancy going to The Winston Churchill for scampi and chips?' It was one of the treats they often took when a morale boost was needed and it wasn't the weekend.

'Actually no; but I could go for a ham toastie and a hug.' Lynn's mum obliged her daughter on both counts.

Lynn's admission two weeks later, again to Harmsworth Ward, was a blessing. Any doubt she may have had melted as her health stumbled. It was as if someone above was underlying the truth of her position; there was no choice to make. Lynn would have her operation and the date was set for the fourth December 1969. The days before then were set by procedure. Soap and water enemas were given for three evenings before operation day. There were visits from doctors and clinical experts to help prepare her mentally for her later new life; all this while dealing with her illness.

Lynn was not alone at this time. She met and made friends with two young girls who were about to have the same operation, though for differing conditions. The older girl, Paula, was married and was suffering with Crohn's disease and Maria, who was engaged to be married, had ulcerative colitis. They all had a lot in common but were very different characters. Although Lynn didn't have a partner she knew she was well loved and would be cared for by a loving family while recovering. The nurses were great and again Lynn was able to form special attachments to some of them. The doctors, too, were sympathetic and understanding; gradually Lynn was nurtured towards her operation.

Doris Stone came into the ward one day to see her. She was a much older woman and was not one of the medical personnel. This gentle and smiling "civilian", employed now as a sympathetic appliance representative for an "ostomy" firm and doubling as a stoma therapist, had been sent to the three girls to explain to them that life would improve and they would adapt to the equipment they would need to wear for the rest of the time necessary for each of them. Doris had had her total colectomy many years before when there were no black rubber bags or cemented flanges; these would have been unheard of. In the pioneering days of the first operations to save lives the patient was confined to bed on their stomachs, with an aperture through the mattress, to enable the collection of natural waste beneath the bed. Lynn didn't want to visualise what it would be like for the patient. Doris was still talking, saying that she had not been in that position, but had been housebound with a cup upon a belt around her waist until clinical improvements advanced. Lynn felt embarrassed for Doris while she related her story, until she saw her smile confidently. She obviously, now, enjoyed life to the full. What right did anyone have to deny the right to live at any cost? For Lynn and the other girls post-operative life would be much better for clinical trials and appliances had improved greatly. Lynn would be active, needing only to maintain the non-disposable rubber bags complete with flanges and cement and elasticated belts. Doris told her she would even be able to wear a costume and go swimming, though she doubted she would have confidence to do that…she couldn't swim anyway! Lynn admired Doris, but she didn't really want to be like her. She was younger and would make her own identity shine through any problems she confronted – of this she was sure.

The evening before the scheduled operation Mr Fairley, a gorgeously handsome houseman, came and sat on her bed. All the girls liked him and by watching the ward social life she knew that he'd taken a fancy to one of the senior student nurses on night duty. Love was obviously in the air and patients and staff alike were happy for them. Now this young surgeon, three classes up from Dr Kildare, who had been her television heart-throb in the sixties, sat on her bed and with a felt-tipped pen marked her tummy for the point of operation and position of the stoma. It could hardly be called a romantic assignation though Lynn enjoyed his concern and brief company. It was only when he had finished that he turned to her and quietly explained something she really didn't expect him to voice. After he had chatted about the necessity of the operation his talk turned to relationships. He was gentle and caring but then he suddenly tried to explain that when she fell in love and chose a partner there might be difficulty. He went on to explain that not every man would be sympathetic to her physical appearance because she would have to wear a bag. Her heart dived; she felt herself shrink within herself. She knew he was just trying to be practical, to prepare her, but to have a man she found attractive convey such things was just too much for Lynn.

'Then he would not be the right man for me,' she denounced his truth, and he sat back a little at her tone and did not continue on that line of conversation.

When he had left her she was hurt and angry, both with herself and him. How dare he think that a man would not love me for who I am. Surely a loving man would wish to know the whole woman? I would be understanding enough to see through a partner's faults and disfigurements if I loved him. If a man felt as the doctor has described then he would not love me enough to deserve me, she thought indignantly.

It was doubly hurtful knowing that the doctor was quite a dishy fellow. She had of course totally misunderstood him. Lynn was still innocent enough to think that she could never fall for a man who was anything other than perfect. She would learn, of course, that the heart ruled the head in such matters and it was from this the doctor was trying to protect her. She tried to put the episode behind her but he had pointed out a fact that would cause her insecurity through much of her adult life. In reality she doubted she would be good enough for anyone! The doctor's caring conversation had done more harm than he could possibly have imagined.

When Lynn climbed into bed that night, exhausted from the enema and subsequent pain, she lifted her nightie and looked beneath the covers. A large round dot marked the right upper quarter of her abdomen. She stared at her stomach, consciously registering that it would be the last time she would see her body as God had made it. She wasn't a 'drama queen', but a very logical young woman. What she regretted most was that she would never be able to wear a bikini. She didn't understand why that should bother her so much… she didn't own a bikini. Perhaps it was because she still desperately wanted to be like every other nineteen-year-old. In later life she would be satisfied with being who she was, and, in fact, never suffered an awkward experience within a relationship because of the ileostomy or having to wear a bag.

The operation was a complete success and Lynn adapted more by trial and error to her new-found friend. She christened her stoma Rosemary and in fact became quite "attached" to her. The three girls compared notes and swapped jokes at their own expense though drew a line at calling themselves the three young bags. The nursing staff realised it was a way of coping and went along with the humour, also drying tears of frustration and disappointment when dressings and healing didn't go to plan.

Christmas was just around the corner and all able patients were set to work making decorations for the ward. Lynn was happy to oblige for anything to do with artistic craft was a joy to her. The others joined in and the whole atmosphere of the ward became lighter and forward thinking.

During that first post-operative week Paula showed symptoms of flu. Lynn and Maria quickly followed suit and a couple of other patients started to sneeze and cough. It was decided to close the ward to all new admissions and send anyone they could home – those who were well enough and not showing signs of the outbreak. The girls were very unwell. Lynn's temperature went up to 104 °F. and all three were prescribed remedial medicines and Friar's Balsam steam inhalations.

'It isn't enough that we have to wipe the stuff on our stomachs, we have to inhale it as well,' said Lynn one morning as she emerged from under the towel covering the heated container of the mixture. Friar's Balsam was a good iodine-based treatment, the colour of old bronze. It was used for sore and irritated skin prior to more soothing lotions later prescribed. The girls were told to use it around their stomas to toughen the skin. Plaster irritation affected them all.

Lynn felt very unwell and her discharge from hospital was delayed until after Christmas. Her recent memories of Christmases at home had not been all that good and she felt somewhat relieved that she was not going home. She missed her family badly and regretted not being able to spend more time with her brother who was home from university for the holiday but lately Christmas had become a rather strained celebration. She knew also that she would miss the companionship of the ward. It had been recognised that Lynn was artistic and the ward staff had quickly involved her in the making of ward decorations. She had become a bit of a star.

The Bart's Hospital Christmas festival started at lights out on Christmas Eve. The nurses of Harmsworth and other wards wore full uniform with their capes reversed to show the scarlet red. In procession they slowly walked from dimly lit ward to ward singing carols in celebration. The sweetness of their combined voices and the impression of heavenly angels singing by candlelight brought tears to the eyes of some of the patients; it was a most moving experience. As they left the ward Lynn strained to hear the last verse of "Silent Night" before the ward doors closed behind them. There were a few muffled sobs in the dark that night as women missed their families at such a poignant time.

Christmas morning began like any other but once the ward routine was hurriedly completed the surgeons made it their role to visit their patients and share a glass or two of sherry with them. Mr Todd chatted to Lynn in a most informal manner and he told her that if he accepted any more sherry from the ward he would not be able to carve the turkey! Everybody laughed a lot that morning. Lynn and the girls were even told off by the vicar who couldn't concentrate on a private communion he was conducting because they were making too much noise. Lynn chided herself that she should have been more thoughtful; after all, they were celebrating Christ's birthday.

The highlight of the Christmas and Boxing Day agenda was the series of short pantomimes that were acted out on specially erected stages on every ward. The student doctors who had volunteered for Christmas duty had worked within their Medical Firms to produce a short pantomime which would tour the wards over the holiday. Harmsworth had their own which the patients supported vigorously. Lynn had a bed near the stage and thought it hilarious how otherwise serious students could look so ridiculously funny in their costume and make-up, which the nurses had obviously had a hand in. The star of their show was a young, short, bespectacled student who always ran last on to the ward at the time of a consultant's round. His curly hair was unruly and his face often wore a confused problematical expression. Charles, however, would one day be a very sympathetic doctor if he didn't turn to a life of show-business! He was hilarious and for those patients who could walk it was a chance to give the Harmsworth panto a standing ovation.

There were several ward-touring productions on the two main afternoons and Lynn's parents and brother had ringside seats when they arrived for visiting. They had just suffered the indignities of a wine waiter at a top London hotel where they had their Christmas lunch. He had almost insisted that they ordered quantities of wine in celebration. Lynn believed her brother had told him in no uncertain terms that the family were hospital visiting in the afternoon. The wine waiter said no more to any of them, probably for the whole of the meal! Her father thought he had been on commission!

The afternoon was great entertainment and Lynn's only complaint was that she was just a little too poorly to get out of bed and join in! The patients had to hold their stomachs through laughter and pulling stitches. Once the student pantomimes had been played to all the wards they were judged by merit and the winning pantomime was then taken to the local theatre. Lynn believed an award was made for the best production. It would have been a job to pick a winner but

Lynn hoped it would be Harmsworth Ward.

After Boxing Day the serious job of running a hospital ward returned. Lynn looked at the young doctors with admiration, trying hard to see if any still carried the remnants of stage-theatre make-up. It went down in Lynn's life as one of the best Christmases ever and it was also a turning point. She was adapting to the management of "Rosemary" and her health was improving. She would never suffer with ulcerative colitis again and neither could she have appendicitis as that part of her bowel had been removed as well. As far as Lynn was concerned things were looking up; not only was she alive but she was also on the mend and almost ready to go home. Paula had been discharged previously and Maria and Lynn were both at about the same stage of recovery and it was likely they would go home within days of each other. Lynn had mixed emotions on the subject, for as much as she wanted to leave the confines of the ward, it had been a caring place to be and once again a hospital had saved her life.

What would it be like at home? she wondered. Would she be able to adapt? It was all very well managing dressings when there was someone on hand to call, but what would it be like in the real world and had things improved at all in her family life?

Lynn would find the answers to all these questions in a very short time. On the next ward round, between Christmas and New Year, Mr Todd asked Lynn if she thought she was ready to go home. She nodded her head vigorously and almost hugged him. Home is where the heart is, she thought, and by the time the surgeon had reached the end of the ward Lynn was out of bed and making her way to the hospital ward telephone to make that long-awaited call to her parents. As she put down the phone she realised not for the first time just how much she missed them and how great it would be to see her brother before he returned to Edinburgh at the end of his university vacation.

The following day Lynn watched for the door of the ward to open. So similar to the hospital ward of The London Hospital, Whitechapel; she wondered if her parents would really come. Her memory came flooding back, but she was a child no longer and as an adult she said goodbye to the friends she had made and the staff she had respected and cared for and as an adult, she eventually walked out of the ward knowing she was going home to continue her recovery. She had decided she would then take up her own challenge of applying to enrol in the career of becoming a State Registered Nurse if her qualifications were sufficient. She had beaten so much in her young life, and wanted to rise as high as her spirit dictated. The idea of becoming a nanny to other people's fit children had faded and though she was unsure if she would be too emotionally involved to care for sick children, she did feel it was within her personality to become a good General Nurse. She thought back to Sister Canon who had become a role model to her as well as her sister angel. Surely all her experiences had not been in vain? She thanked her "child within" for showing courage, for that is what she would now need to walk her chosen path towards such a dedicated caring profession and, like Sister Canon, to prove to others that she was fit enough to do so.

Chapter 33

She knew it wouldn't be easy, but Lynn doggedly persevered in managing the changes of her body and her bathroom routine. The black rubber bags with screw openings were not pleasant and remembering to carry a penny in her pocket to turn the screw when needing to empty the bag while away from home was a habit she sometimes failed to remember. She looked at the Britannic penny, twelve to a shilling, as a sense of security instead of as one to spend. But she managed – managed very well. Her weight was now nine stone and her strength was returning and over the course of the following year her hospital appointments monitored her condition, bearing in mind that she still had the remaining five or so inches of her large bowel in the hopes of the original operation being reversed. Alas it was not to be. Within eighteen months, Lynn returned to hospital for her final operation. Her rectum was removed, the operation site made neat and aesthetically satisfactory. She realised she would always carry Rosemary but she also knew she had done with haemorrhaging and bowel problems for ever. Now, finally, she could look forward.

Two weeks after the operation she flew with her parents to Edinburgh to witness her brother graduating. He became a Bachelor of Science in the field of Astrophysics. She was very proud of him. The fact that she was there at the McEwan Hall, seated on a cushion, positioned high in the gods, was in itself a mark of personal achievement. Bill would go on to gain his doctorate and marry his Scottish sweetheart before making their life firstly in Edinburgh and then Australia and Hawaii, eventually returning to Wollongong, New South Wales.

Bill would never live in Dunstable again. One fledgling had flown and Lynn was desperate for the time that she could take to the skies of life as well.

It was a slow crawl first of all. The appliance she wore was satisfactory – however, it gave her little confidence. The composite flange was rigid and the paste cement would hold for a limited period, letting her down at the most inopportune time. The rubber bag was heavy and the belt ugly; Lynn might be living a life but not the life she wanted.

Lynn attended the Ileostomy Association's meetings held at the local Luton and Dunstable hospital. She didn't go to many, finding she preferred to deny her involvement rather than learning from it. However, at one such meeting which she went to with her mother she discovered that clinical "engineering" had moved on. It was unnecessary now to wear a black rubber surgical appliance. Plastic was on the scene at last. Slim, flesh-coloured and simple, the bags were one-piece and disposable. For patients like Lynn it was a breakthrough. Once she had used the sample she had been given there was no turning back and, over the years, the surgical products were reformed and refashioned to the slim versions that are on prescription today. At last Lynn's life would totally change for ever.

It was at this time Lynn remembered Doris Stone, and the emotional and practical support that lady had given so many patients, herself included. Although Lynn was unqualified to give advice on appliances, she knew she would be able to support younger "ostomists" like herself in adapting to their new lives. Her offer of voluntary help was gratefully accepted and Lynn paid many visits to London hospitals as well as her local one, dispelling negative attitudes and myths surrounding the operation.

Lynn also became involved with the Stoma Department at Barts. Her illustrative skills were called for regarding illustrations for an article in the *Nursing Times* about the surgical operation and the department's after-care. She produced many illustrations, which were also useful to the teaching school. Lynn felt, at last, she was giving something back to the hospital that had helped her start a new life.

The summer of her twenty-first birthday was full of hope. She celebrated it with her family in Jersey, yet looked forward more to her future than the celebrations that were organised for her. Birthdays were always strange affairs, they never came up to their expectations and this one was no different. Her mother, celebrating her own birthday the day before Lynn's twenty-first, fell down the stairs at the family's hotel. She was shocked but not badly hurt but it put a doubt and shadow on Lynn's own celebrations. Lynn would have no friends of her own celebrating with her; as she was away from home it would be a family affair. She hoped for little on such a special birthday but everybody pulled all the stops out for party drinks and eats at the hotel. Her father did not come across to the island to join them. There had been a cheque left on the mantelpiece for her, before she travelled to Jersey, but secretly Lynn would have still preferred a card and a big hug from her dad.

By now Lynn had researched the possibility of commencing S.R.N. training but things were not so simple. She had not been able to gain sufficient GCE O-Levels and had insufficient time to study A-levels because of her faltered education. Through no fault of her own it looked as though her career would fail at the first fence. She needed a nursing school that still accepted students through the sitting and passing of an entrance examination. In this matter her luck improved; the Jersey General Hospital at that time enrolled students through this alternative method; she felt success to be within her grasp. With the support of her mother and her family's Jersey GP she was accepted by the Jersey General Hospital to sit an entrance examination. She was nervous yet determined and, not long afterwards, she heard that she had been successful. Because the matron, Miss Renouf, and, no doubt, the committee, were unsure if the new candidate would be physically strong enough to take up her career, it was suggested that Lynn joined the hospital team firstly as a pre-nurse for three months. Her mother pointed out to Lynn that they had asked her for assurance that if her daughter failed in health the medical establishment would not be held wholly responsible.

Lynn would start her full General Training in January the following year. She had indeed deserved the college prize she had received many years before for "*The Best Endeavour in the Face of Adversity.*"

Lynn left home in 1971, in the September of her twenty-first year. Like a fledgling leaving the nest she already knew she could fly – she had been testing her wings since childhood. What she didn't know was how far.

She joined the female surgical ward "Rayner" wearing a white dress uniform but without the nurse's white apron. On her head she wore the white starched cap synonymous to nursing, though she didn't own a cape. This was her pre-nurse's uniform, which apart from the cap seemed to her to be very "down market" in the uniform stakes, and a small disappointment.

It was first thought sensible that she should lodge with her Uncle Peter and Pat in St Helier. They ran their guest house on the lines of a boarding house and this gave Lynn a certain independence from the family. After a short period and with Matron's approval, Lynn then moved in to the Nurses Home in Gloucester Street, attached to the main hospital. Gradually she was taking on the mantle of her chosen profession. While pre-nursing she acted as general carer, helping on the ward with the day-to-day routine. She was enthusiastic and, as she worked alongside trained staff and students, she learned quickly. As the more senior nurses took time to show her some of the basic procedures Lynn became one of the team. She felt at home on the wards and was sympathetic to the patients, having experienced so much of what they were going through. One lovely elderly lady had been operated on and given an ileostomy. She was recovering fairly well but remained on Rayner Ward over Christmas. Lynn was able to give her great encouragement, aided by her own experience. Looking back at the Christmas photographs taken on the ward Lynn was shocked to find she looked as pale and as fragile as the patient she was nursing. Lynn knew she had set herself a huge challenge by choosing a nursing career so soon after her own recovery.

That first Christmas on the ward was a milestone in Lynn's life and achievement. Two Christmases before, as a patient, she had listened to carols as nurses glided through Harmsworth in the glow of subdued ward lighting before midnight. The next day she had been laughing at the ward pantomimes having no notion of what the following two years would bring. Lynn now stood in the entrance hall of The Jersey General Hospital on Christmas Eve, preparing for the carol service. A senior sister came up to her as she stood in her white uniform among the blues and striped greys.

'Lynn; wear this for the service, I'd be pleased for you to borrow it.' The thoughtful sister threw her cloak over Lynn's shoulders, having turned it inside out. Lynn stood, the red of the nurse's cape matching the others along the line. It would seem to her that it was the moment Lynn had been accepted into the honoured profession of nursing. On Christmas Eve 1972 she took her place in the choir and walked the wards singing traditional carols and for every note she sang her heart and spirit sang more sweetly. She had achieved what she had almost never thought possible.

That year she played her part in the hospital pantomime and filled her ward with cartoons for Christmas. Her only disappointment was that when she went back on the ward on Twelfth Night all her art work had been taken by approving student nurses. Peggy, the Nurses Home cleaner, who was a good sort and who looked after her girls, said that they were in other students' rooms hanging on the walls as souvenirs of Christmas! It was a compliment really.

Lynn joined her relatives around the Christmas Day dinner table and returned to Dunstable on Boxing Day for one last festive celebration with her own family. She was, in fact, exhausted but ready to start her new nursing career upon her return.

In January 1972 she was deemed fit enough to commence her full S.R.N. training and did so proudly, unsure as any of the new intake of student nurses just what the future would hold.

Lynn the child was no more. It had taken her a long time to grow out of childhood but each step along the way was in itself an experience of a lifetime.

Chapter 34

Lynn went on to achieve many things in life which she thought important, and failed in many more, for such is life. She banned all thoughts of childhood to the past and marched on through years and experiences, trying hard to look forward and not back at her past. She never acknowledged "little Lynn". The experiences of her childhood were buried, suffocated and drowned, emerging only in controlled memories. Lynn the adult wanted to move on and to deny the traumatic past. Instead of admitting the battles won and the small successes of such a childhood, she harboured to herself the pain, weakness and failure of what she thought of as a negative youth. She carried through to adulthood the need to be approved of, to be loved and yet she thought herself unworthy of either of these. She wished someone would listen when she stood up for herself, not realising that she was only whispering her defence. Despite achieving so much in her adult life she only saw her failures and resigned herself to being only half successful. She was proud of her creative talent but looked upon it as God's gift; not a bad thing in itself, but she denied she had much part in it.

Just as in her school reports Lynn tried hard throughout her life; sometimes too hard. Married and divorced nineteen years later, the only child she had was not of flesh but was the child within who cried to be heard; but Lynn denied her. Lynn preferred to climb the steepest path, do everything the hard way as if it was what she deserved. She had always battled with life and fought for her right to struggle! She didn't allow herself to realise that her biggest strengths, just like her greatest weaknesses, came from her childhood, though she would admit openly that her greatest strengths were brought to her from her love of God.

After contracting glandular fever, a recurrent illness which leaves the patient debilitated for months, Lynn could not maintain her stamina. Eventually, having collapsed with exhaustion during a ward night duty, she knew she could no longer continue the strenuous role of nursing. With the advice and genuine concern of her superiors she took the heart-breaking decision to leave nursing. Once again she looked on this as failure but not defeat, for it was the inner strength from childhood that made her fight and regain her path. Her life moved restlessly on; the highs and lows likened to tidal flow were marked by an encouraging sense of spirit.

Later in life her continuing understanding of people and circumstances enabled her to express their pain and longing rather than her own through her artistic talent. She coupled her childhood skills in handwriting and drawing, moulding them into creative illustrative verse to encompass prayer, comfort and the personal ideals of others. She discovered her words could help and aid healing far more effectively than her tired physical self. Her child within had given her all the gifts to help her in her work and gave her strength to battle the periods of traumatic health she was to encounter all her life as well as to reach out to others less fortunate.

Lynn became a published poet and illustrator of seven anthologies of inspired verse. She became known for the work of sympathetic words and branched into many fields of creative writing, making a successful and satisfying career; but Lynn still denied herself. She valued everything but not herself. She smiled a lot and people loved her, but she could not believe it, nor understand it. Perhaps Lynn had never tried to love or understand herself, preferring to love and understand others. The child within waited patiently for the time she would be accepted back into Lynn's life.

Lynn was now five months from her sixtieth birthday. The major operation she had waited for had finally been carried out. Her dark days of winter were now over.

The recovery nurse watched her patient as she took her observations. Lynn seemed to be sleeping, though the rhythm of her breathing and the flicker of her eyelids would indicate she was dreaming or shortly would be returning to consciousness. She looked at her chart. "Lynn New, age 59". She would have to look at her notes for more detailed information but under the theatre team's care her patient had undergone a five-hour operation for the dividing of internal adhesions, caused through her history of major abdominal surgery. A hernia had also trapped her small bowel, squeezing it between heavy abdominal muscles. Another chapter could be added to Lynn's extensive medical notes. The nurse checked the intra-venous drip and watched her patient from a distance.

Something disturbed her. Lynn gradually awoke; a thought drifted through her semi-consciousness. How could she be heavy and light at the same time? she wondered. The ethereal lightness from administered pain relief and post-anaesthetic euphoria lifted her from her recovery bed. The heaviness of spasmodic deep pain pushed her heavily back into reality. Lynn did not have the energy to be frightened. The nurse told her to breathe in the gas and air and repositioned the mask over her patient's face. Lynn opened her eyes; the light was bright, too bright. She was about to close her eyes again and drift back to her darkness, when some part of her brain became aware of another presence standing by her prone figure. She was not an adult.

Whose child is this? thought Lynn, wanting to drift on; but the child would not let her.

'Don't leave me now you have found me,' the child whispered.

'Found you?' Lynn slurred, the mist of cotton wool trying to encroach upon her senses.

'You have searched for me for a long time, knowing something in your life was missing, like a piece of jig-saw. Without it you could not see the full picture; without me you could not be complete or make full sense of your life. You denied me for so long thinking, as all adults do, that you could manage without me.'

'But you are a child!'

'Exactly!'

'But I have left my childhood behind so long ago.'

'Yet lately you have recalled it and in doing so you have called me.' The child stood closer, touching Lynn's uncovered arm, above the cannula in her wrist. Lynn felt nothing, her mind and body confused, tired.

Recognition slowly dawned. She remembered feeling caught and trapped in her life; asking questions of herself without having the answers; feeling inadequate, the fear of failure over-riding the ambition of success. The need for approval dominated the focus of her adult life. Had she called the child? She did not know, but a child was standing before her now.

Lynn turned her head towards her and looked up, just a little, into her hazel eyes, so much like her own. She let her guard down, still searching for answers to her unspoken questions.

'It's true I've been trying to make sense of my life, sort out who I am and why I behave the way I do. That is all, I did not call you; you are my past.' Lynn wanted to sleep but could not let go of her chain of thought. 'I know I make the same mistakes over and over again yet I am unable to break the coding; it seems I am victim of my own vicious circle.' She spoke her thought.

'Is it that vicious?' whispered the child.

'Oh yes.'

'Then we must break it,' the child retorted.

'Who are you to help me?'

'I have always helped you, that is why you are who you are; because of me. Because of me you have experience of character. Because of what I have done, you have become; we are one. Without each other we could not be whole.'

'You are but a child.'

'And you merely an adult.' The child was forthright. 'Without me your soul would shine with the weakest of light, for without childhood experience an adult would be shallow and without substance.'

'And without me you would remain childlike and vulnerable.' Their attitude towards each other was very similar.

Lynn rested back against the pillow and closed her eyes. The effort she had demanded of herself had been exhausting, but the child stood resolute.

'What is your name child?' Lynn asked.

'My name is Lynn.'

'Mine also,' she murmured and then the mists cleared in recognition. She opened her eyes to see the child smile. The child was so familiar; she was no stranger.

The child stood back so Lynn could see her more clearly, 'I am Lynn, your *inner child*. All I asked of you was recognition, without denial. When you called for the answers to your life you called me. Just as you are part of me, I am also part of you... your child within. Together we are as one and in recognising the child and the memories of that child, however painful or joyous, you can add to your store of experience to benefit your life instead of denying the growth of it. Let go of the bad memories, by all means, but know that it is through all experiences, good and bad, that you have become who you are. It is up to you what you make of it.' The child smiled. 'I'll let you rest.' She reached up; her head level with Lynn's own as she lay on the trolley. 'Accept me and you accept life.'

Little Lynn touched Lynn's hand; the patient hardly felt it. It was as light as a swallow's feather upon her arm. Her eyelids dropped and opened again for a moment only. Lynn the child had gone and yet the woman knew they would never be parted again.

'Goodnight, my child,' she whispered to herself and fell back into the sleep of healing.

Biography of Author

Brought up in Dunstable where much of "The Child Within" is based, Lynn New was born in Jersey in 1950, returning to the island to commence S.R.N. training. Following the curtailment of her nursing career through ill health she moved to Guernsey with her husband and then on to the Isle of Wight where she still resides. She began to express her caring of others through her uniquely illustrated poetry and found sympathetic island life was conducive to her creativity which continues to flourish. She managed her own retail outlet and by 1996 began her published career in the form of illustrated anthologies and greeting cards. The popularity and distribution of her work grew nationally and internationally.

Her spiritual understanding is important to her and although not blessed with children she identifies with their struggle for personal identity. She utilises her wicked sense of humour by occasionally script writing for local hospital radio. Now independent, Lynn enjoys the inspiration she gains from friends and travel, yet importantly takes time out to appreciate the smaller miracles in life.